Global Markets and Local Crafts

Johns Hopkins Studies in Globalization

Christopher Chase-Dunn, *Series Editor*

Consulting editors: Volker Bornschier, Christine Gailey, Walter L. Goldfrank, Su-Hoon Lee, William R. Thompson, Immanuel Wallerstein, and David Wilkinson

Global Markets and Local Crafts

Thailand and Costa Rica Compared

FREDERICK F. WHERRY

The Johns Hopkins University Press

Baltimore

© 2008 The Johns Hopkins University Press
All rights reserved. Published 2008
Printed in the United States of America on acid-free paper
2 4 6 8 9 7 5 3 1

The Johns Hopkins University Press
2715 North Charles Street
Baltimore, Maryland 21218-4363
www.press.jhu.edu

Library of Congress Cataloging-in-Publication Data

Wherry, Frederick F.
Global markets and local crafts : Thailand and Costa Rica compared /
Frederick F. Wherry.
p. cm. — (Johns Hopkins studies in globalization)
Includes bibliographical references and index.
ISBN-13: 978-0-8018-8794-9 (hardcover : alk. paper)
ISBN-10: 0-8018-8794-1 (hardcover : alk. paper)
1. Handicraft industries—Thailand. 2. Handicraft industries—Costa Rica.
3. Export marketing—Management. 4. International business
enterprises—Marketing. I. Title.
HD9999.H363T58 2008
338.4'77455—dc22
2007033663

A catalog record for this book is available from the British Library.

*Special discounts are available for bulk purchases of this book. For more
information, please contact Special Sales at 410-516-6936 or
specialsales@press.jhu.edu.*

For Charlie and Peggy, my parents

Contents

Preface

Despite the predictions of doomsayers, the global market has not smashed the artisan's workbench. On the contrary, the artisan has acquired a cultural cachet, fetching a price and a place in the global market. Whereas artisans once were an endangered species, they now have begun to propagate apprentices. The consumption of their handiwork has found demand among consumers seeking products that represent different cultural traditions and local histories. Rich cultures and the local industries they inspire hold great promise for countries and communities unable to compete in the market for cheap labor. Such countries as Thailand and Costa Rica have therefore found within their sociocultural heritage the source of their own global competitiveness. Although global capitalism has increased competition in the low-cost labor market, the creative industries that have surfaced from the currents of capitalist destruction have opened new pathways from the economic periphery toward the global core. The kernel of this development is not the factory but the fantasy of the authentic, the unadulterated, and the exotic, which draw international tourists and corporate buyers into villages and communities across the globe in order to experience the real and to source the nearly lost. In this way, globalization revives economies and thrives as a means of trading culture and cultural symbols. As artisans and buyers mark distinctions between what is authentic and what not, between the singular and the mass-produced, they sometimes infuse their commercial market transactions with information on relations of exchange using specialized media, as Viviana Zelizer predicted. Examination of how artisans produce their handcrafted objects within circuits of commerce, as well as the distribution of these objects through such circuits, shows the pitfalls and possibilities for making cultural traditions work to the advantage of local producers in the global marketplace.

This book is about the narratives and rituals that generate the allure held by local cultural industries in Southeast Asia and Central America. What one usually encounters in studies on globalization is a regional comparison of two communities within the same country, or communities in neighboring countries. This book compares communities in Thailand and Costa Rica. The comparative strategy employed here is a global one because it studies and contrasts the experiences of countries on opposite sides of the globe. What unites these countries is the fact that they use international tourism as the pathway through which to join the global market.

The handicraft sector, in which micro and small entrepreneurs export their souvenirs, their hand-carved furniture, or their handmade pottery, offers a strategic research site, in the sense outlined by Robert K. Merton, in that the cultural capital of handicraft traditions and the process of converting that value into economic profit can be seen, qualified, and analyzed with remarkable clarity. Instead of a dysfunctional bazaar where the language of scarcity and information asymmetry increases economic values, this study depicts a marketplace where different selling situations correspond to different price tags negotiated in light of concerns for the authentic and the singular. In these situations, which resemble the interaction ritual chains described by Randall Collins, the power of symbols resonates with buyers and producers, placing constraints on and opening opportunities for each set of actors as some objects and some producers become framed as authentic while others do not. Artisans and their objects do not generate economic value independently of the circuit of other individuals, objects, and histories in which they are embedded. An artisan who carves or molds an object may be merely doing it for the pleasure of creating, or preparing an object for a religious/spiritual purpose, or perhaps working the object according to the specifications of a buyer, or even engaging in a household chore. When buyers encounter these artisans, the buyers themselves may be primarily engaging in a leisure activity or may eventually have sought out the artisan for specific commercial purposes, looking for specific sizes, volumes, quality levels, and styles. What the actors think they are doing affects what they bargain about and how much emotional and culturally charged intensity the bargaining generates.

This process of defining the situation (framing) and of generating intensity and opportunity based on those definitions in the micro-situation also manifests itself at the macro-level. Just as the local histories and social relationships among entrepreneurs make it easier for some entrepreneurs to export their products, these same histories and relationships may limit the export opportunities for other artisans whose work does not represent the character of the nation as understood by international tourists, buying agents, and cultural institutions within and outside of these countries. The artisans in Thailand operate in environments favorable to their local cultural productions, but the artisans in Costa Rica may confront either hostile or indifferent environments. For Thailand, a nation proud of its cultural distinction and the fact that it has never been colonized, local cultural industries that exemplify the country's cultural independence are to be materially supported and socially extolled. In the national imagination of Costa Rica, indigenous artisans hardly exist, and by extension into the imaginations of international tourists and cultural institutions, indigenous arts are a surprise to be met with skepticism, if met at all. Nation-states create favorable or unfavorable environments for exporting cultural commodities, for attracting international tourist and corporate buyers, and for facilitating the outflow of products ready for sale.

Individuals caught up in these markets are not hapless victims to the forces and frames shaping their private lives, however. Artisans and other business entrepreneurs take advantage of the flow of people, information, and ideas from within and outside of their communities in order to open new pathways leading into the global market. They make personal connections with corporate buyers, who assist some of them to become independent exporters; the instrumental use of social ties can make or break these small businesses, confirming the importance of social capital, as argued by Alejandro Portes and his collaborators studying micro- and small-scale businesses. What is most remarkable about the cases presented in this book is the extent to which some corporate buyers cut themselves out of the exporting process as middlemen when dealing with artisans deemed to glow with the aura of authenticity. The power that framing infuses in the artisan's business and personal networks contributes to some of the positive outcomes that artisans experience in the global marketplace.

My attention to forces, frames, and flows (what I call the Three Fs of globalization) shows how grounded research helps us understand the effects of globalization on local cultures. This typology of the Three Fs corresponds to Michael Burawoy's discussion of forces, connections, and imaginations, but my focus on framing in the marketplace and on the movement (rather than the static ties and nodes implied by the word *connection*) illustrates the micro-interactions and the situational emergence of power that operate in some transactions and in some market spaces but not in others.

Some questions are bound to remain unanswered. While the economic forces of the market have created the premises for the death of one set of industries and the opportunities for the rise of local cultural industries, the gale of destruction still blows. Can local cultures protect these local industries without forsaking themselves? Under what conditions do authentic cultural representations and commercial market engagements coexist without the latter overcoming and ultimately erasing the creative distinctiveness of the former? While this book offers no definitive answers to these critical issues, the approach I have taken points to ways of identifying the empirical marks of authenticity and the potential sources of their destruction.

This book would not have been possible without the willingness of artisans to open their workshops and their homes to me, and I hope that in turn it will offer a medium for their voices, allowing their integrity to be more broadly recognized.

This book sprang from my dissertation in the Department of Sociology at Princeton University. I owe a great intellectual debt to Alejandro Portes and Viviana Zelizer, my mentors. I am deeply grateful to Sara Curran, Miguel Centeno, Patricia Fernández-Kelly, Paul DiMaggio, Juan Pablo Pérez-Sáinz (FLACSO, Costa Rica), and Luechai Chulasai (Chiang Mai University, Thailand). These individuals anchored me as I wrote my dissertation at Princeton, along with Dean Joy Montero, Dean David Redmond, Provost Joanne Mitchell, Elaine Wiley, and Sandy Sussman at the Graduate School, as well as Maria DiBattista, Pat Heslin, John Templeton, and Ann Corwin. For financial support, I am grateful for the generosity of the Center for Migration and Development (and its director, Alejandro Portes), the Hannah Fund administered by the Princeton University Graduate School, the Urbanization and Development Program, the MacArthur Fellowship administered by the Center for International Studies, and the Mellon Postdoctoral Fellowship for the Humanities and Social Sciences at the University of Pennsylvania (and a special thanks to Randall Collins and Elijah Anderson for helping me while there). At the University of Michigan I have found the longed-for serenity to complete the final manuscript revisions.

In the field site, I greatly benefited from numerous meetings with Juan Pablo Pérez-Sáinz in Costa Rica and Luechai Chulasai in Thailand. Associate Professor Busabong Jamroendararasame, the director of the Chiang Mai University International Center, invited me to work under the supervision Dr. Luechai Chulasai. Before traveling to Thailand, I received help in the intricacies of the Thai language from Nongpoth Sternstein (Penn Language Center) and Ajarn Janpanith (Chulalongkorn; visiting professor, University of Wisconsin at Madison, SEASSI). While in Thailand, I continued to meet with Ajarn Janpanith and I also met with Kruu Amara (AUA Language Center, Chiang Mai). In the field sites I received research assistance from Gustavo Coronado at the University of

Costa Rica and from Khun Aey, Khun Burt, Khun Pak, Khun Jiab, and Khun Lek at Chiang Mai University. In Thailand I benefited from the generosity of Andrew Coyle, Patrick Pierce, Clyde Fowles, Vittaras Teetaa (Khun Tom), Libby Saul, Kevin Kettle, Anuchit Jittrathanakul (Neung), Sheila Taylor, Hanscom Smith, Dave Streckfuss, Pii Daychaa, and Pii Gowit. Max Iacono at the International Labor Organization, Jim Klein and Poonsook Pantitanonta at the Asia Foundation in Bangkok, Mark Narongsak at the Northern Organization of Handicraft Manufacturers and Exporters (NOHMEX), Helene Redelle (along with Hank Luce, Kit Luce, Terry Lautz, and Michelle Douenias) at the Henry Luce Foundation, and Pam Tansanguanwong at the Asia Foundation and then the World Bank were wonderful in offering me contacts and encouragement along the way.

During the writing stage, Paolo Asso, Rachel Havrelock, Wendy Cadge, and Claiborne Kenneth Hutchins Smith offered their insights and their encouragement. Barbara McCabe and Melanie Adams helped me stay on track as I negotiated my graduate school schedule. Henry Tom and Claire McCabe Tamberino at the Johns Hopkins University Press offered guidance in keeping the manuscript moving, and Marie Blanchard carefully edited the final copy. Any flaws contained therein are entirely of my own making. I thank Eric Frierson for helping me format the figures for the book.

I dedicate this work to my parents, Charlie and Peggy, who were always ready to sacrifice so that I could pursue my educational goals. My brothers (Bernard, Sam, Reggie, and Scott) and especially my twin sister, Frances, have been a constant source of joy. Larry Poston, Ross Advincula, Jeff Schulden, Shelley Senterfitt, James Wilson, Reuel Rogers, Bill Wood, Clay Smith, Peter Barberie, Nana Bogis, John Moon, Helima Croft, Gauti Eggertsson, Pat Egan, and Dylan Penningroth have functioned as extended family. Jan Boxill, Kenneth Janken, and Donna LeFevre nudged me toward academia, and Ell Close and Katherine Marshall remained wonderful mentors before and after my "academic turn." Finally, Paolo Asso has become a part of my family and has helped me remain on the sunny side of life.

Global Markets and Local Crafts

CHAPTER ONE

Introduction
Making Culture or Making Work?

This book explores the contradictions in the creative destructions wrought by globalization—the new freedoms (Cowen 2002) and the cruel fates (Bauman 1998). Examining how the global market for handicrafts has affected the cultural traditions and the economic lives of artisans in Thailand and Costa Rica, I ask: Are handicraft artisans globalization's victors, reviving their local cultural traditions and generating pride along with income for their families and communities, or are they globalization's victims, turned into de-centrally sited proletariats, selling the only thing available that enables survival? Are handicraft artisans who are caught up in these global commercial webs actually making authentic culture, or are they turning their cultural traditions into another depersonalized work product—a widget easily packaged to represent whatever "authentic" trend is catching the buyer's eye? As handicraft retailers have proliferated in the United States, artisans across the world have acquired new commercial connections and proffered old (noncommercial, culturally authentic) narratives. This commercial expansion and the narratives of authenticity they carry raise four pressing questions: How do those commercial connections emerge and who makes them? Once established, how do they work? How do they affect the well-being, social ties, and social standing of the artisans? And, finally, what is the effect on local economic development and on the intergenerational transfer of authentic local traditions?

Large retailers such as Pier 1 Imports, World Market, and Ten Thousand Villages, to name but a few, have emerged as major players in the market for handicrafts. According to the database of artisanal products maintained by the World

Trade Organization (WTO) and the United Nations Commission on Trade and Development (UNCTAD), in 2003 the global export of wooden furniture generated US$14.6 billion; ceramics, $1.4 billion; candles and tapers, $1.4 billion; and artificial flowers, $1.3 billion. Although handicraft artisans constitute a significant segment of the world economy, little is known about the creation of this artisan market or about how artisans have fared and will fare as they intensify their participation in global markets. Has the global demand for handicrafts empowered craft communities, preserved cultural traditions, and revitalized local economies? Or, instead, has the global market exploited artisans and quashed their creativity for the sake of profits?

Handicraft communities are rife with controversies over authenticity, globalization, and the viability of local economic life. This book contributes to our understanding of how cultural traditions (the "real" thing) become empowering for some local economies in the global market. This study goes beyond previous investigations of how cultural traditions are deployed in the service of local economic development (Cohen 2000; Colloredo-Mansfeld 2002; Graburn 1976; Herzfeld 2004; Nash 1993; Pérez-Sáinz and Andrade-Eekhoff 2003) by examining how authenticity gets generated in different social situations. By focusing on Viviana Zelizer's concept of circuits of commerce and Randall Collins's concept of interaction ritual chains, this book locates the study of culture and economic development primarily within the economic sociology and secondarily within the sociology of culture literatures so that it may untangle how cultural resources are generated and maintained as well as how these resources may be converted into economic and political assets.

Circuits of commerce refer to the multiple types of relationships, sentiments, emotions, meanings, and media that may be transferred between and among persons in definite patterns of exchange. These circuits have a well-defined boundary (which is not necessarily spatial) whose contours are incessantly negotiated and enforced. The actors within these circuits exchange various media that match their various definitions of the situation (namely, what type of relationship the actor is in and what would be appropriate given the relationship). This concept helps us understand how the commercial market for handicrafts might simultaneously involve the creation and export of objects that are devoid of meaningful local content alongside objects that reflect sacred rituals and that remain full of local content infused with symbolic, sentimental, and other noneconomic values.

The concept of interaction ritual chains refers to the series of actions or the types of behavior that seem to be prescribed because they are followed with regularity and involve reciprocal influence between (or among) persons. What happens in one set of interactions is linked to what happens in subsequent interactions because earlier "wins" generate energy for a group and make its members more enthusiastic about future interactions of the same sort. Interaction ritual chains remind us that culture and other macro-level social forces emerge from identifiable local situations and that the key to understanding how artisans or others become advantaged (or disadvantaged) in the global marketplace requires an examination of the seemingly prescribed patterns of behavior that generate (or diminish) the power and prestige of persons and groups in different types of encounters. In this way, we might better understand the heterogeneous outcomes wrought by globalization—how a community of artisans might be disadvantaged in some but not other types of selling situations.

Having cultural resources does not automatically translate into an empowering cultural tradition that gives the artisan an advantage when negotiating with buying agents and with representatives of the nation-state. If not the cultural resources themselves, this book asks, what other factors lead to empowering cultural symbols that the artisans themselves may utilize? And how do the social conditions under which the artisans work affect their dedication to and protection of authentic forms and traditional processes of production? What is "real" and authentic depends on the social context in which its manifestations are performed and argued over. I will argue that one has to observe the interaction rituals in which authenticity gets defined by various actors to understand the variability in what gets defined as authentic in one situation but not another. While this view highlights the socially constructed nature of authenticity, the micro-interactions in which authenticity is put to the test and the international and national contexts in which these interactions take place help us better understand why some artisans and villages succeed in framing their work as authentic cultural expressions while others do not.

To address these concerns, I interviewed 123 handicraft artisans running workshops in Thailand and Costa Rica between 2002 and 2003. I used other methods as well to provide systematic comparison: direct observation, a field survey of handicraft workshops, interviews with key informants, and archival research. My language facility in Thai and Spanish allowed me not only to conduct interviews but to incorporate documents written in those languages. These documents and my interviews uncovered significant differences in the experiences of artisans and their communities in the global market. I illustrate some of these variations by describing the dramatically different experiences of two Thai artisans living in nearby villages. The first artisan, Nopphadol, was initially reluctant to participate in global markets but succeeded in it; the second artisan, a woman who will remain anonymous, wanted to participate in global markets but found herself unable to overcome the barriers to entry. After reviewing the experiences of these two Thai artisans, I contrast the fates of two Costa Rican artisans living in neighboring villages. From these four stories we will begin to see how culture works to the advantage of some (but not others) within the same country as well as how the global market opportunities to be seized in Thailand differ from those in Costa Rica.

FOUR STORIES

As a handicraft artisan in the global market, the reluctant Nopphadol discovered that one of the few ways to excel in cultural commerce is to shun it. He tried to say no. Why would he, a wood carver with limited financial means living in northern Thailand, take the risk? He was satisfied that he could make a living by carving Thai pastoral scenes. When he was not carving scenes to be hung on the wall, he was meeting the requests of local Thai temples for wooden doors carved with lotus flowers in relief, the entangled stems nearly indistinguishable from one another, their mesh constituting the door's surface. These were the local traditions that generated work and pride for the talented. The thought of turning his artwork into work appropriated by Europeans, Americans, or any other outsiders triggered an automatic response: No, thank you. The German fellow who had come to give Nopphadol the chance to "go global" was not accustomed to such refusals. He had traveled throughout Asia to identify and purchase high-quality, authentic handicrafts. En route to Bali, he stopped in Chiang Mai, a region well known for the craft villages scattered across its territory. Like many others before him, the German searched for only those villages aglow with the aura of authenticity, where he would seek out the most talented artisans.

Ironically, Nopphadol's refusal to go global and his sincere reticence might have been exactly what the German sought. Not money, not fame, but caution blocked the deal. The artisan wanted to protect a socially valued tradition and seemed savvy enough to understand how messy and duplicitous commercial relationships could be in the modern world (Wuthnow 1996; Zelizer 2001). Here was an artisan who would not lay waste his local traditions nor cheapen them for sale. In the local environment, the artisan found all he needed (materials, handmade equipment and tools, consumers, civic pride, and regional fame). The German did not doubt that Nopphadol was an authentic local artisan worthy of pursuit, but Nopphadol's refusal clinched the deal. He now hosts his own website selling his carvings and conducts workshops on wood carving attended by international tourists and wood carving enthusiasts. Well respected at home and abroad, this humble man has reaped the profits of global markets. ⏌

While such success stories multiply in the Baan Thawai handicraft village, they do not manifest themselves with regularity in the Sanpatong handicraft area, thirteen kilometers away. In Sanpatong, refusing a good-enough deal is not so frequently done. I traveled there by car with my research team of four students from the economics department of Chiang Mai University. We stopped near a house where impressionistic directions indicated a handicraft artisan would be found. A woman seemingly in her thirties appeared from behind her house as one of my research assistants overcame the noise of a chain saw to announce our presence. Heavy-set and dark-complexioned (for a northerner), she sported dull black mud boots and toted a chainsaw. She asked, "Have you come to buy?" Before handing her my university business card bearing the Princeton seal, I wrote my name and mobile phone number in Thai script to reassure her that I knew her language. Although she was relieved that we would not have to struggle with language, she seemed disappointed: *If not to buy,* her eyes pleaded, *maybe to publicize?* She led us to the back of the house, where a makeshift canopy covered her workbench and her handiwork. She had been busy, she told us, making lots of the same thing. By her feet, we saw the evidence: a stack of miniature wooden elephants and jewelry boxes to be collected by a middleman who would have them painted elsewhere then sold for a much higher price to a large souvenir shop in the city of Chiang Mai. She informed us, "You won't find the same situation here as in Baan Thawai. Everyone knows about Baan Thawai, but not about us. Here in Sanpatong, we make the same things [as they do in Baan Thawai], but the buyers, the tourists don't come." She was not the first, and would not be the last, to tell us this.

Though the villages share the same craft traditions and operate in the same province, the artisans, village leaders, and foreign buying agents have come to a general consensus that Baan Thawai is not like the other craft villages nearby. Baan Thawai has the aura of authenticity—a feeling that the practices and crafts represent an original tradition. Aura is the subtle emanation of the imagined essences of persons, things, or places. The emanation envelops its source and permeates its surroundings by enthralling the onlookers with a sense that the space and its elements are worthy of deference. When potential buyers in the handicraft market become mesmerized by the artisans, the environment of the workshop and the daily practices of the village inhabitants, and the products and

the histories they represent, the buyer begins to evaluate the products more favorably. Held in high regard, the local artisans can negotiate better terms of
trade with outsiders, making them more successful than other economies in
the area. What draws people to Baan Thawai and, more generally, how artisans
across northern Thailand participate in the global market for crafts are the subjects of my investigation.

Carrying the same questions and concepts, I compared the lessons learned
in Thailand with those learned from studying pottery artisans in neighboring
villages in Costa Rica. I entered the first village, Guaitil, on an aging yellow
school bus that carried passengers reliably from the town of Santa Cruz up a
paved road with pasture on the left and pasture on the right. The closer we came
to the center of Guaitil, the more we confronted what must have been motifs
of the Chorotega cultural tradition. Lest there be any doubt, "Chorotega pottery"
was hand painted on wooden signs posted at the sides of the road and on a billboard sponsored by the National Bank of Costa Rica, set solitary in the field.
Anxious, I had to ask the bus driver if we were "there," because I increasingly
saw large kilns between the houses as well as bamboo and wooden kiosks displaying colorfully decorated pottery just in front of some homes. At the center
of the village, I got off the bus in front of the soccer field, which was encircled
by the school, the half-burned-down church, the women's cooperative store
(painted pink), and numerous kiosks.

Over the next four months I began to take notice of how two communities
within two kilometers of one another experienced the global tourist market for
handicrafts in rather different ways. The villages claim the same cultural heritage (Chorotega), produce the same goods (pottery), but do not reap the same
economic benefits. In the first village (Guaitil), where sales are swifter, the artisans enjoy higher incomes and better living standards than do the artisans in
the second village (San Vicente). I witnessed a woman from the United States
engage in a spirited conversation with an artisan in Guaitil about her family's
biography: how many children, which children have what gifts for painting or
for molding pottery, what a shame it would be to let the Chorotegan traditions
fall into extinction. The price seemed to be the last thing on the woman's mind,
and when she asked the artisan how much one of the vases was, she didn't
bother to haggle.

On another day, I heard (before I saw) a potential buyer overcome by frustration. "Why can't they get more support services out here? It doesn't make
good business sense!" From the looks of me, she knew that I had not grown up
there and said so. Having caught my attention and drawn me into her confi-

dence with her outspoken recognition of my difference, she was now ready to express the outrage of having her generosity thwarted. She had come from Los Angeles and really wanted to buy this handmade vase. She hadn't known these ethnic crafts were available in Costa Rica and had just happened upon a description of the village and its crafts while at the beach, over an hour away. Now that she was here and had seen the craftspeople at work, she was hooked. She didn't care about the price: One hundred and fifty dollars, what's that? Certainly, it was not a lot of money. Even though the shipping costs would probably make the vase cost as much, if not more, than anything she could buy in Los Angeles, she had a singular relationship with *this vase.* She would carry the memory of this day—the artisans seen at work, the things touched, the sentiments stirred. She had been here, in this out-of-the-way spot, and found something that she liked and wanted to carry home—but no; no shipping services here; no way to get it back. Did that make any sense? How could there not be some entrepreneur ready to take advantage of the opportunities to ship things of such high value, she asked. Surely, there was money to be made, yet the opportunities were being passed by. Why?

A similar question might be asked of the tourists themselves. Guaitil is not the only place to buy Chorotega crafts, yet in the Nicoya Peninsula where Guaitil and San Vicente are located, the Costa Rican Tourism Board only recognizes Guaitil as a center for handicrafts (Costa Rican Tourism Board 2002). Several artisans in San Vicente remarked, "We are not on the tourist map. People always visit Guaitil but not us. We make the same things." San Vicente's failure to capture as much attention as Guaitil seems more curious when one considers that the clay deposits for production come from San Vicente and that the old "Indian" burial ground is also located in San Vicente's territory. Indeed, having cultural resources does not automatically translate into an empowering cultural tradition or into the aura that gives the artisan's community an advantage when negotiating with buying agents and with representatives of the nation-state. If not the cultural resources themselves, what factors lead to empowering cultural symbols that the artisans may deploy with profit?

I argue that artisan economies do not thrive in countries that have been historically stigmatized by the "backwardness" that some ethnic products have been thought to represent. The most successful communities and regions of artisans become branded as the most authentic and important centers of cultural production because of, principally, the political mobilization of the community and the extra-community connections that the artisans make. If communities have mobilized against perceived external threats, they have signaled to outsiders that they hold traditions worth fighting for and have generated an aura of authenticity for the artisans residing in the locale. The inordinate attention paid to these communities by the government, nongovernmental organizations, international tourists, and retail brokers results from aura's attraction and enables these locales to become regions of dynamic local economies. Finally, I find that social capital (the capacity to mobilize scarce resources based on one's social relationships) will be limited in its effects on local economic development, given the aforementioned dynamics of the country's orientation toward the cultural heritage of these locales and given the emergence of aura in some communities but not others.

The aura of authenticity occupies a central place in my argument because the successful artisans have found that their status as the assumed purveyors of authentic cultural traditions has protected them from the most competitive pressures of the market. In defense of culture, they sometimes rejected requests to distort the designs of their handiwork. Rather than scoff at the idiosyncrasies of the culturally empowered artisans, some retailers have praised the artisans' dedication to authenticity. The retailers have found consumers willing to pay more and to wait longer for the "real" thing. In their market experiences, some artisans have learned that culture protects.

To use the language of cultural pragmatics, developed by Jeffrey Alexander, cultural representations offer the raw materials necessary for the performance of authenticity and sincerity in a marketplace that depends on it. Alexander (2004: 530) writes: "Marx . . . observed that 'just when they seem engaged in revolutionizing themselves and things, in creating something that has never yet existed,' social actors 'anxiously conjure up the spirits of the past to their service and borrow from them names, battle cries, and costumes in order to present the new scene of world history in this time-honored disguise and this borrowed language.' Marx is describing here the systems of collective representations that background every performative act." It would be a mistake to view the success of authenticity as the result of the individual's cunning or the resources and power that facilitate a more believable performance. Sincerity and authenticity are tied to the historical representations that cling to individuals within a particular territory, the power relations that generate the audience for the artisans, and the contingencies of enactment and negotiation.

This book takes a novel approach by bridging the theoretical frameworks from cultural sociology (associated with Jeffrey Alexander and Randall Collins) with theories from economic sociology and the sociology of development. The theoretical syntheses in this book and the discoveries this approach has made possible depart significantly from past research. First, this is one of the few books examining how culture can shield infant industries in national and global markets. Contrary to standard economic expectations, the social significance of cultural traditions protects the sellers from the more venal interests of buyers and distributors. Because the seller and the buyer are not likely to meet again, it would seem that the buyer has an incentive to bargain for the lowest price, yet the buyer is more reluctant to discuss price and talks much more about the traditional techniques of production and the importance of maintaining those traditions. Although the buyer and seller do not have a long-term relationship, the importance of the artisan's long-held tradition seems to restrict opportunism. Likewise, the importance of these traditions for the nation's social identity leads, in some cases, the central government and private-sector individuals to privilege cultural activities by providing material resources and by setting up official barriers to prevent better capitalized outsiders from entering and overtaking the handicraft sector.

In this exploration of how artisans engage in "culture work" to navigate the dangers and opportunities in the global market my approach was informed by past sociological studies. In particular I looked to David Kyle's *Transnational Peasants* (2000) as a model for understanding the diverse outcomes wrought by globalization through a comparative perspective. Kyle found handicraft artisans who had cut out the middleman by traveling back and forth to Western countries to sell their goods directly to consumers. This phenomenon is remarkable because an economically weak group of people used their authentic cultural identity as a means to navigate the global market. While Kyle's study focuses on the new ways that these entrepreneurs were migrating in the age of globalization, his work also glimpsed the dynamic of performance in the marketplace: "The same handicrafts sold by an Otavalan family in native dress in a street fair in San Francisco are more valuable and attract more attention than when they are sold in an ethnic novelty shop in the same neighborhood and are worth less still when sold by a large transnational firm such as Pier One Imports" (Kyle 2000: 205). Not only the artisan's position within the distribution channel (cutting out the middleman) but also the artisan's performance of authenticity (native dress and circumstance) enabled the artisan's successful engagement with the global market. My analysis goes beyond Kyle's in my use of Zelizer circuits and interaction ritual chains to understand how the performance of authenticity works well in some situations but not others. Kyle's analysis does not account for how the power and prestige of artisans varies from one situation to another.

A more obvious difference between my work and Kyle's is the nature of the artisans we study. Not all artisans can be transnational migrants, nor do they have to be in order to take advantage of cultural commerce in the global market. International tourists act as cultural brokers. For cultural commodities whose authenticity grants the good its social and economic value, cross-cultural brokers themselves become part of the package; they give the buyers the right cues for understanding the authenticity of the good in the act of discussion, negotiation, and sale. Philip Curtin (1984), an economic historian, reminds us that foreign merchants spread across the globe and act as cross-cultural brokers for the trade of goods. The trade diasporas generated by the merchants' social ties have been spurred by the rise of the great empires throughout history, creating the impetus for new contacts and the demand for more and different forms of consumption.

Since the publication of Kyle's book, the fields of economic sociology that Kyle directly addresses and the sociology of culture to which he indirectly alludes have emerged as lively arenas for examining the roles that identity and authenticity play in obtaining power—sometimes derived from the deference that others extend but always based on the performances that take place—within commercial encounters. Cultural sociologists such as Randall Collins and Jeffrey Alexander remind us that the myths that enable (ritual) performance and that are re-created through it can shift the balance of power in an interaction. And Michael Schudson (1989) pushes us to go beyond the question of whether culture might create advantages for some and disadvantages for others and to ask how culture creates these differences. I have more explicitly incorporated these insights from cultural sociology and have benefited from the mounting theoretical clarity enjoyed in both cultural and economic sociology. I discuss these theoretical perspectives in much greater depth in the chapters that follow.

Aside from these theoretical innovations, this study advances a methodological innovation. Comparative studies have been largely executed in the same geographic region of the world. The underlying assumption of such studies is either that the handicraft entrepreneurs around the world face similar constraints to succeeding in the global market or that general patterns cannot be discerned across local handicraft economies. By contrast, my comparative research design enables me to examine the experiences of handicraft artisans in two dramatically different parts of the world. To the extent that these findings confirm the importance of aura, outside actors, and the community's social networks in such diverse cultural contexts, the findings hold greater theoretical importance than they would if the fieldwork had been limited to a single region.

The comparison between Thailand and Costa Rica enables me to consider the historical circumstances peculiar to each region that might explain how participation in national and global markets affects the ways in which the artisans understand, adapt, and utilize their cultural traditions. By separating idiosyncratic circumstances from more nearly universal factors, the study can clarify the sociological processes that contribute to and limit success in both countries, thereby appealing to readers more concerned with the theoretical questions posed than with the national, regional, or community specifics (Portes, Dore-Cabral, and Landolt 1997; Przeworski and Teune 1970; Ragin 1987).

How can artisans making the same thing encounter such different fates in the global market, in spite of the fact that they come from the same region of the same country? How do artisans in one part of the world find themselves in near obscurity relative to those in other parts of the world?

THE STUDY SITES

From one side of the world to the other, I researched handicraft artisans closely tied to the global economy through tourism. Both Costa Rica and Thailand share the rank of the number one recipient of tourist expenditures in their respective regions. The World Tourism Organization publishes information on tourist expenditures by country. Figure 1.1 shows the growing importance of tourism in Central America, and Figure 1.2 shows the same information for Southeast Asia. Costa Rica receives more than twice as much as Panama from tourism expenditure. Trailing all the Central American countries pictured here is Nicaragua, no

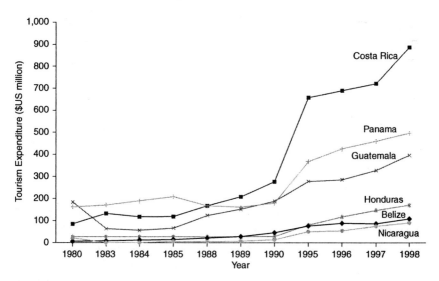

Figure 1.1. Tourism Expenditure in Selected Central American Countries, 1980–1998. *Source:* World Tourism Organization.

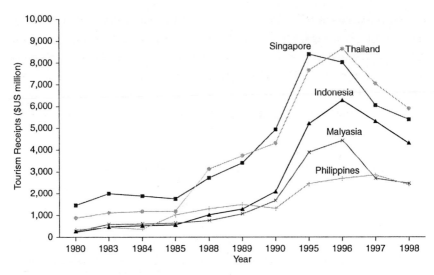

Figure 1.2. Tourism Expenditure in Selected Southeast Asian Countries, 1980–1998.
Source: World Tourism Organization.

doubt because of its history of political instability and violence. Just as Costa Rica leads the Central American countries, Thailand leads the Southeast Asian ones (World Tourism Organization 2005). In 2001 tourism revenues accounted for 7.8 percent of GDP in Costa Rica and 5.8 percent of GDP in Thailand. These figures indicate the extent to which Costa Rica and Thailand are tied to global tourism.

In handicrafts, Costa Rica differs from Thailand. Whereas the handicraft sector in Costa Rica does not find itself represented in the nation-state's economic development strategy, the Thai state has recently focused considerable energies in promoting handicraft production as a means to replace the jobs lost as factories have migrated to China to take advantage of the lower costs of production there. The attention given to handicrafts by the Thai prime minister, Thaksin Shinawatra, and the amount of money given to villages to promote the production and export of the cottage industry products (US$1.58 billion) mark Thailand as an activist state.

A brief look at how artisans' products from Thailand fare in global markets indicates the privileged place of Thai cultural commodities worldwide. The World Trade Organization and the United Nations Conference on Trade and Development jointly maintain a database of cultural commodity export flows for ninety-eight countries. In 2003 Thailand exported US$377 million in furniture made by artisans. Brazil's export totals were US$235 million and Mexico's were US$198 million. Italy and China account for nearly a quarter of the world's export totals. Interestingly, no African or Arab country accounts for 1 percent of world trade or higher in this sector. In the African region of the world, South Africa registers just under 1 percent of the world's export totals for wooden furniture at US$71 million, just behind Portugal (US$78.8 million) and Belarus (US$82.5 million), which find themselves represented among the key players in the sector. (Figure 1.3) In the export of ceramics, Thailand ranked fourth in

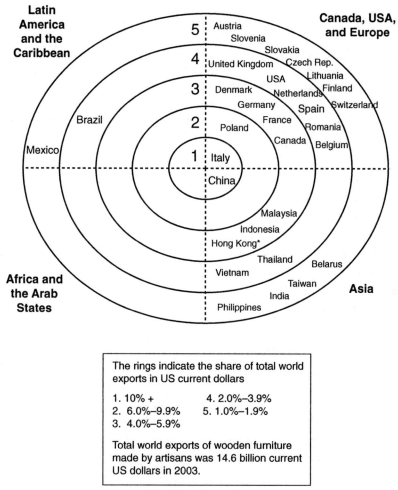

The rings indicate the share of total world exports in US current dollars

1. 10% +   4. 2.0%–3.9%
2. 6.0%–9.9%   5. 1.0%–1.9%
3. 4.0%–5.9%

Total world exports of wooden furniture made by artisans was 14.6 billion current US dollars in 2003.

*Note: Hong Kong re-exports

Figure 1.3. The Regional Structure of Wooden Furniture Exports Made by Artisans in 2003. *Source:* Product Map, International Trade Centre UNCTAD/WTO (www.p-maps.org/Client/index.aspx)

the world in 2003. Thailand's ceramics exports totaled US$137 million; Italy, $149 million; Portugal, $157 million; and the United Kingdom, $1.4 billion. China trailed at number five with $102 million. Mexico stood at $19 million and Brazil $17 million. (Figure 1.4) And in the export of artificial flowers, Hong Kong ($742 million in re-exports) and China ($357 million) led the list. Thailand ranked third in the world at $25 million. Mexico fell to the bottom of the top quartile with just over a million, and Spain performed only slightly better at $5.6 million. (Figure 1.4)

Thailand and Costa Rica have other obvious differences. The Republic of Costa Rica is a small country located in the middle of Central America. (Figure 1.5) To its north is Nicaragua; southwest, the Pacific Ocean; northeast, the Caribbean Sea; and southeast, Panama. The population totals 4.3 million; life expectancy in 2005 was 75 years for males and 80 for females. Having been colonized by the Spanish, the country realized independence in 1821. The official language is Spanish, and the official religion is Roman Catholicism. Since 1949 Costa Rica has been a unitary multiparty republic with one legislative house. Every four years, there is a vigorous election that thus far has resulted each time

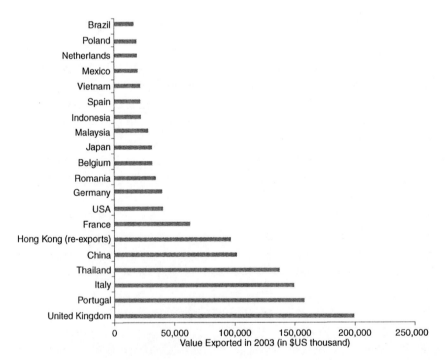

Figure 1.4. Ceramics Exported from Countries in the Top Quintile in 2003 (World Total $US 1.4 billion). *Source:* TradeMap (www.trademap.net.mds/world_trade.htm;Product).

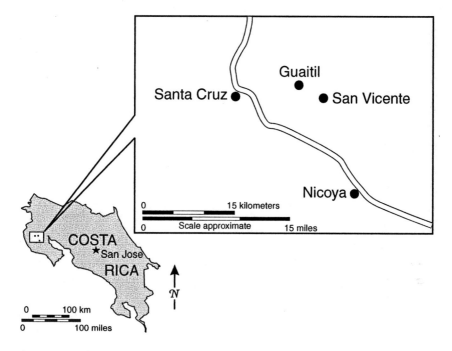

Figure 1.5. Northwest Costa Rica

in a change of the ruling party. In the agricultural sector Costa Rica exports coffee and bananas. In the manufacturing sector, it exports clothing and cloth, medicines, and electrical appliances. Manufacturing for domestic consumption includes food and beverage processing and textile, shoe, and furniture making. Costa Rica's GDP was US$20 billion in 2005.

By contrast, the Kingdom of Thailand is a medium-sized country located in the middle of mainland Southeast Asia. (Figure 1.6) Along its western border is Myanmar (Burma), to its north and northeast is the People's Republic of Laos, to its eastern border is Cambodia, and to the south is Malaysia. The population totaled 65.1 million in 2005, with a life expectancy of 67 years for males and 73 years for females. Thailand is a constitutional monarchy; the prime minister dissolves parliament or faces a no-confidence vote every one to two years. Having acquired a new constitution in 1997, Thailand is considered a stable democracy; it has had some form of constitutional democracy since 1932 (with a military-coup attempt from time to time). However, Thailand means "land of the free" and its people distinguish themselves from their neighbors because they have never been colonized. The official language is Thai, and the official religion is Buddhism. In the agricultural sector Thailand exports rice, cassava,

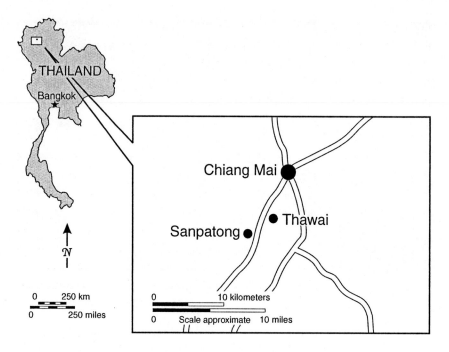

Figure 1.6. Northern Thailand

and tin. In the manufacturing sector, it exports clothing, canned goods, and electrical circuits. The GDP was US$178.6 billion in 2005, more than eight times the GDP of Costa Rica. With all of these differences, the countries share some significant similarities. Namely, they are middle-income democracies that excel all other countries in their respective regions for the percentage of their GDP that comes from the travel and tourism sector. These similarities and differences make the cases of the two countries relevant for understanding how the global market for handicrafts, along with international tourism, has affected local economic development in two different regions of the world, in two different language and religious groups, and in states with very different attitudes toward the cultures that these handicraft artisans represent.

THE ROADMAP

To understand the fate of local artisans and their traditions in global markets, I focus on three general processes characterizing globalization: forces, flows, and frames (the Three Fs of globalization). These processes recast Michael

Burawoy (2000) and his collaborators' ethnographic investigations of forces, imaginations, and connections. The first (forces) refers to large-scale economic processes to which artisans respond. Macroeconomic changes in the economy spur reactions from the nation-states, private industry, and private citizens in their efforts to fend off threats and to take advantage of opportunities. The second (flows) emphasizes the interactions among actors and institutions as well as their exchanges of information, materials, money, and status. Circumspect investigations of these flows unveil the third dimension of globalization (frames): how actors and institutions make sense of their maneuvers and with what consequences. I ask how the aura of authentic local traditions becomes amplified or diminished by government policies or by other external interventions and how the demand environment abroad for different cultural traditions limits the artisan's capacity to "go global." The three countervailing forces of globalization make it possible for differently situated artisans to make culture while also making work. The circumstances facilitating the intermingling of culture and commerce animate the chapters that follow.

CHAPTER TWO

The Frames and Forces of the Market

From our encounters with artisans from Thailand and Costa Rica we see that more than individual talent, good luck, and the dedication to honing traditional practices is involved in explaining the different outcomes that artisans experience in the same country. As far as differences between the countries are concerned, international tourists might say, Thai artisans do better in global markets than Costa Rican artisans because Thailand has more stocks of cultural heritage than Costa Rica does. Thailand lays claim to uninterrupted cultural traditions, free from the stain of colonialism, but Costa Rica seems to have been a virgin wilderness before the Spaniards seized hold of it. One crafts broker from the United States remarked that buying crafts and furniture from Chiang Mai was nearly risk-free because his pool of clients had a pretty good idea about what to expect from "Amazing Thailand": the land of gold-roofed Buddhist temples, the spectacle of saffron robes suspended in morning mist (a barely perceptible procession of cloaked monks carrying silver alms bowls), white sand beaches, teakwood furniture, hill-tribe and local crafts, and sex on sale.

By contrast, in surveys of international tourists to Costa Rica, it becomes clear that most people know, before ever arriving, that Costa Rica is a great place for lounging on the beach and for visiting the jungle, but ask what they know about Costa Rica's indigenous cultures and expect to draw a blank, because, it is vaguely believed, the indigenous groups reside in those other countries around there—you know, Guatemala and places like that. In Costa Rica, one finds the lush jungle, the carefully manicured coffee plantations cooperatively owned by small-scale landowners, brilliantly plumaged parrots, oversized butterflies, clean seas, and an even cleaner social conscience. (They abolished their military to invest in people rather than bloodshed.) As the visitor takes home a bag of Costa Rican coffee or pictures of her jungle trek, she confirms what everyone already believed to be true about what Costa Rica is and, by extension, what the country and its citizens produce.

This chapter focuses on how these public expectations about a country affect (and are affected by) the stances that artisans, brokers, governments, and other actors take with regard to the production of cultural commodities such as handicrafts. The way that brokers and consumers make sense of their handicraft purchases relies on their patched-together understanding of these public perceptions. When one hears "Made in Thailand," one conjures a different set of images about the types of products and the character of its producers than one does upon hearing "Made in Costa Rica." These images connect the item to its country of origin and to similar goods around the world. These images also evoke historical myths, symbols, and practices. The way that one makes sense of the purchase is often a mishmash, as if from a rag drawer: Just as a person pieces together different fragments of cloth from different sources to make a quilt, so too does an observer piece disparate elements together to formulate an account of what something is and why a particular kind of response may be called for (Wuthnow 1996: 95-96). In the handicraft market, buyers stitch together the rationale for purchasing cultural commodities from bits and pieces of history: travel accounts, posters, pamphlets, museum visits, *National Geographic*, the *New York Times* (travel and arts sections), other magazines and newspapers, and direct experience with a place, a person, or a thing. The accumulation of these rags in memory's drawer enable artisans, brokers, and buyers to make sense of what they do, what they sell, and what they buy.

In both these nations, one sees how the country's overall reputation for cultural heritage corresponds, in part, with the comparative advantages that its handicrafts obtain in global markets. Going back to the roots of each country's traditions, one finds that the comparative advantage that Thai artisans enjoy in cultural markets and the comparative disadvantage that the Costa Rican artisans endure do not emerge "naturally." Each country "worked" its reputation for culture according to how the nation-state defined itself and in response to a set of historical contingencies. Frank Dobbin's understanding of how the United States, Britain, and France developed their industrial railroad policies is pertinent to the market for cultural commodities: "History has produced distinct ideas about order and rationality in different nations and modern industrial policies are organized around those ideas" (Dobbin 1994: 2). In Thailand, for example, the imperative to define the national identity emerged in reaction to the threat of colonization, as a response to pressures within the nation-state for social unity and political control, and with concern for the nation's status within the world community of nations. The ideas about national identity that emerged from these histories shaped the state's export promotion policies for handicrafts and the contours of its appeal for international tourism.

The two countries have worked their cultural images, in part, through the identity of their exported products. Thailand's exports justified its freedom from colonization, and Costa Rica's exports affirmed its worthiness to act independently of its colonial master after decolonization. Exports confirmed that not only was Thailand unique among nations (in the exotic items it produced) but also that it was on a par with the European powers in its adaptation of modern practices and in its production of modern commodities for export; therefore, the Thai were in no need of being civilized by outsiders. Costa Rica's export platform tried to eliminate any hint that the country was unique in indigenous exotica. In order to be *en par* with its former colonial master, the country insisted it was as modern in its practices and products as any European nation. To prove itself a member of the global mainstream, Costa Rica was willing to shed indigenous identities and practices for universal (read: white European) ones. These orientations to national identity—one culturally independent, the other assimilated—shaped the opportunities available for the promotion and export of indigenous handicrafts.

As these states developed symbolic boundaries to define their own social identities and to differentiate themselves from the identities of their neighbors and of other outsiders, they created niches for some types of cultural commodities but made other types nearly unthinkable. Cultural objects conforming to the state's self-image were more likely to escape state-imposed restrictions, if not to enjoy state-sponsored supports. By sketching the biographical moments in which these cultural commodities were born, one can understand why some handicraft economies are better able than others to use their cultural traditions effectively in the global crafts market.

A state's promotion of cultural commodity exports (e.g., handicrafts, ethnic food, etc.) resembles an individual engaging in face-work to create and maintain a favorable self image: the state works on the impression that others have of it by putting on a "face" that confirms its favorable self-image. As an actor on the world stage, the state "takes a line" in the international division of labor by portraying itself as possessing a modern (as defined by prestige symbols: high technology exports, industrial production) or traditional economy (as defined by stigma symbols: low technology exports, extractive industries). The state and private-sector agents are not always aware that they too are taking a line. Indeed, the rationale for promoting export in one sector but not another is justified in technical terms. However, Frank Dobbin's study of the railroad promotion policies demonstrates that there are numerous ways to achieve the same sense of technical efficiency in constructing railroads, but the selection of the most appropriate option depends on the shared understandings (the public culture) within the nation. Likewise, an earlier assessment by Jacques Maquet (1993) describes the design of trains produced in the United States, Britain, and France as signs of each country's public culture that also take technical efficiency concerns into account. In short, the shared understandings of a nation-state become refracted in the state's way of seeing which economic policies may be viable, in spite of efficiency and profit considerations.

THICK INSTITUTIONALISM

A symbolic realm of the marketplace exists along with the material reality of macroeconomic forces. Within the realm of symbols and cognitive frameworks, different nation-states have different levels of interest in promoting the export of cultural commodities. By emphasizing the different (and changing) capacities of nation-states to realize these symbolic interests, I am moving away from the "thin" institutionalist approach that offers such commonplace notions as "context matters" and undertaking with thick description to show how context matters. The accumulated knowledge about a country's cultural heritage and the relative status of the country in a global status hierarchy orients the country's definition of situation. Defining cultural resources as valuable (sometimes priceless) nearly makes them so. Definitions of the situation must confront the material reality that allows some actors to support their claims with physical or legal force, if not with monetary persuasion alone. Export strategies of nation-states do not emerge ex nihilo but from their state histories, their bureaucratic capacities, and the alliances of capitalists within each country. More importantly, these seemingly obvious influences on national export strategies demonstrate surprising dynamics, such as public narratives about the nation's history steering bureaucratic capacities and private alliances toward some opportunities in the global marketplace but away from others.

In *Ethnic and Tourist Arts: Cultural Expressions from the Fourth World* (1976), Nelson H. H. Graburn argues that although the world economy made it necessary for local people to commodify their craft traditions as a means for survival, the motivation for economic survival was not the only logic in play. The state selected which products to support based on its own image of the national identity. Take Mexico, for example: "The government concerns include . . . promoting a favorable image of regional Mexico. . . . Mexico has long differentiated itself from European Spain and from other Latin American countries; it has glorified the arts of the conquered civilizations . . . . [and] supports many exhibitions, collections, and museums" (117-18). When the Mexican government proudly supports expressions of *indigenismo*, "that which is Indian and not European" (115), the Mexican government is promoting the country's national image as distinct as possible from that of the European invader, yet such a distinction makes the promotion of Mexico's hybrid identity more durable. In other words, not a mixture of mixtures but a combination of distinct, proud, and long-held traditions distinguishes the Mexican identity. The government uses export incentives as a means to manage the impression that the country has of itself and that outsiders have of it—different but proud of it.

The cultural politics of the state offer a lens through which business people within and outside of the nation-state frame their evaluations of the cultural goods produced therein. Margaret Somers and Fred Block highlight the importance of public narratives in their study of government policies and the principles justifying them: "Every nation has a story—a public narrative it tells to explain its place . . . in the flow of history, to justify its normative principles, to delineate the boundaries of rational political decision-making, and to give meaning to its economic policies and practices" (Somers and Block 2005: 280). I am arguing that these narratives matter for the export strategies of nation-states and their entrepreneurs. In short, the "ideational embeddedness" identified by Somers and Block help us see the social orientation of a government's export promotion policies. At the same time, I am steering away from a facile means-end account of identity and action. Economic development remains at the forefront of policy debates on export promotion, and debates about cultural traditions or about the identity of the nation-state need not be explicit to be implicated in the image management in which the state (sometimes unknowingly) engages. Although government administrations may change and the governing coalition has to appease various elite factions within society, governments nonetheless find themselves responding to an overarching realm of ideas about what the nation represents, and these ideas are reflected in enduring state policies toward the state-sanctioned representatives of national culture.

Some scholars have identified the state's support for cultural commodity exports as an epiphenomenon of a larger political and economic struggle. Shea butter, an indigenous commodity, became popularized through advertisements by The Body Shop and L'Occitane showing Ghanaian and other West African women gathering shea nuts, pulverizing them, and putting the lotion to traditional uses, just as these women have done for generations. In Ghana, this indigenous commodity reflects, in part, former president J. J. Rawlings's attempt to incorporate the regional identity of the north (where shea nuts are gathered) into the national identity, as a response to pressures from economic interests within and outside of the country, and as a means of satisfying the conditions of structural adjustment imposed by the international financial institutions (Chalfin 2004). Likewise, the government's provision of infrastructure and other support for indigenous textile artisans in Otavalo, Ecuador, results from the historical construction of the Otavaleños as the noble Indians worthy of international exposure versus the "dirty Indians" in other parts of the territory best left, as it were, in the dark (Colloredo-Mansfeld 2002; Kyle 2000; Meisch 2002).

That government orientations toward the economy are socially conditioned is well known. In *Economy and Society* ([1922-23] 1978), Max Weber identifies transcendental beliefs (based in cultural traditions or religious belief) and social conventions (collective practices and rituals) as two orienting factors for economic life. Institutionally oriented studies in sociology have demonstrated how collective understandings shape the institutions that, in turn, affect economic outcomes (Biggart and Orrú 1997; Biggart and Guillén 1999; Powell and DiMaggio 1991). Collective understandings about the national identity and the way that exports represent that identity inform the country's cultural tool kit—"symbols, stories, rituals, and world-views, which people may use in varying configurations to solve different kinds of problems" (Swidler 1986: 273). The tool kit shapes the strategies that actors are likely to pursue as well as the manner of pursuit.

Similar to Biggart and Guillén's account of how institutional logics organize industries within a country, I argue that historical events and the understandings that result from them influence "the types, availability, and legitimacy of actors [and symbols]" (Biggart and Guillén 1999: 728) in the economy for cultural commodities. I call these orientations cultural rather than institutional because they depend on shared understandings about one's membership in a group characterized by distinct practices, traditions, and outlooks. The government's cultural orientation affects how it interprets the meanings (sign-vehicles) carried by economic action, such as what it means to export cultural commodities depicting courtly traditions rather than (or in conjunction with) indigenous commodities evoking images of the savannah or the wild jungle. Cultural orientations reflect the response of the nation-state to the society of world opinion (Meyer, Boli, Thomas, and Ramírez 1997), the response of world society to the nation's dramaturgical performance, and the adjustments made by the image management team of the nation-state in response to how the performance is being taken (Goffman 1959).

The nation-state's cultural orientation influences the scripts the relevant government agencies and the country's capitalists will select for enactment. The collective understandings within the nation-state about its own social identity compared with the social identities of other nation-states have shaped commercial opportunities for handicrafts and other local products in Ecuador (Kyle 2000; Colloredo-Mansfeld 2002; Meisch 2002); Mexico (Carruthers 2001; Cohen 1998; García Canclini 1990); Guatemala (Little 2002; Pérez-Sáinz 1997; Pérez-Sáinz and Andrade-Eekhoff 2003); Indonesia (Alexander and Alexander 2000; Causey 2003); Mali (Rovine 2001); Ghana and West Africa (Chalfin 2004; Terrio 1996); Nigeria (Allen 1983); Costa Rica (Wherry 2006); throughout Central America; and around the globe.

Cultural orientation conditions the likelihood that a country's capitalists will pursue opportunities in the global handicraft market. In other words, it is not enough to possess stocks of symbolic capital; the capitalist inherits a collective understanding (orientation) of the uses (appropriation) to which different types of symbolic capital ought to be put. It is not only that former agricultural workers are pushed out of farm, factory, and government employment while being pulled into handicraft production and tourist services, but it is also that both the workers and the capitalists "see" (e.g., Scott 1998) the production of some types of cultural commodities as a means to protect cultural traditions and to validate a favorable cultural identity for themselves as a nation. There is a deep structure of inequality in the relative social statuses of different nation-states based on the interstate comparison of prestige and stigma symbols. Historians have identified the status hierarchies at the world's fairs (Breckenridge 1989; Mitchell 1989; Rydell, Gwinn, and Gilbert 1994), and a recent study of foreign direct investment decisions suggests that stigma and prestige symbols may trump objective economic indicators for Western capitalists choosing among different countries to select for investment (Bandelj 2002). This enduring set of status perceptions orients the course of the country's economic development. These perceptions sometimes divert economic development energies away from those stocks of symbolic capital easily appropriated but socially stigmatized. At other times, these perceptions intensify the state's motivation to support material culture and to protect cultural traditions in order to promote both economic development and a favorable social identity for the nation-state.

CULTURAL FRAMES AND STRUCTURAL FORCES

Material gain is not enough for most individuals making decisions about how best to make money. A set of principles guides these individuals, indicating what "ought" and what "ought not" be done. The sense of right and wrong is so ingrained in the individual that there is no need to articulate the principle. Indeed, when a conflict emerges, the actors involved articulate these principles through the constraints they place on their own actions and through the abhorrence they express at the actions of others. These norms are expressed in ritual, in law, and in everyday behavior. In cultural markets, they impinge directly on what entrepreneurs "see" as profitable opportunities and what entrepreneurs might not consider at all or might consider abhorrent. For example, countries with an excess of orphaned children might not actively promote the sale of these children in the global market. A country whose citizens believe that abortion is murder might prohibit the medical practice, even though there is a large demand for and supply of the service. Even the donation of blood might be organized commercially in some countries but not in others (e.g., Healy 2006), based on the value orientation of the society.

Values and the normative constraints on behavior congeal in the roles that countries and their representatives play. These roles are themselves bundles of norms, indicating what some countries and individuals ought to do and how they ought to do it. The country's perceived role might make that country more attractive to investors, all other things being equal. It is said that everybody knows that country X is good at Y things and rich in Z traditions. These taken-for-granted notions affect how both demanders and suppliers evaluate objective opportunities for gain. In the sociology of work, one sees these different evaluations occurring when employers assess the performance of employees. The employee's mistake is usually considered to be a fluke if the employee is a member of the in-group (white male), but the mistake is attributed the inherent characteristics of the employee if the employee is not a member of the in-group. Barbara Reskin writes: "We automatically pursue, prefer, and remember 'evidence' that supports our stereotypes (including untrue 'evidence') and ignore, discount, and forget facts that challenge them" (Reskin 2002: 223). These collective representations of a group prime the buyer to give the benefit of the doubt to some and to exercise extreme caution with others. Similarly, Roger Waldinger and Michael Lichter (2003) find in their interviews with over two hundred employers in Los Angeles that employers are looking for workers who have the right set of nonobjective characteristics. In other words, for some types of jobs, certain types of people are good at dealing with people but certain other types of people have "too much attitude" to be effective workers. Some people don't mind doing dirty jobs, some employers said, because it's what they're used to, back home.

I highlight these findings because I will focus on how importers take objective information into account and how other indicators of cultural heritage, skill, and advantage are taken for granted in the decision makers' minds. In other words, the structure of inequality in the demand market exists before the individual suppliers come into play to contend with that demand market. We begin to see this with Nina Bandelj's discovery that there is a great deal of variation in where foreign direct investment flows in central Eastern Europe, even though the objective criteria for investment would predict much less variation in the region. She finds that the investor's familiarity with and affinity for different cultures in the region account for their selection of investment sites.

I argue that the public narratives that cling to a country's identity affect what types of cultural commodities the country's entrepreneurs produce and the level of material support that the government extends in promoting these exports. Either through cultural matching and elective affinities (Bandelj 2002) or through the suspension of disbelief about things that everyone should know, social processes shape what cultural commodities a country's entrepreneurs can export, and with what ease. We will explore these processes by first witnessing each of our case countries engage in the arts of image management at the world's fair, with an eye toward what (social identity) roles these countries play in the global community. Then we will see how geopolitical issues and changes in the macroeconomic environment further shape the public's understanding of what it means to be Thai or Costa Rican and what types of goods and services might make the most sense to government agencies selecting which economic sectors to encourage and which cultural endeavors to promote to local producers and exporters as well as their potential consumers. It is this sense-making about the meanings invested in physical locations that must complement structural analyses of national economic development.

FRAMING CULTURAL CHARACTERISTICS: WHAT MAKES SENSE AT THE WORLD'S FAIR

World's fairs offer strategic research materials for understanding how countries get framed as being rich (or poor) in particular cultural traditions, since such representations are the manifest function of the fairs. World's fairs began in 1851 when Great Britain at the height of its industrial revolution hosted the event in London's Crystal Palace, designed by Sir Joseph Paxton, reportedly in ten days, and constructed in six months. With over a million feet of glass slated across iron limbs, the Crystal Palace conveyed the power of the great colonizers of the West and the cultural differences existing between the West and the rest of the world. Some 6.2 million visitors came to the fair to witness its 13,000 exhibitions. The Western countries boasted of their technological progress; the non-Western countries entertained Western spectators with their careful reconstructions of disorderly bazaars where even the dirt, peeling plaster, and scuff marks on the originals reappeared vibrantly on the copies. Donkeys and their stink along with half-clad villagers donning exotica in their supposed simplicity offered definitive proof of the new world order in which the race to economic and social progress belonged to the naturally gifted and the strong (Breckenridge 1989; Karp and Lavine 1991; Mitchell 1989).

We can see how, starting in the mid-nineteenth century, Thailand became branded as a source of cultural goods and how the country's export agency and local entrepreneurs now have built on that existing cultural resource to compete in global markets; by contrast, we can see how Costa Rica became branded as a bland, Western country, high in human and social rights (as any civilized country ought to be) but low in the exotica associated with the savage, barbaric, and half-civilized. The irony of the Costa Rican case is that the powerful Western nation-states wanted to mark the Costa Ricans with exotic and "primitive" designations, but the Costa Rican government resisted being distinguished with such stigma and hid some of its cultural resources from view. The contrast between the Thai and the Costa Rican cases demonstrates that a country needs to have both the raw cultural materials and the desire to be portrayed as a particular stock cultural character for the international community to designate the country as an authentic source for cultural goods.

Thailand

In Thailand, the monarchy understood that a global hierarchy existed among nations, based not only on economic wealth and military power but also on scientific progress and cultural richness. The leaders of Siam reasoned that they could influence how the world saw the nation's position within the global hierarchy, and perhaps move upwards in that hierarchy, by participating strategically in the world's fairs. The Thais entered the world's fair in order to do symbolic battle. They acted as if the fair offered a tournament in which the "savage," "barbaric," "civilized," and "enlightened" represented the four stages of cultural development (Rydell, Gwinn, and Gilbert 1994: 160-61). As much as possible, Thailand wanted outsiders to consider their kingdom as civilized, but to accomplish this goal the Thais had to distinguish themselves from the barbaric and the savage. They had to tantalize outsiders with Thailand's exotica while also gaining recognition for Thailand's scientific progress and its similarities with the "civilized" world.

To walk this fine line between the exotic and the scientifically advanced, Thailand participated in world's fairs even when the state could not easily afford it. The Kingdom of Siam did not shy away from sending "a village, people, and a dancing troupe" whenever the funds could be spared: "In most cases, Siam displayed crafts, arts, and natural products from all over the country. . . . On the other hand, Siam usually took the opportunity to show its technological progress in such areas as postal and telegraphic services, railways, or the first modern map made in Siam" (Thongchai 2000: 541). Although the fair offered the colonizing powers justification for subjugating "savage" peoples, the Thai proudly participated because they had never been colonized and had achieved economic and social development on their own terms, marking them as a civilized country. Thongchai, a prominent historian of Thailand, notes that the Thai government persisted in presenting Thailand as constituting a multidimensional cultural character, even though some Westerners did not understand (or perhaps even respect) Thailand's efforts to designate itself also as scientifically progressive: "The organizers of the fair at St. Louis in 1904 were obviously disappointed at the exhibit that displayed technological progress in Siam because the exhibit did not show the 'national characteristics' of Siam. . . . Presumably, that is to say, Siam should have been an exotic, half-civilized country on the progressing course" [Thongchai 2000: 541-42]. Perhaps Siam did not win any immediate symbolic battles in transforming the country's image in the West, yet Thailand's participation in such international conventions served local political interests. It affirmed for the Thais themselves that their country occupied its rightful place among the civilized countries of the world community.

To guard their status as a civilized country, the Thai delegation remained vigilant over the location of its exhibit relative to other types of nation-states at the world's fairs. Usually, Thailand found itself among the independent countries of the Far East, but sometimes it exhibited alongside "the exotic, the half-civilized, or the inferior civilizations, such as among Haiti and the Caribbean islands at the Chicago Fair" (Thongchai 2000: 541). Only when the Paris fair organizers assigned Thailand a place among the colonies in 1900 did the Thai delegation insist on being moved. And moved it was to a place among the non-colonized nations (ibid. 541). That Thailand was *never* colonized, there could be no confusion.

Costa Rica

By contrast, Christopher Columbus's "discovery" of the Americas marked the Costa Ricans and their neighbors with a designation of the formerly colonized. In the cultural arena of world's fairs, this designation found emphasis. In 1893 the world's fair commemorated Columbus's discovery, and at the Columbian Historical Exhibition, signs of the premodern were in abundance. The archeological artifacts on display included works from Mexico, Guatemala, Nicaragua, Costa Rica, Columbia, Ecuador, and Peru. For today's international traveler, the inclusion of Costa Rica as a major contributor of archeological artifacts might come as a surprise, since those cultural contributions have been largely erased in public discussions about Costa Rica. However, one should keep in mind that Costa Rica contributed several thousand pieces to the exhibition and that the experts at the fair praised the Costa Rican exhibition for being well organized and for being original and tasteful in its ornamentation (Hough 1893; Peralta and Alfaro 1893).

The fact that Costa Rica's exhibition of ceramics and other cultural objects attracted so much attention highlights the insufficiency of having stocks of cultural capital as a condition for participating in global cultural markets, but it, also prompts the question: What cultural traditions did these objects represent? Many Costa Rican archeological artifacts come from the Chorotega, an indigenous people who settled in the Nicoya Peninsula of northwest Costa Rica (Scott 1999). The artifacts of the Chorotega have strong family resemblances with both the Olmec (Lowe 1989; Sharer 1989; Soustelle 1984) and the Maya (Lines 1978). However, it is believed that the Chorotega were neither a peripheral element of the Olmec nor an outpost of the Maya. Instead, the Chorotega in what is now northwest Costa Rica occupied a lively trading zone between the Olmec and the Maya where neither of the large empires dominated (Pohorilenko 1981).

The description of northwest Costa Rica as a trading zone where no one group dominated emphasizes Nicoya's contested place within Mesoamerica. Based on his analysis of fifteen pre-Columbian artifacts found in Costa Rica, Anatole Pohorilenko (1981: 310-11) argues that "the presence of Olmec-related material found in Costa Rica does not warrant the incorporation of the Nicoya Peninsula within the Mesoamerican cultural sphere." Pohorilenko adds that some of the Olmec pieces found their way into Costa Rica through trade with the Maya and that some of the Olmec-style glyphs became incorporated into Costa Rican artifacts before the arrival of the Olmec. Costa Rica remains a contested cultural space in the periphery of Mesoamerica (Creamer 1987). To climb out of the periphery of the world system, the Costa Rica state obscured these indigenous contributions to the national identity and thereby disabled handicraft artisans and others who might have benefited from the market for ethnic commodities. Those constructing the Costa Rican nation wanted to belong to the European cultural sphere and measured themselves by European cultural standards. What Aníbal Quijano calls the "coloniality of power" manifests itself in the Costa Rican case, as the nation builders continued the colonial cultural and social matrices of power even after formal independence (Quijano 2000). In short, the cultural politics of Costa Rica de-emphasized indigenous culture, while the cultural politics of Thailand made the distinguishing exotica integral components of the nation-state's identity.

POLITICAL FORCES

The cultural politics of nation-states cannot be understood without reference to the larger geopolitical challenges confronting them. As the country's leaders and the government's bureaucratic agencies forge their public narratives about the national character and as they offer material support to operations confirming those narratives, these leaders and agencies also navigate broader geopolitical threats. To be or not to be colonized by Western powers and to be or not to be recognized as a member of the civilized set are the political concerns that give emphasis to the cultural politics of the state. I contrast these concerns in Thailand and Costa Rica, whose "national images" as enacted on the global stage served both expressive and instrumental ends.

Thailand

The national image of Thailand can be traced, in part, to its success in never being colonized and to the embodiment of the nation's cultural heritage in the benevolent and widely respected Thai monarchy (Thongchai 2000). Since its founding in A.D. 1257, the Kingdom of Siam (Thailand) has never been colonized, and Thai politicians sprinkle references to this fact in their speeches, as do tour guides in their tours. At the train station and in the movie theater, the national obsession with freedom takes the form of song: government buildings broadcast the national anthem daily over loudspeakers, and movie theaters play the national anthem while paying homage to the king. Before the feature presentation begins, the theater audience stands to attention and remains silent as the anthem proclaims (in Thai with English subtitles) that the Thai are a free people willing to sacrifice anything to stay that way.

The Thai have much to defend. According to the travel lore, the territory abounds in natural resources, nearly robbing labor of its toil. For centuries visitors to the territory have remarked upon the country's fecundity: "During his eighteenth-century sojourn there, Captain Alexander Hamilton . . . elaborated: 'The river abounds in many species of excellent fish, which plentifully indulge the inhabitants, and make them indolent and lazy, and consequently proud, superstitious and wanton' [1811]. . . . Similarly, the French naturalist Henri Mouhot wrote that 'bountiful nature, that second mother, treats them as her spoilt children and does all for them' [1864]. . . . The Norwegian naturalist Carl Bock observed that the northern Thai were 'naturally lazy, and, with a fertile soil which provides them with all the necessities of life without any appreciable effort on their part, their indolence is encouraged' [1884]" (Bowie 1992: 799). In the minds of the colonial powers, much had been given to the Thais by Mother Nature; by the same token, much should have been required.

Published reports indicate that the colonial powers coveted the natives' "underutilized" resources. The Portuguese traveler Fernão Pinto regarded the possession of Siam to be far more valuable than all of Portugal's estates in India. And the British explorer Francis Edward Younghusband considered Siam to be a goldmine, an Eldorado waiting for an "enterprising and energetic nation" to take possession of it (Bowie 1992: 799). The only way to harness these natural resources, the agents of the colonial powers reasoned, was to subjugate the Thais. In their quest to conquer the Kingdom of Siam, the colonial powers encountered a collective action problem, in that each pursued its own interest, creating a deadlock. With the French holding the territories in Indo-China (east of Siam) and Laos (to the north), but the English in Burma (to the west) and in the Malay Peninsula (to the south), the Dutch further south in Indonesia, and the English further west in India, too many unrelated actors crowded the scene. The king of Siam could play one colonial power against the other in trade negotiations and could placate them by ceding parcels of land on occasion. Strategically located in the center of mainland Southeast Asia at the confluence of these colonial powers, Siam could be assured that no one country would attempt to seize the kingdom (Thongchai 1994; Warr 1993; Wyatt 2003).

With unilateral military action too costly and unpredictable, the colonial powers resorted to cultural justifications for extending their territories into Siam.

The French system of the protectorate meant that in territories where ethnic Laotians lived, they enjoyed the protection of the French state. Therefore, if large groups of French (ethnic Lao) lived in northeastern Siam, those groups and the territories they occupied fell under the protection of the French. With most of the residents of the northeast claiming Lao ethnicity, the Thai state had to define what it means to be Thai and had to extend that definition to those threatened territories. The Thai kings realized that to maintain their territorial integrity, they would have to mark their subjects as *culturally* distinct from the colonial subjects in nearby countries. Colonial incursions required the peoples of Southeast Asia to put aside their differences and to consider themselves as a group sharing a common way of life, facing a common adversary. King Chulalongkorn (r. 1868-1910) expressed this sentiment to his representative commissioner in Luang Prabang in 1888: "We must . . . describ[e] the fact that the Thai and Lao belong to the same soil. . . . France is merely an alien who looks down on the Lao race as savage. Whatever the French do to please the rulers of Luang Phrabang is merely bait on a hook. . . . Although the Lao people habitually regard Lao as We and Thai as They when only the two peoples are considered, comparing the Thai and the French, however, it would be natural that they regard the Thai as We and the French as They" (quoted in Thongchai 1994: 102). Developing standard definitions of what it means to be Thai became a question of territorial survival (Pasuk and Baker 1995: 233).

Before the 1890s, the territories in the periphery of Siam held names that corresponded with their ethnic affiliations. The Lao, the Khmer, the Malay, and the Khaek states did possess the same characteristics of the "Thai race" until colonial penetration made these ethnic distinctions a danger to the survival of Siam. At a public dinner in 1902, the Bangkok commissioner in Lampang announced: "The distinction between Siamese and Lao no longer exists—we are all subjects of His Majesty [the Thai king]" (cited in Pasuk and Baker 1995: 234). The absolutist Thai state became the tie that binds. However, in the 1950s there could be no confusion between the modernizing, market-loving Thais and their backward, communist-sympathizing neighbors. The military-led government of the period secured Thailand this distinction by imposing mandates on how Thais should behave and what they should wear, especially in the presence of foreigners. By the time of Prime Minister Sarit's rule, the state outlawed pedicabs because they represented a premodern era. Moreover, the army-sponsored radio stations would instruct the Thai citizens daily in the virtues of cleanliness and orderliness. Men were to kiss their wives good-bye in the morning. People were to greet one another with "hello" instead of "Where are you going?" Visitors to government buildings were to wear Western-style clothing rather than the now-outlawed traditional dress. In short, Sarit visibly revived the push from the old era (*samai gon,* literally the period that is past) to the new one (*samai mai,* literally the new period) (Wyatt 1984: 280-81).

Just as transportation, greetings, and dress had to be transformed, so too did the national economic structure. Economic development and social protection became part of the state's way of promoting modernity and of justifying its authority. Under the authoritarian rule of Sarit, development, modernization, and democracy came to mean that the government was responsive to the needs and aspirations of the population. Sarit used the spoils of development to justify his rule. He also deployed the symbol of the king as justification for authoritarianism. Like a father, the king and the government cared for the citizenry: "Sarit made a deliberate attempt to fit the traditional Thai image of a paternal ruler— pho muang—and found a Thai term (phattana) for the ideology of capitalist development. . . . He won approval as a capable ruler, and his notions of development 'captured the fancy of the public'" (Pasuk 1980: 445). Evidence of this care was presented in "progress," "development," and clear progression from "samai gon" to "samai mai."

Although the Thai state began moving away from the primitive and exotica in its modernizing push, those primal elements remained in the country, waiting merely to be activated. More importantly, the Thai monarchy actively promoted courtly craft traditions and local craft practices as legitimate and respectable ways of affirming Thai identity (Peleggi 2002; Van Esterik 2000). Thailand's uncolonized history gave the Thais cultural continuity with their past. Finally, the national preoccupation with culture led the state to establish its legitimacy through its capacity to provide social protections and to promote economic development.

Costa Rica

Although geopolitical pressures led to emphasizing the exotic along with the modern in Thai identity, similar pressures had the opposite effect in Costa Rica. The colonial period there began in the early 1500s, after Columbus landed on its Caribbean coast in 1502. In 1522 Captain Gil González called this region "the rich coast" because he believed that great gold deposits awaited exploitation; in 1539 the Spaniards officially named the territory Costa Rica (Biesanz, Biesanz, and Biesanz 1999). Ironically, Costa Rica did not enjoy the natural abundance of gold and other natural materials that its neighbors offered for extraction. As the "poorest" of the Spanish holdings in Central America and the territory with the lowest stocks of "naturally" endowed wealth, Costa Rica encountered less coercion from the Spaniards relative to the forced extraction experienced in other parts of the Central American isthmus. The country's supposed misnomer gave the country a great deal of autonomy and a historical claim to being unlike its neighbors.

The general pattern of colonization was the *encomienda*. The Spanish crown would assign a designated group of indigenous inhabitants to a colonizing landowner, who was responsible for teaching them the Castellan language, converting them to Catholicism, and protecting them from the sin of idleness. The indigenous inhabitants had to learn the importance of productive work, checking in with their patrons for an assigned number of workdays per year. Such a system worked well where large, docile pockets of indigenous people could be found (Yashar 1997). This was not the case for Costa Rica (Edelman and Seligson 1994; Kincaid 1989; Yashar 1997).

Unlike the rest of Central and Latin America, this settlement did not encounter large, docile indigenous populations to subdue, nor did they find large deposits of gold. Because labor was scarce and land plentiful, the society was not highly stratified. The landed elite and the merchant classes could not practice occupational differentiation among themselves because they lacked a large labor supply. Government officials and landowners assumed mercantile roles in multiplex networks of exchange. A German businessman traveling through Costa Rica in the 1850s, Wilhelm Marr, reported: "On market day the president of the Republic does not disdain to cut some yards of gingham for a peasant; the Treasury Minister becomes hoarse in his efforts to prove to a purchaser that he ought to buy a miserable glass. Behind the improvised counters there are Officials, captains, and Majors selling nails, feather cutters, and scissors; Magistrates of the Supreme Court sell cotton socks; lawyers find buyers for underwear" (quoted in Wilson 1998: 16). Furthermore, with too few workers, large labor estates could not be maintained. Agricultural production occurred on smaller plots of land, precluding the concentration of landownership into the hands of a few, politically powerful families. With the means of survival more evenly distributed in the society, the masses attenuated oligarchic domination, and the seeds of democracy found more fertile beginnings.

The "agrarian democracy thesis" refers to the notion that agrarian egalitarianism laid the foundations for democracy in Costa Rica. According to the thesis, political participation is easier in Costa Rica compared to other Latin American countries because wealth was more evenly distributed in the population during colonization, giving more of its citizens a material stake in the well-being of the polity. The same land distribution patterns created a more civil, co-operative set of citizens. For example, to the extent that land was more evenly distributed, large plantations could not define the economic landscape. In or-der to realize economies of scale, medium-sized and larger farms had to co-operate with one another and with small landholders. The rural, modest, cooperating folk therefore became the dominant image of the Costa Rican char-acter, and it has made its way into the handicrafts of Costa Rica. The most suc-cessful community of handicraft artisans resides in the Central Valley in the town of Sarchí, but they are not associated with Costa Rica's indigenous past. Quite the contrary, these artisans produce brightly colored oxcarts and other folks arts that represent the agrarian democracy thesis. The oxcarts were used to transport coffee and other agricultural products and the bright colors reflect the lush flora inspiring these hard-working people in their land of plenty.

These images are powerful in that they validate the choices that artisans make and the policies that the state chooses to deploy in support of these artisans (and in support of itself through their success). The historical validity of the myth matters less than the belief and its visible manifestation in everyday life. Marc Edelman and Mitchell A. Seligson (1994) argue, however, that the agrarian democracy thesis overstates the initial conditions found in Costa Rica. Using different data sources that report the same phenomenon (landownership), they refute the widely held belief that land distribution was relatively egalitarian. In southern Costa Rica, they compared census data with land records. They find that the census excludes most or all of the large properties, but that it does mea-sure the sizes of small farms. In contrast, the land registry captured most or all of the large properties but failed to measure the sizes of the small farms. Their explanation for the discrepancy: the large *finca* (plantation) owners had an in-terest in reporting their property holdings accurately for the land registry be-cause banks referred to the registry to verify that loan seekers had collateral property. The small landowners did not have an incentive to report their land holdings accurately to the census takers, nor is there evidence that the census takers inquired any further into the matter. Adjusting the Gini index of 1955, the authors find that this measure of inequity would have been 82 rather than the reported 55. In other words, in the early stages of colonization in Coto Brus in southern Costa Rica, there were extreme concentrations of land (Edelman and Seligson 1994: 467; Wilson 1998). Yet the myth of the egalitarian society remains remarkably resilient in the face of evidence to the contrary.

A second myth that persists is that of Costa Rica as a white, European country situated in the middle of Central America. Indeed, United States President Taft validated the myth when he famously referred to Costa Rica as the Switzerland of Central America: a stable, social democracy that remained neutral when its neighbors quarreled. With Taft's declaration, the world audience of nations had recognized Costa Rica to be just like a European nation. And under General Tomás Guardia's administration (1870-82), policies were implemented to make the myth accord more closely with reality. Borrowing from the classical tradition, Guardia and his followers became known as "The Olympians." They envisioned a racially pure (white) nation and aspired to civilization's highest standards of secular education, hygiene, science, and patriotism (Molina and Palmer 1990: 65-66). Although the Costa Rican state took antiracist positions in the United Nations, its municipal governments practiced widespread racial discrimination against those lacking *piel claro*, light-complexioned skin (Bourgois 1986; Harpelle 1993; Purcell and Sawyers 1993). As we will see, the state's self-image of an enlightened nation precluded promoting sectors of the economy or elements of cultural life that might draw the attention to the exotic or indigenous elements of the past.

ECONOMIC FORCES
Thailand

In addition to the political forces that Thailand and Costa Rica faced, a set of global economic forces also pushed these countries to commodify other endowments that neither country was fully aware it had. As Thailand began to lose its advantage of cheap labor in the early 1990s, it had to find new ways to compete in the global market. This pushed the Thai state to search for new ways to compete in exports at the same time that it forced workers to use whatever resources they could muster to create alternative sources of income. Earlier, in the seventies and eighties, Thailand had pursued import substitution industrialization (ISI). Instead of buying foreign imports, the country restricted imports and provided financial support for national industries to make those same products for domestic consumption. To finance its import substitution strategy and later its export-oriented program, the Thai government took money away from agricultural initiatives and heavily taxed rice exports. The state's policies toward rice eventually pushed agricultural workers off their farms into urban factories. Later, as manufacturing could no longer compete with the cheaper labor offered by such countries as China, Thailand's workers found themselves having to squeeze out economic opportunities wherever they might be found.

The taxation of rice exports effectively depressed the domestic price of rice compared to that prevailing in the international market: by 35 percent from 1955 to 1974, by 28 percent from 1975 to 1979, and by 15 percent from 1980 to 1985. The adverse impact of the rice premium on the incomes of rice growers was reinforced from the mid-1970s onward by the overvaluation of the baht (Dixon 1999: 141). As a result of government intervention, the agricultural sector presented a paradox: the largest rice exporter in the world registered very low rural incomes. At the same time, the government did not invest in agriculture to improve its productivity. The National Economic and Social Development Plan explicitly stated its vision of Thailand's future. Agriculture was something of the past. Thailand was on the road to convergence with Western industrial societies. In order for Thailand to progress, it needed to gain a reputation for manufacturing, not agriculture.

With agriculture's decline came a rise in internal migration to Thailand's major cities. By the early 1990s, nearly four million workers left agriculture in the off season for manufacturing and construction jobs in the cities. And an estimated 16 percent of the workers in Bangkok and other major cities had migrated from rural areas within the previous five years (Pasuk and Baker 1995: 198). Three million out of a total agricultural labor force of twenty million left farming in the early 1990s and headed for the cities in search of more lucrative incomes (Coxhead 1999). The Thai National Migration Survey of 1992 indicates that a quarter of Bangkok's population had migrated within the last two years (Chamratrithirong et al. 1995).

While opportunities became scarce in agriculture, new economic opportunities became available through tourism. The World Tourism Organization's estimates of tourism receipts show the increasing importance of this sector for Thailand's economic livelihood. In 1980 Thailand received low receipts from tourism at US$867 million, while Singapore led the region in tourism receipts at US$1.4 billion. Between 1985 and 1988 receipts from tourism nearly tripled in Thailand. At US$3.1 billion, Thailand's receipts from tourism surpassed those of Singapore. From 1995 to 1998 Thailand established itself as the leader in tourism for Southeast Asia.

This rise in the tourism sector came not a moment too soon. Those familiar with Bangkok both before and after the financial crisis of 1997 will, no doubt, remember the construction cranes that symbolized the country's economic boom and that later became emblems of the bust. Before the crisis, the cranes swayed among newly built and half-constructed towers, while at their clawed feet, taxis, tuk-tuks, and motorbikes negotiated roads, alleys, and sidewalks. A symbol of modernity before the financial crisis, construction activity later became the evidence of ad hoc development and an old-fashioned mess.

Foreign direct investment had fueled Thailand's economic growth in the mid-1980s. After the country shifted its industrialization platform to an export-oriented one in the late 1980s, foreign direct investment in Thailand in 1990 increased to US$ 2.5 billion, more than fourteen times the foreign direct investment recorded in 1985. Japanese capital accounted for nearly half that amount in 1990 (Bello, Cunningham, and Li 1998: 17). Regrettably, most of the foreign investment could leave more quickly than it came. Capital's freedom to move in search of higher returns, unpredictably and en masse, resulted from the high interest rates, pegged exchange rate, and the financial-sector deregulation policies of the Thai state. After giving Thailand boasting rights for its rapid economic growth, these three factors contributed to the economy's downturn. The slowdown in Thai exports, the rise in nonperforming loans, and the decline in productive investments sent foreign investors away in herds. With an estimated US$24 billion of mobile ("hot") capital invested in the country, speculators (such as George Soros) saw the Thai baht weakening and speculated that it would not withstand an attack. The speculators did not forgo the opportunity to benefit from the Thai baht's ruin. The Bank of Thailand saw its reserves dwindle from a high of US$39 billion in January 1997 to a low of about $7 billion seven months later (Bello, Cunningham, and Li 1998: 33-36). Thailand's economic "miracle" had come to an end.

The bust in the financial and real estate sector freed entrepreneurs who knew a great deal about export but little about handicrafts to respond creatively to the crisis. No official figures exist to indicate which entrepreneurs left other sectors of the economy for the handicraft sector; however, a number of informants and feature stories in the English-language newspapers indicate that some entrepreneurs had moved into handicraft production or sales in response to the uncertainties in the mainstream economy: An architect now designed Thai-style furniture for export (Mazurkewich 2002); a mid-level employee of a private firm now exported ceramics (Luechai and Wherry 2003); a farmer now sold his handbags in Paris, Milan, and Tokyo (Crispin 2003). As one set of opportunities disappeared, the industrious responded with creativity. Though it is difficult to estimate the size of the handicraft sector in terms of export volume, these initial estimates demonstrate that the handicraft sector is not insignificant to the national economy, nor is the sector likely to disappear in the near future.

The Royal Thai Government has responded to these new opportunities in the global crafts market by creating programs to support handicraft producers directly. The state is providing US$23,250 to each of 68,000 villages to finance micro- and small-sized business enterprises (Economist Intelligence Unit 2003). The Thai prime minister has erected his own website to promote cottage industries and other pillars of national economic dynamism. The website, Thaksinomics.com, plays on the Chinese ethnicity in the prime minister's family line (and in the families of the country's merchant class). The name also harkens to the trickle-down philosophy of Ronald Reagan. In addition to the prime minister's strong vocal and financial support for cottage industries, the queen of Thailand has long promoted the arts and crafts of the nation. With the state's financial backing and the queen's encouragement, creative destruction might benefit some communities of peasant artisans.

Although changes in the global economy pushed workers out of agriculture into cultural industries and motivated the state to support craft exports, the question remains: Why do some cultural traditions become appropriated in the service of market capitalism while other traditions lie untouched? In the coming chapters I will show how outsiders (anthropologists, international tourists, and international organizations) have served as early explorers who have identified the cultural forms that have come to be known widely as authentic representations of specific peoples living in specific places. These travelers are not biased by concerns for profit and are therefore the legitimate certifiers of material culture. Nations and their certifying institutions take their cues from these outsiders for the kinds of identity that the state can project, given the received ideas that outsiders already hold about the culture. For now, suffice it to say that the internal dynamics growing out of a nation's history as well as interactions with outsiders orient the nation-state in seeing some cultural forms as beneficial to its international image, which can act as a legitimate cultural commodity. Simply having stocks of material culture is not enough.

Costa Rica

The stocks and beauty of indigenous crafts in Costa Rica's Nicoya Peninsula did not become reason enough for their export promotion in the eyes of the state. Officials pursued strategies dictated by their pride in their social democracy, their deference to Western European norms and practices, and their obligations to the international financial institutions. In the rush to leave reputations of backwardness behind, Costa Rica did what it could to become a fully industrialized country. In 1963 it joined the Central American Common Market (CACM). The CACM imposed high tariffs on goods coming from outside of Central America but low ones on goods produced and sold within the region. As part of the ISI strategy, government incentives and import duties created a greenhouse to promote local industries while protecting them from competition. As developed by Raúl Prebisch at the Latin American Economic Commission (ECLAC), the ISI strategy would speed the country's approach to industrialization.

Reaping the benefits of readily available loans and of 1977 coffee prices that stood at four times their 1975 levels, the state offered a win-win solution for exporters and workers. Agricultural exporters who feared the volatility of the market for their products were happy to diversify their economic base. Moving into other export markets and becoming more integrated with their neighboring countries lessened their risks and increased their payoffs for market participation. Workers were happy because the state employed a fifth of the workforce and produced nearly a quarter of all goods and services (Edelman 1985: 38). The country would soon learn that it was skating on thin ice.

In 1979 Costa Rica was jolted for a second time in that decade by an oil price hike. Two years later, Costa Rica defaulted on its debt. A year later, so did Mexico. After Mexico coughed, so to speak, the rest of Latin America caught the cold. In the meantime, the military struggles within the Central American isthmus undermined the cooperative trade agreements among the Central American states by restricting the movement of goods, services, and capital (Fallas Venegas 1989). Strapped with a large debt and lacking enough buyers in the world market able to pay for Costa Rican products, the neoliberal factions within the country declared the social democracy over. The neoliberal technocrats tried to convince the electorate that Costa Rica's domestic policies were governed from without. If the country's international economic position was weak, the state lacked the funds to implement social legislation. With state funds growing scarce, it was time to dismantle the welfare state, as much as institutional inertia would allow.

Between 1980 and 1982 the inflation rate doubled and the currency lost value at a rate of 450 percent. The nation's 3 percent GDP growth in 1978 fell to a nadir of -9.8 percent four years later (Edelman 1985: 40). Meanwhile, "the cost of servicing the debt had risen from a manageable US $60 million in 1977 to US $510 million in 1982" (Wilson 1998: 153). Costa Rica had no choice but to turn to the International Monetary Fund (IMF), and it appealed to the IMF for a bailout loan in 1981. In return for the bailout, the government agreed to devalue its currency, decrease spending on social programs, remove price controls, reform the tax code, and increase tax collections. The conditions of the loan exceeded the expectations of the Costa Rican electorate. President Carazo "expelled the IMF's Costa Rica mission, stating that given the choice 'between eating and paying the external debt, we cannot accept anything other than the first option'" (Wilson 1998: 105). Carazo's position was untenable. Without loans from the international financial institutions, the government fell apart. In 1982, Luis Alberto Monge took control, imposing the orthodox economic stabilization measures required by the IMF. With external loans now flowing into the government's coffers and with the approval of the core countries, Monge saw results. The deficit fell from 17.4 percent of GDP in 1980 to 14 percent in 1981. Costa Rica's GDP grew by 7 percent in 1984 (Wilson 1998: 116).

The country's import substitution strategy had exhausted its possibilities. In order to revive its economic health, Costa Rica turned to export-oriented industrialization. In the early 1990s export promotion in Costa Rica relied increasingly on export-processing zones (EPZs). The export-processing zones were located in nine sites across the country. Within the zone, a firm could import and export financial capital as well as inputs for production (e.g., machine parts, equipment) without paying customs duties. With approval these firms could also sell up to 40 percent of their products in local markets. There were no requirements for local inputs or for national value added imports (Clark 1995). The working conditions within these processing zones have deteriorated, rendering them almost indistinguishable from the wage and working conditions in the informal economy (Pérez-Sáinz 1996).

This export regimen affected state-society coalitions by strengthening some civil society groups while debilitating others. A significant group within the upper classes favored the neoliberal turn. They hoped that their products would find lucrative foreign markets, and they disparaged the growing public sector. Ironically, those industrialists who had benefited from the special protections of the ISI platform identified with the upper classes, who were most likely to benefit from laissez-faire trade.

The irony did not end there. It was not a neoliberal president whose administration promoted neoliberal economic reforms. The president from 1994 through 1998 and the opponent of market-driven policies, José María Figueres, soon learned the limits of state sovereignty. Although his Liberation Party (PLN) won the elections based on his opposition to the IMF–World Bank austerity measures, he could not obtain loans from international lenders after taking office. After public opinion turned against Figueres, he struck a deal with Rafael Calderón, the former president and leader of the conservative Christian Socialists Party. On April 28, 1995, Figueres and Calderón signed a pact that would reduce the government deficit, eliminate some social services, deregulate the market, and privatize some state-run industries. The Calderón-Figueres pact dismantled the apparatus on which the poor had heavily relied and created a new set of economic opportunities.

The benefits of economic openness showed themselves with the advent of Intel. Instead of relying on low-cost labor (with which Costa Rica could not compete in the global economy), the national economy turned to the more lucrative knowledge economy. In 1997 Intel (the computer microprocessor producer) did not have a plant in Costa Rica, and textile exports accounted for the lion's share of exports at US$788 million, with bananas and coffee trailing at $560 and $391 million, respectively. Two years later, Intel accounted for "8 percent of Costa Rica's GDP and about 40 percent of the country's export value" (Luxner 2000: 3). In 1999 the company's microchips surpassed by almost 100 percent the export value of textiles, bananas, and coffee combined. And in 1998 and 1999 Costa Rica's GDP growth increased by 8 and 8.3 percent compared with the average for Latin America of 2.3 and 0.3 percent for those years. Intel accounted for 3.5 percent of GDP and almost 40 percent of exports in 2000 (Swenson 2001: 45). When Intel entered Costa Rica, the country's position in the global economy fundamentally changed.

In addition to becoming a knowledge economy, Costa Rica had already transformed itself into a tourist economy. While the 1990s saw the decline of low-cost manufacturing jobs, it also witnessed the creation of new economic opportunities in tourism. With few resources, the state could promote tourism by simply offering tax breaks to tour operators within the country. Before the 1990s, Costa Rica was not well known as a major vacation spot. It had retained its reputation from the colonial days as a country whose resources belied its name: There was no gold and there were few Indians.

Tourism brought the state into contact with travelers who brought in money along with preconceived notions about the environmental (primarily) and cultural (secondarily) riches the country held. Tourism brought in $600 million in foreign exchange in 1995. Between 1984 and 1994 tourism increased by 178 percent. Over that ten-year period, North American tourists—the largest group of travelers to Costa Rica—increased from 88,360 to 332,602 persons, representing a 276 percent increase (Costa Rican Tourism Board 2000a). Tourism became a mainstay of the economy. In 1991 the revenue from this source accounted for nearly one-fifth of the value generated by exports. Although the tourism sector declined relative to other exports with the advent of Intel, the total revenues garnered by tourism continued to climb. By 1999 it generated

US$917 million. In the Institute for Costa Rican Tourism's survey of 1,500 international tourists to Costa Rica in 1999, a significant proportion came to enjoy the beaches or to engage in ecotourism, but the survey neither found nor inquired about tourists coming to see cultural heritage sites or to visit handicraft artisans (Costa Rican Tourism Board 2000b). The potential for Costa Rican handicraft artisans to enter global markets has been limited by the state's inability to see them as legitimate competitors in the (modern) global market. The state sees itself as promoting industries that might have a comparative advantage in the global market but it does not recognize the latent function that participation in the global market serves—to distinguish the nation as modern, progressive, and progressing.

If the presence of material culture were sufficient for a state to promote cultural commodities, Costa Rica would be well known for its indigenous crafts. In the late 1800s Costa Rica demonstrated that it possesses stocks of material culture when it participated in the 1893 World's Fair. Then a leader in material culture, the country now has transformed itself into a "green" leader with environmental riches. The state's political and economic history helps us better understand why a reputation for indigenous cultures did not take hold.

ASSESSING CULTURE AND SOCIAL STRUCTURE IN COMPARATIVE PERSPECTIVE

The geopolitics of colonization and the global economic pressures that threatened Thailand and Costa Rica have oriented the goals and strategies of each nation-state as it sought a comparative advantage in the global market. Two ideal-typical cultural orientations toward cultural commodities manifest themselves in the strategies that these states pursued to promote cultural or other commodities and in the groups of actors placed at a relative advantage or disadvantage: a selectively acculturated and an assimilated orientation to world society. These concepts of selective acculturation and assimilation come out of the immigration literature (Portes and Rumbaut 1996) and refer to the relationship of less powerful actors to "mainstream" society. I use the terms to denote a world standard which lies largely with the dominating empire, be it the European empires of the past or the United States empire of the present day. In the Thai case, the selectively acculturated state takes pride in its movement from and preservation of tradition, but the state also pushes its citizens and its cultural institutions to be more like and more understandable to Westerners. The state's premodern traditions act as symbols of national identity, unique to the nation.

After the state develops a modern bureaucracy, it might keep or revive its traditions as a source of pride rather than treating them as residue from a past to be forgotten. The state actively certifies its cultural traditions through its museums, its schools, and its tourism promotion agency. With open arms, the state invites outsiders to be in awe of sights never before seen. These certifying agents of culture help generate the foreign demand for handicrafts and signal to domestic producers that handicraft production is a modern, legitimate, and significant economic undertaking. Later in the chapter we will see how the assimilated identity of the Costa Ricans tended toward the erasure of difference.

A Selectively Acculturated Identity

The Thais' sense of themselves as a nation never colonized affected how they saw their role in the global economy. The products that the Thai made for themselves through import substitution and those goods made for export symbolized Thailand's relative position among developing nations. On the one hand, Thailand looked to its stocks of natural resources as a means to industrialize and to lessen the country's dependence on agricultural exports. On the other, the country exported goods that represented a proud cultural heritage. At first, that pride resided in how similar Thai products were to Western-made products in terms of technology and quality. Later, the Thai decided to celebrate diversity in the global market. As the new year began in 2005, Pansak Vinyaratn, the prime minister's chief policy adviser, suggested: "Producers and retailers [should] add 'Thainess' to the designs of their products to attract both domestic and international consumers, and differentiate the products from imported ones. 'Thainess in design here doesn't mean something like Lai Kanok [traditional Thai craft patterns], but the attributes of Thai culture that could be reflected in the design of a product'. . . . [T]he charms of Thai culture could create a kind of 'mysterious allure' to attract consumers. . . . Things will continue to sell as long as the 'seductive force' of a product or service is not yet clearly identified" (Sujintana 2005). Over the last ten years, Thai columnists have noted this new orientation toward cultural goods. At one time, such cultural products were associated with a backward past but were exalted as indicators of a distinct people that could not be subjugated. What brought the exotic to the fore as an important image for the nation-state were transformations in the global markets.

States that have an acculturated orientation toward the global community are more likely to assist suppliers in exporting objects that represent a favorable national identity. Such states are also more likely to disseminate officially sanctioned cultural exhibitions that confirm the nation's cultural uniqueness and its legitimate place as a modern entity. The state's intention to support cultural institutions must confront the existing coalitions within and outside of the national territory intent on promoting particular cultural representations as well as market forces that may make the supply of raw materials or the distribution of goods abroad more difficult.

An Assimilated Identity

In the case of Costa Rica, the orientation to assimilate as a "white" nation-state leads Costa Rica to mimic the cultural institutions found in core Western countries. The Costa Rican elites explicitly outlined an assimilation strategy as their nation-building project—privileging the classical tradition of the "Old World" and civilizing the untamed of the new. Exotic traditions are deemphasized as the state highlights its movement from its traditional roots into its proper place as a modern, enlightened society. The museums, schools, and tourism organizations do not highlight indigenous groups or local traditions that appear to be backward or, in some other way, embarrassing. As Pierre Bourdieu (1977) rightly points out, being in the position to act must be coupled with having the disposition to act in a particular way; if the markets are relatively free but the disposition of nation-states and entrepreneurs are disinclined to create an audience for their goods, cultural goods that might be lucrative are not likely to be exported. Such orientations may work well for countries in the core of the world-system that are relatively wealthy, with a diversified economy, and with a great deal of political autonomy. More diversified economies have positive spillovers in shipping and in communications technologies that aid cultural industries in distributing their products. Such countries also have a "business reputation" for reliability and a "cultural reputation" that is widely recognized. However, countries on the periphery find themselves engaged in ideological values about their intrinsic cultural wealth. These structural positions of advantage or disadvantage interact with the orientation of nation-states to structure the opportunities available in the handicraft market.

FORCES AND FRAMES IN GLOBAL CULTURAL MARKETS

The state's orientation toward indigenous cultures changes over time and it may arise from the same set of circumstances that lead the state to promote indigenous cultural industries. In other words, changes in the global economy (material conditions) might unleash new opportunities for cultural industries by providing a ready set of consumers for the product while making it more difficult for producers in other sectors of the economy to survive. The state simply abandons the losing horse for the winning one. If this were the only explanation, we would return to the truism: the most creative countries succeed in the creative sectors of the economy. Similarly, path dependency arguments would note the cumulative advantages of operating in the creative economy in which a country's entrepreneurs have already learned the ropes and built the right connections with distributors around the globe. To account for these competing explanations, one would need more comparative cases to see whether the state's orientation toward cultural heritage preceded the state's promotion of cultural commodity exports, all other things being equal. One would also have to account for negative evidence: What happens when one sees a selectively acculturated state ignore opportunities in the cultural economy? Would such a state be said to lack the pertinent evidence for promoting the sector? Would such a state simply lack the organizational capacity to do what it would have done otherwise? Such questions themselves warn of the circular reasoning that one's commitment to a particular theory can bring about. What this chapter has done is to take clear-cut cases of state orientations toward culture as ideal types for building a theory about the likelihood of the state supporting some types of cultural commodity exports over other available ones.

FRAMING THE SITUATION, CONCLUDING REMARKS

This chapter has explored the historical construction of the impressions that Western buyers as well as the Thai and Costa Rican citizens have about their country's cultural character. These definitions of the situation orient the course of the country's economic development and reinforce the other sources of state power. In the Costa Rican case, I have argued that the government's fear of being associated with a stigmatized identity has sometimes diverted economic development energies away from those stocks of symbolic capital associated with indigenous peoples that might have been easily appropriated. In the Thai case, the government actively promoted a multidimensional image of its national character by supporting the production of material culture that also conveyed a favorable social identity for the nation-state in the eyes of Westerners. Therefore, to understand the success of artisans in global markets, it is not enough to think about the individual qualities of the artisans or of the particular cultural contributions of their group to world culture; one must also think about the public culture that makes the promotion of particular cultural sectors of the economy thinkable. How a nation's identity is framed affects the likelihood that capital, labor, and knowledge will be mobilized in the service of particular cultural productions.

This chapter has focused on the economic and political differences between Thailand and Costa Rica to explain the more favorable position that Thai artisans occupy in handicraft markets. I have also drawn our attention to how opportunities in cultural markets are more obvious for Thai government officials and for Thai entrepreneurs than they have been for Costa Rican officials and entrepreneurs. However, what holds true for these countries overall does not hold for the diverse range of individual artisans and their communities within each country. As the stories of individual artisans in the first chapter indicate, some artisans in Thailand have been able to go global (export their goods directly or find favorable terms of trade) but others have not; similarly, some artisans in Costa Rica have profited much more than other artisans making the same style of pottery. Because each country studied has one village in which the artisans have largely succeeded economically and another in which the artisans continue to struggle for survival, the case studies emphasize that the artisans are embedded in the histories and politics of their local communities. These artisans contend with local and national-level factors that generate diverse outcomes on the ground. Living in a country such as Thailand confers collective advantages for artisans wishing to enter the global market, but the dynamics among the local community contexts, the situations in which artisans negotiate new and old business propositions, and the types of actors from outside of the nation-state who become tied to these communities greatly influence the fortune of these artisans. What the cultural orientation of the nation-state can tell us is whether an artisan living in Thailand is more likely to enjoy the support of the nation-state and the recognition of outsiders compared with an artisan living in Costa Rica. To understand how some communities have made their cultural traditions work to their economic advantage requires observations of the flows of people, resources, and ideas at close range. With qualitative data we can also explore the cultural implications of participating in global markets. Does market participation necessarily cheapen cultural traditions or render inauthentic creative expression? Questions about the social connections that artisans make, how these connections facilitate their business transactions, and the meanings embedded in these transactions motivate the coming chapters.

CHAPTER THREE

Same Local Traditions, Different Frames

If understanding how government officials and entrepreneurs frame the cultural identity of their national locales explains why international tourists and the buying agents for large retail stores are drawn to particular country sites of cultural production, analysis of the differences among the sites of production within each country explains the diverging fates of communities that share the same local traditions and that are in close proximity to one another. Local artisans use their social connections (a social capital explanation), assistance from government programs (a political economy explanation), and their nearly inimitable craft traditions (a cultural capital explanation) to frame the image of their workshops, and by extension their communities, as authentic sites of cultural production. As we observe the interactive process of framing, we discover one of the mechanisms whereby cultural capital becomes convertible into economic capital; these conversions affect the cultural capital derived from local craft traditions. The advantage of studying communities in such different parts of the world is that we can see how well the concepts of social and cultural capital travel. Because the empirical realities make it possible to modify existing theories and to develop new ones (in this case, the aura of authenticity as a collective resource), we can transcend regional boundaries in studying comparative development.

SOCIAL CAPITAL EXPLANATIONS

In encounters with artisans operating small workshops in an economically dynamic business cluster, the example of the Italian region of Emilia-Romagna provides a celebrated case of a successful industrial district that was aided by social capital and government interventions. An industrial district is a collection of firms united by "a complex [web] of external economies and diseconomies, inter-related costs and historical and cultural links which influence both business and personal relationship[s]" (Solinas 1982: 332). Such districts contain many small enterprises that are able to realize economies of scale and economies of scope. Economies of scale are achieved through collective action such as buying supplies in bulk. Economies of scope refers to the complementarities achieved by bringing different products together to form a single basket of goods. Social capital plays an important role in achieving economies of scope and scale because the artisans can share tools, equipment, labor, and information, enabling them to produce with greater efficiency and at higher quality than they could acting alone. Therefore, the expectation would be that the more economically successful handicraft communities in Thailand and Costa Rica are those exhibiting cooperation and solidarity within their inter-workshop networks.

Robert Putnam (1993) and his collaborators have made such an argument, citing the differences between northern and southern Italy as an example of how civic engagement and social solidarity lead to positive economic outcomes for entire communities and regions: In communities where there is more solidarity and trust to facilitate inter-firm cooperation, local economies thrive. Subsequent scholarship led by Alejandro Portes and his collaborators has called into question the usefulness of thinking about social capital at such a high level of aggregation as a nation-state or a geographically vast region; worse, the benefits of sociability sometimes become confused as both predictor and outcome. Unable to see how interpersonal relationships work at the ground level and the different forms that these relationships take, social scientists using social capital to explain local economic development may confuse more than they explain by ignoring the heterogeneous social relationships and the extreme outcomes apparent in these regions.

Portes and his collaborators offer a remedy for this confusion. While local solidarity, acts of reciprocity, shared values, and trust (backed up by the capacity to sanction wrongdoers) are all manifestations of social capital, they remain analytically distinct in their constitution and in their effects. The type of social capital that proves decisive for framing handicraft communities as authentic is bounded solidarity. Portes and Sensenbrenner (1993) offer a comprehensive scope of variables that promote bounded solidarity in their exploration of immigrant communities. These variables include the following: (1) distinct phenotypic or cultural characteristics and (often) the existence of prejudice against these characteristics, (2) blockage of exit opportunities, and (3) situational confrontations. The authors offer a passage from *The Communist Manifesto* to illustrate how bounded solidarity emerges: "With the development of industry the proletariat not only increases in number; it becomes concentrated in greater masses, its strength grows, and it feels that strength more. The various interests and conditions of life within the ranks of the proletariat are more and more equalized. . . . The collisions between individual workmen and individual bourgeois take more and more the character of collisions between two classes" (Marx and Engels [1848] cited in Portes and Sensenbrenner 1993: 1324). Marx and Engels's treatment of solidarity as a sense of belonging to a group based on confrontations with an identifiable Other defines solidarity in structural terms. While structural shifts in the mode of production explain how these collisions between classes were possible, the collision itself is the explanatory variable for the rise of bounded solidarity and is analytically distinct from a structural change in the economy. In the Thai community of Baan Thawai, the local artisans will be shown to collide with outside investors coming to take advantage of the international demand for Thai handicrafts. The collision between the individual artisans and the bourgeois entrepreneurs from Bangkok and elsewhere will spark a sense of "we-ness" among the artisans, and this sense of unity will have economic consequences for the development of the locale. In short, the community's cultural capital and external threats to the survival of that cultural capital will be shown to spark the emergence of bounded solidarity (e.g., Pérez-Sáinz and Andrade-Eekhoff 2003).

As a member of a group with a strong sense of belonging, one may mobilize resources from among the group's membership. In this way, one may achieve economies of scale and scope and may better coordinate the presentation of the village's image as an authentic site of cultural production. "Submerged in social relationships . . . [the individual artisan] acts so as to safeguard his social standing, his social claims, his social assets. He values material goods only in so far as they serve this end" (Polanyi [1944] 1957: 46). In fact, when potential buyers perceive that the artisans are valuing their social assets (authenticity) over economic profits, the buyers are more likely to grant privileges to their favorite artisans. It stands to reason that for these buyers the authentic products are somehow worth more than inauthentic ones, even if those products come from the same geographic region and are made with more or less the same raw materials. As the community of artisans seemingly concerns itself more with the integrity of their traditions than with making money, that community becomes better able to turn a profit and to make demands on the regional and national governments to provide the types of infrastructure and material resources that no amount of group solidarity could obtain.

POLITICAL ECONOMY EXPLANATIONS

Indeed, there are some things that sociability cannot do. A critical reading of the Emilia-Romagna case offers a strong corrective to the notion that community solidarity leads to dynamic local economic development without the support of the regional or the national government. Vittorio Capecchi explains that the region's solidarity emerged as a byproduct of the ongoing conflict between the regional government, headed by the Communist Party, and the central government, headed by the Christian Democratic Party. The political disjunction between the party heading Emilia-Romagna and the party heading the central government served as a symbol of binary opposition around which the locality could rally.

Likewise, the political culture of the socialist state promoted the kind of social organization that facilitates the emergence of bounded solidarity. Namely, there were numerous leagues and cooperatives. Moreover, the regional government provided training programs for artisans and child care for parents. The government programs lowered the artisans' costs of living (food, shelter, education). As a result, starting a business or suffering financial losses while trying to innovate had less severe consequences for the artisans and their families (Brusco 1982; Capecchi 1989). In short, the state provided both the physical infrastructure for entrepreneurial development and the political conditions that spurred the emergence of the social infrastructure (solidarity and reciprocity) generating the region's economic dynamism.

While the state, especially the regional government, spurred entrepreneurship even among those who did not have enterprises, dynamic economic activity occurred mostly among those who already owned property and held some wealth. Capecchi stresses that the Emilia-Romagna case does not represent the peasant class realizing their entrepreneurial dream of moving out of rags into riches. Because those who practiced subsistence agriculture later found themselves engaged in subsistence-level enterprises, Capecchi confirms the old adage that those who have are indeed the ones who get more. Therefore, most entrepreneurial activities in the handicraft sector will be undertaken as a survival strategy if most of the entrepreneurs have little to no financial resources.

As we explore political economy explanations for local economic development in handicraft communities, we will be attentive to how community leaders use their political connections to get their villages marked as tourist destinations and how festivals become advertised through the government's tourism agency, especially in the Thai case studies. We will also see in the Costa Rican cases how the decision to pave a road connecting a village to the main highway can ease commercial intercourse and facilitate social connections with international tourists and buying agents for small boutiques and large retail stores. We will have to go beyond the usual political economy explanations, however, to understand how these political favors flow to some of the communities under study.

THE FRAMING EXPLANATION

To understand how communities of handicraft artisans become dynamic economic clusters without having wealthy families able to invest in artistic endeavors or politically well-connected individuals to attract government programs, better transportation, and more modern communications infrastructure, one should understand how the community's identity becomes framed. In other words, how does the community's image enable it to attract inordinate amounts of attention (compared with neighboring communities) from researchers, activists, Peace Corps volunteers, buyers, government officials, and others?

In their study of how communities engaged in tourism and handicraft production become inserted in global markets, Juan Pablo Pérez-Sáinz and Katharine Andrade-Eekhoff pay attention to how geographic locales become framed in the imagination of outsiders. In San Pedro Sacatepéquez, Guatemala, where textile subcontracting is common, the authors interviewed one maquila subcontract facilitator who emphasized the importance of managing the impressions of the communities where the factory subcontracts: "We realized that we could not sell a contract without selling the town, showing the contractors that San Pedro was an industrious town and not just a group. In 1987 we started this, selling San Pedro as an industry. Just imagine—there were eleven thousand sewing machines, a small Taiwan. You knocked on a door and found three or four sewing machines" (2003: 79). Global actors recognize the reputations of the local territories. The benefits that accrue from the reputation of one's locality are available to all who operate therein.

Likewise, David Kyle shows how the more favorably framed a community's image is, the more material resources the community obtains from extra-community sources. In this way, Kyle can explain how the indigenous Quichua speakers from Otavalo have become more successful handicraft merchants in the global market than have the artisans in Azuay, although both groups come from the Andean highlands of Ecuador. Kyle suggests a method for separating how a community has been framed in the national imagination (favorably, neutrally, or not at all) from whether the community obtains more resources from extra-community sources than do other communities. In his analysis, Kyle digs through the colonial history of Ecuador and discovers that the Otavalans were considered the most civilized of the indigenous peoples in Ecuador. The comparatively favorable status of the Otavalans may be understood as the outcome of the colonial government's "divide and conquer" strategy meant to legitimize the cultural boundaries among indigenous groups as well as the objective economic and social conditions associated with the different indigenous identities. The colonial government exacerbated the material inequalities among different ethnic groups to affirm the system of status hierarchies that facilitated colonial rule (Kyle 2000; Colloredo-Mansfeld 2003; Meisch 2002).

While this historical account sensitizes us to the history of boundary work in Ecuador, it does not explain the advantages that Otavalan artisans have in global markets by virtue of their community of origin. The interactions of local and international actors lead to these location advantages. Upstage an anthropologist; downstage some cultural capital: In the 1940s Elsie Clews Parsons conducted an anthropological study in Otavalo and chose Rosita Lema as her informant. Rosita (also called Rosa) had a reputation among the British and US Embassy crowd as being the most intelligent Indian in the area, and based on this cultural capital, she was able to "network," casually engaging with politicians and businesspeople. After Parsons's study showcased Rosa Lema and her community, the spotlight intensified on the locale. Kyle quotes Linda D'Amico's account of the progression: "The first temporary migration was set up by the U.S. Embassy in Quito . . . in 1949. Because of her relation with anthropologist Elsie Clews Parsons, she had become well acquainted with U.S. Embassy people, who recognized the quality of Peguche textiles. . . . An entourage of 70 people came to her house in the late 1940s. This paved the way for her subsequent invitation to the White House . . . and then on to 5th Avenue in New York where she exhibited textile handicrafts" (quoted in Kyle 2000: 130). Further piquing outsiders' interest was the photographic book *The Awakening Valley*, by Collier and Buitrón, which created an a historical but magical portrait of the local crafts and the communities producing them. These accounts played up the social values of dedication to one's calling and of hard work that so resonated with the Protestant ethic and the spirit of capitalism.

By coming to the valley as it awakened, tourists could enjoy and contribute to that miracle. The aura of authenticity glowed like a dome encapsulating the valley, drawing to its heart external interventions and outside interest not otherwise forthcoming. Fourteen years after Lema's goodwill cultural tour to the United Nations in 1949, the Ecuadorian government paved the way for the global articulation of the Otavalan valley into the global market by constructing the Pan American highway and building the "Poncho Plaza" for tourists in the heart of Otavalo. The plaza served as an important meeting point where tourists, buying agents, and others could "discover" the marvel of the Otavalans and could affirm (through their presence and their reports) the legitimacy of the artisans' claims to authenticity.

SAME PLACE, DIFFERENT FRAMES: THE COMPARISONS

Along with having a reputation for authenticity, the community's physical attributes also influence how the community will fare in global markets. The physical attributes most important for my study communities are proximity to major tourist attractions and transportation and communication infrastructures (paved roads, shipping services, and reliable phone lines). However, the comparative advantage of one community over another derives from its aura of authenticity generating the motivation among buyers to come to the village and the rationale among governmental and nongovernmental organizations to provide the village with the desired infrastructures.

The chainsaw-wielding woman from Sanpatong that we encountered in the first chapter—who carves figurines from wood and drives them in her pickup truck to such villages as Baan Thawai to sell to other artisans for final finishing and distribution—might have earned a higher income if she had been born (and still lived) *in* Baan Thawai. Without customers coming in abundance to her doorstep, she entered the commercial market as a price taker, not a price setter. Likewise, the man in San Vicente who complained of having much product to supply but few customers to demand it might have had fewer complaints had he lived in Guaitil, where tour buses brought buyers to experience and support indigenous traditions. It is not necessarily the talent or the individual initiative that prevents some artisans from succeeding in commercial markets but rather the location where buyer and sellers meet. Just as the previous chapter explained the importance of the artisan's country of origin for success in global markets for handicrafts and international tourism, this chapter explains how the community characteristics affect the likelihood that the artisan will succeed in global markets. More importantly, this chapter explores how this collective resource emerges in the first place.

THE THAI COMPARISONS
Baan Thawai

Drive twelve kilometers down the Hangdong Road out of the city of Chiang Mai just past the international airport, and you encounter the Baan Thawai Handicraft Center. One would not think to venture further, having just arrived at the handicraft market—a destination of repute in Chiang Mai—where women dab their paint brushes with acrylic and adorn banana leaf patterns on wooden bowls, while men hammer handmade chisels to carve scenes from Thai folklore into mango wood. The market stretches from the main road, already heavily populated with furniture and home décor shops, into a dense agglomeration of vending stalls. The larger shops bristle with modernity but retain a sense of tradition at their core. Motifs in the Lanna kingdom style enmesh the buildings with curved points and decorative spirals, inviting the customer to experience the authenticity of place, while in the act of shopping. The shop windows read RETAIL AND WHOLESALE, WE EXPORT; in the windows the Visa, Mastercard, and American Express symbols stack as if they are the abstractly rendered heads of a totem pole. Outside the shop, a spirit house contains soon-to-rot fruit, cooked rice, and the ash of burnt joss sticks. Most of the shops in the handicraft market are not the enclosed structures found at Western shopping malls, but are quaint, open-air stalls. Approximately six by eight feet, they stand side by side and constitute zones. Each zone carries a number so that one can buy a carved bed in zone 12 and find the wall hangings in zone 6.

The vendors seem distracted with their own banter or with finishing the intricate details of a painted bowl. Caught in the music of chisels knocking wood, observers marvel at the care taken to create a three-dimensional relief on a panel of teak. Interspersed along the main road cutting through the market one finds packaging and shipping services. Buy crafts and furniture in several different shops, and a shipping agent will collect, package, and ship the purchases with great convenience, if not great haste. In this market, the tour buses unload. Trucks depart burdened by wooden crates headed for the train station, the airport, the freight truck, the port. Hand-held phones vibrate with new orders. Faxes and email accounts deliver buyer specifications. In the center of the shopping area, the Thai tourist police occupy a booth that monitors the Siam Commercial Bank's automatic teller machine, ready to dispense Thai baht or US dollars. It is in front of the ATM machine that the tour buses park and deposit their passengers.

For some buyers, the large handicraft market seems too assembled, too staged. The buyer wants to be able to tell a story about having gotten away from the "tourist" area, having courageously ventured further in order to have a more authentic encounter with the real artisans rather than with their simulated counterparts. If keenly observant while in the middle of the shopping area, one might notice the faded billboard advertising the Baan Thawai Song Fang Khlong Handicraft Market, 500 meters away, where one might find a cheaper (misspelled "chipper") price. Perhaps heeding the advice of someone who has already been there or following the annual wood carving festival parade, one might leave the main market area for the village crafts market. The din of the large market subsides; the main road veers left; two large houses flank the entrance. The road forks, both sides winding past modest homes and a few small shops. The cement roads lead to the irrigation canal and the handicraft shops lining both its shores. This is the "real" Baan Thawai, the community whose name adorns the larger commercial market. In the "real" Baan Thawai, business remains swift, though the pace of getting and spending slows. Baan Thawai village shares a primary school with the village of Dthon Kaew. Therefore, this study included enterprises in Dthon Kaew near handicraft workshops in Baan Thawai. The village has about 220 households (735 persons) and the Dthon Kaew village has 80 households (290 persons). Both villages are located in the Hang Dong district.

In the early 1980s Baan Thawai had not yet established itself as a major wood carving sales center. All of the handicraft businesses were concentrated in the Sankampaeng district on the other side of the city of Chiang Mai. The Thawai village was certainly known for its expertise in wood carving, but most villagers earned their livelihood from farming. In their spare time, they would produce carvings to be sold in Sankampaeng. By 1996 wood carving had become the local cash cow. Though most of the villagers in Baan Thawai were still farmers, earning from 20,000 to 30,000 baht, or 800 to 1,200 US dollars, they supplemented their farming incomes by engaging in handicrafts, operating a small food/commodities store, or selling their labor as nonskilled workers or as construction workers. About 156 families were involved in the handicraft and wood carving sector, earning 100 to 550 baht per day (US$4 to US$22) with annual incomes reaching 198,000 baht (US$7,920), more than twice the provincial average. About 32 families worked small food stores earning between 100 and 250 baht per day (US$4 to US$10) for annual incomes reaching 75,000 baht (US$3,000). And about 20 families engaged in nonskilled labor and construction, earning annual incomes in the same range as the small food store operators (Luechai and Siroros 2002). The surge in incomes occurred after the government established the large Baan Thawai Handicraft Center and the villagers responded to this government initiative by establishing their own handicraft center. As the artisans in this village market would readily admit, being an artisan in Baan Thawai makes their economic lives much better than they would have been were they working out of another handicraft village nearby. One such area where tourists and other buyers do not always think to venture is in the Sanpatong area.

The Sanpatong District

Instead of turning left from the Hang Dong–Chiang Mai road at the sign for Baan Thawai Handicraft Center, continue straight for Sanpatong, where you will find two handicraft cooperatives within two kilometers of each other. The first is by Baan Kew Ler Luang and the other is by Baan Kew Ler Noi. My primary comparison with Baan Thawai is Baan Kew Ler Noi, where the Sanpatong Handicraft Center is located. The two village handicraft centers are so similar that I talk about them almost interchangeably as the Sanpatong handicraft cluster. At the Sanpatong Handicraft Center in front of the Kew Ler Noi village, the market's center replicates the layout of the Baan Thawai Handicraft Center in miniature. As in Baan Thawai, the wood carvers here pride themselves on their craftsmanship, displaying mostly elephants and wall hangings. The artisans send many of these carvings to such places as Baan Thawai to be decorated (with gold leafing and paint) and sold. Though they boast that some of their work is sold in the Baan Thawai handicraft center, they lament the loss of value-added income. Aside from the handicraft workshops at the two "strip malls," other handicraft workshops are located within the villages of Kew Ler Noi and Kew Ler Luang, long known for their wood carvings. The Kew Ler Noi village has 281 households (849 persons); the Kew Ler Luang, 402 households (1,334 persons).

Unlike in Baan Thawai, the Thai government did not establish a large handicraft center in the Sanpatong district to promote rural economic development. Rather, the government and a nongovernmental organization gave the villagers of Kew Ler Noi and Kew Ler Luang resources to establish a handicraft cooperative. The assistance came in response to the 1997 financial crisis in Thailand. Because the Sanpatong cluster had largely grown without government aid until that time, when the financial crisis hit, the state and nongovernmental actors decided to take advantage of the talent for wood carving, recognized as a local endowment. Complementing the provincial government's assistance, the

W. P. Schmidt Foundation, which concerns itself with rural development and economic projects, contributed the start-up funds to promote wood carving as an income-generating project. The villagers left their home workshops and came under one roof to carve at the Sanpatong Wood Carving Center.

The provincial government of Chiang Mai provided the Sanpatong Wood Carving Center with marketing assistance and established the Chiang Mai Brand to promote products representing the special character of the province. The Chiang Mai Brand covers a select group of enterprises selling agricultural products popular in the region as well as a select group of manufacturers distributing wood carvings, basket work, and ceramics.

Different Starting Points

Before venturing into how different communities obtained an aura of authenticity that benefits the community's artisans in the marketplace, I want to emphasize the demographic advantages that Baan Thawai had before it became framed as an authentic site of production. The prior existence of material and demographic advantage suggests that cultural resources are more easily constructed in localities with greater material advantages. The Thai study communities occupy districts with strikingly different population characteristics in terms of population density, fertility, and household income. The population of Sanpatong was more densely concentrated than that of Hang Dong (where Baan Thawai is located) in 1990 and 2000. The difference stood at 439.29 people per square kilometer in Sanpatong compared with 252.19 in Hang Dong. Ten years later, these population densities had hardly changed (Chiang Mai Provincial Statistical Office, various years).

A second demographic difference has been the number of births in each district. In Hang Dong there were thirty-three reported births in 1990, but Sanpatong boasted eight times that amount. In 2000 there were more than twice as many births in Hang Dong as there had been in 1990, but there were fewer births in Sanpatong than there had been ten years earlier. Out-migration declined in both districts, although the percentage of out-migrants was greater in Hang Dong. These trends suggest that there were more subsistence-level enterprises in Sanpatong. Indeed, the household incomes in Hang Dong exceed those in Sanpatong. In 1992 a larger share of the population of Sanpatong (31 percent) earned incomes less than 10,000 baht per year, while a larger share of Hang Dong's population (38 percent) earned incomes of more than 10,000 baht. Seven years later the percentage of Hang Dong's population (46 percent) earning in the upper income category was nearly double Sanpatong's share (23.77 percent).

These differences in household income by district indicates that the villages in Hang Dong have had more material resources than those in Sanpatong. However, there does not seem to have been a big difference in out-migration. Moreover, housing tenure data from 1993 indicate that a larger percentage of Sanpatong's rural households owned their land whereas a larger percentage of Hang Dong's household rented or share-cropped. What these data show is that the community that has benefited most from the global handicraft market has had not only more material resources but also more favorable demographic conditions. But it takes more than favorable economic and geographic conditions to become framed as an authentic site of cultural production.

Constructing the Aura of Authenticity

Given the importance of the aura of authenticity for handicraft sales, one might think that the artisans along with their local and national governments would deliberately generate such an aura. What we find in Thailand (and will find later in Costa Rica) is that aura emerges because of a set of events that neither the artisans nor their local and national government leaders had in mind. Ironically, the state has been most helpful to local artisans in generating aura when the state's plans have backfired.

A living testament to how the state's good intentions can go wrong (before going right) is the presence of two Baan Thawai handicraft centers located back-to-back. Most international tourists enter the big Baan Thawai Handicraft Center in front of the village and assume that the large center is operated by the local villagers. The faded billboard in the large market indicates that there is a second market, the Baan Thawai Song Fang Khlong Handicraft Center, just five hundred meters beyond the large one. The proximity of these similarly named handicraft centers is a result of a past and present struggle. In 1990 the government established the large Baan Thawai Handicraft Center with the best of intentions. It would serve as a job training center so that villagers could find an alternative source of livelihood. The Baan Thawai villagers had held a wood carving festival on the district government's land since 1988. With migration to Bangkok on the rise, the national government wanted to encourage villagers to find alternatives to farming that would not require migration to industrial centers. At the same time, Queen Sirikit had begun emphasizing the fine arts and handicraft traditions of Thailand. On a visit to the handicraft center, the queen implored the nation to preserve these local crafts. In her stead, Prime Minister Chatchai came to the opening of the center in 1991. From outside of the Thawai village, it seemed that a local government initiative (with national government support) had realized its intended benefits.

From inside the market, the view was rather different. Instead of a center for training, the handicraft center served as a concentration for handicraft retail shops. As business people from Bangkok and elsewhere moved into the center, shop rents rose. When rents ranged from US$250 to more than US$1,000 per month, many of the local villagers could no longer afford to operate their shops. Squeezed out of the handicraft center bearing the village's name, the residents of Baan Thawai began to consider themselves to be a distinct group, confronted by an outside enemy and pushed into the economic margins of the handicraft sector. The contrast between who could and could not pay the high rents in the gentrified market (Herzfeld 2004) served as a symbol of what the village artisans held in common. Squeezed out of the handicraft center bearing the village's name, they decided to establish their own marketplace.

When the village committee informed the local irrigation group, a branch of the government charged with implementing the national development plan and creating commitment to that plan among the local residents, of its decision to build its own handicraft center in the middle of the village, the development group reportedly objected; such a center was not part of the local economic development plan. The local school curriculum explains the history of the village: "The village market did not result from the initiative of civil servants in the government or of business people but of the vision of the village's leader who worked so that people in the village could earn a living by working in the village" (Payung ca. 2001: 10-11). Suwan (the Thawai village leader) recounts that he and the other villagers acted appropriately by making three unanswered requests to government officials for permission to begin building the handicraft center before taking matters into their own hands: "We didn't do anything illegal. We knew what the building codes were. . . . The only thing we lacked was official permission, but what could they say? If you want to walk, there is the walkway, go ahead. If you want to drive, there are the roadways, drive as you like. We have followed all the necessary procedures, adhered to the right building codes, paid attention to traffic flows. We even looked after sanitation requirements. Where had we erred? Nowhere" (interview with author, 22 November 2002, Thailand). The irrigation group served as an ordering institution for how the villagers could proceed. And the villagers' recognition of the legitimacy of the institution's rules marked the steps that their cooperative actions would need to accomplish. The

irrigation development group fell silent upon seeing the new center being constructed, and the government acted as if the village had conducted business as
usual. I privilege Suwan's account of these events because he speaks for his
community and for its point of view, whatever the official version of the conflict might be, if there is one.

The collective identity of the village's authenticity was not a conscious strategy on the part of the village head or any other institution. This emergent social resource induced the artisans and others in their community to shift from
one set of goals to another, while in midcourse. With their own handicraft center, the villagers insisted on their own authenticity as producers and on their
birthright to the village name, as if the village name were a marketing brand
and the community's family inheritance, simultaneously.

No longer related to the space and time of the object's original use, authenticity becomes tied to the current set of social relations, the historical struggles
the space evokes, and the dynamic reenactment and embodiment of the simulated production processes by the artisans. The real-ness of the artisans' crafts
does not emerge from the discovery of a historical precedent of craft production. Indeed, wood carving began in the village in the 1960s when three village
men, Pho Naan Daeng Phanthusa, Pho Jaima Inkewa, and Pho Huen
Phuntusart, went to the city of Chiang Mai to learn wood carving from 1957 to
1962. Their exit from the village coincides with the land act of the 1950s which
transformed agricultural land into a commodity and denied its unrestricted use
to farmers (Jamaree 1996). Unable to farm open lands after the enclosures and
facing drought, villagers began seeking other ways to supplement their farm
incomes.

As international tourists began asking shopkeepers in Sankampaeng in the
1980s about where the wood carvings were being produced, the Thawai village
began to earn its reputation as a center of traditional wood carvings. After the
flow of buyers redirected itself toward Baan Thawai, they made it possible for a
superstar village to come to life. However, just as global tourism elevated the
artisan community onto a pedestal, the market forces it unleashed threatened
the village artisans with eviction. Authenticity based in a reactive identity, therefore, reveals itself to be highly vulnerable to global market forces. To maintain
reactive authenticity against gentrification, the artisans depend on the strength
of their own political mobilization, the sustained interest of outsiders in their
well-being, and the lucky turn of events in their favor.

By contrast, no rebellion was required for the emergence of the Sanpatong
market. One finds historical evidence of the market's emergence on a small

white piece of paper taped to the wall of the market's open-air office that also serves as the village savings group, the handicraft group, and the socializing salon. The undated sheet of paper on the wall tells the history of the Sanpatong Wood Carving Handicraft Center: "In 1954 the village suffered from poverty. There was no easy access to good roads or to telephone lines as one finds nowadays. Mr. Bunmii Taobintaa, who lived in the Chiang Mai district, married a local woman, Lekhaa, and they built their home in the village. At that time the village was poor. Bunmii decided to start carving wooden figures of elephants and to put these elephants on sale."[1] As more villagers followed Mr. Bunmii's example, engaging in wood carving as a means to supplement or replace their farming incomes, a cluster of wood carving artisans emerged.

In contrast to the Baan Thawai center, the Sanpatong center seems to have resulted from a straightforward set of events. In the 1950s Bunmii would reportedly sell a three-foot wooden elephant for 4,000 baht. (To show how significant 4,000 baht was, the anthropologist Jamaree Pitackwong remarks that a junior government official would earn only 2,700 baht over a six-month period.) Moreover, the way that Bunmii earned the money carried prestige because he did not have to work outdoors, where his skin would darken. As a successful wood carver, Mr. Bunmii increased both his monthly income and his social standing within the community (Jamaree 1996: 129-31).

In 1972 two large firms in Bangkok, the Narai Shop and the Central Department Store, contacted Mr. Bunmii and asked to buy his work. Because Mr. Bunmii already had established his reputation as a wood carver, when teak sales increased exponentially in the 1970s and the demand for wood carvings rose in tandem, Mr. Bunmii found himself well poised to take advantage of these new market opportunities. His success in the retail market had a demonstration effect. The other villagers who had practiced different forms of handicraft as a hobby now saw its potential as full-time employment. In Sanpatong the halo effect that bathes a few artisans in the glories of their accomplishment does not overflow onto the general reputation of all the artisans in the community. The halo effect refers to the intangible qualities (not easily identified, measured, or valued) that increase or decrease an object or a person's value, *ceteris paribus* (Thorndike 1920). The person assessing the value of an object or service has a general feeling about how good or bad the object or service is. This general feeling sometimes overrides observable evidence to the contrary. The assessor ex-

---

1. Two-page mimeographed document, unsigned, not dated, found 10 November 2002, translated by author.

plains away the difference between what the evidence suggests and what the general feeling asserts (Nesbitt and Wilson 1977). In this way, the halo effect introduces error into rational calculations of value (Bernardin 1977; Borman 1975; Jacobs and Kozlowski 1985). By contrast, the aura effect inheres at the level of small groups or communities. As a collective resource that operates at the level of small groups or communities, the aura effect differs from the halo in its public goods character. Individuals without a halo coming from aura-less places nonetheless can benefit from it by becoming a resident in a community with an aura of authenticity. Most importantly, as a collective characteristic, aura changes the calculation of the government and of private sector actors with regard to the collectivity. While Sanpatong has the raw materials (a tradition of wood carving) for the aura effect to operate, Sanpatong lacks the history of social mobilization among its artisan population that might have marked it as a place worth fighting for. Sanpatong offers an excellent comparison to Baan Thawai because the Sanpatong case emphasizes how the aura of a locality emerges from on-the-ground political struggles as much as it does from local traditions. These struggles (or the absence thereof) have changed the evaluations by governmental and nongovernmental actors and have enabled the collectivity to obtain valuable resources that otherwise might have been given to the economically well off or to the politically well connected.

HANDICRAFT VILLAGES IN COSTA RICA

The aura of authenticity may not be the initial or the overriding consideration of a government in its decision to promote local cultural industries. This becomes apparent in the neighboring Costa Rican communities of Guaitil and San Vicente, whose handicraft artisans benefited initially from programs in rural development and concerns with gender equity, rather than from any concerns for losing a cultural heritage that, quite frankly, many Costa Ricans might not miss. Just as we saw in the Thai case, state policies were somewhat successful in promoting one of the community's cultural industries, and some plans go awry.

Guaitil

The communities of Guaitil and San Vicente are home to about 1,200 individuals and are located two kilometers apart in the Nicoya Peninsula. With high levels of intermarriage between indigenous Chorotega and the general Costa

Rican population and with no one in the village speaking the group's indigenous tongue, they affirm their nativeness through their craft arts. These artisans represent communities that have been swept up into global networks of commerce and exchange by way of tourism. The artisans create ceramics ranging from small works the size of saucers to large vases standing three feet tall. Most of the pottery is meant for tourists who spend between US$5 and US$30 per items, many of them replicas of the artifacts discovered in the Chorotegan ancestral zones. In the tourist season, most workshops earn between US$100 and US$300 each month. Most earnings cluster near the US$100 or the US$300 level. The artisans operate out of their homes and work in groups of two or three (sometimes more). The home workshops are sometimes detached from the house and are often open-air structures, a roof with no walls. Some of the artisans arrange their pottery on the dirt in front of the house, where they would have set flowers or shrubs otherwise. The artisans also build kiosks from bamboo, thin trees, and plywood to display and sell their goods.

Although the artisans in Guaitil and San Vicente highly regard each other's pottery, both sides recognize that sharing the same cultural tradition has not translated into having the same level of economic performance among the artisans. Ask an artisan from Guaitil about the artisans in San Vicente, and he or she would probably tell you that the people of San Vicente are poor. Then the person would probably qualify that statement: "It is not that we *aren't* poor. It's just that we are *less poor* than they are." The difference in economic development between the two villages manifests itself in the local food shop. In the center of Guaitil the corner store (*pulpería*) offers juices, sodas, bread, canned food, household cleaners, and other goods. Periodically, small delivery trucks visit the store to replenish its stocks. By contrast, the corner store in the center of San Vicente has few items on its shelves, cannot easily make change for bank notes, and does not stock its shelves with food that will spoil.

The original settlers of Guaitil possessed small plots of land on which they farmed. After the village was settled, Joaquín Sánchez, a rich man from neighboring Santa Barbara, arrived. He bought much of the surrounding plantations and gave the village men needed work. What is known of those early days was told to anthropologists twenty-five years ago by the children of the first settlers:

Doña Carmen Briceño Villareal, who is ninety-five years old, and doña Cata Villa-fuerte González, who is ninety-four, are the oldest women in the village and are related by marriage. They assert that their families were the first to arrive in Guaitil from Santa Bárbara. First came don Jesús Villafuerte and doña Paulina González.

Many of don Jesús' brothers also moved into the village and married women from outside of the village. Doña Paulina was a native of Liberia, the daughter of a Nicaraguan man and a Los Angeles [Costa Rica] woman. . . . Other early settlers came from Santa Bárbara, San Vicente, Florida, Chira, and other villages near Guaitil. . . . These first settlers were happy to receive new settlers so that the village would grow. (Hernández and Marín 1975: 12-13)

This pattern of outside settlement with the wealthiest persons arriving last is the opposite of how San Vicente was settled.

The first two families in San Vicente in the early 1900s were the Grijalbas and the Acostas. They owned some four hundred hectares of land between them. Arriving later were the Ruiz, López, and Chavarría families. In contrast to the Grijalbas and Acostas, these latecomers had been dispossessed of their land and had come to San Vicente to settle anew. In the center of the village the landed families are found today; the dispossessed are dotted along the periphery (Román 1994). The maps depicting Guaitil and San Vicente show how the houses and artisan workshops surround the soccer field at the center of Guaitil but how the workshops and homes cluster less tightly in San Vicente.

These early settlement patterns in Guaitil and San Vicente are notable because they have shaped the way that new opportunities for local economic development would be shared. In Guaitil the physical center of the village was not also its economic center because the village was settled before the wealthiest inhabitants arrived. By contrast, the physical center of San Vicente is also its economic center because the landowning villagers first settled its center, and those without land later settled its outskirts. As a result, when tourism promoted the economic development of Guaitil's center, these infusions of cash were shared more widely between the village's physical periphery and its physical center. In San Vicente, on the other hand, those on the periphery physically remained on the periphery economically. Fifty years ago, there were fewer pottery artisans in Guaitil than in San Vicente: only ten could be found among the twenty-one houses in Guaitil, while fifteen potters could be found among the forty households in San Vicente (Stone 1950: 270). Therefore, it cannot be said that Guaitil became the more important pottery village because it has always been dominant.

In 1957 the first communal house in San Vicente was built by several families, mainly the Sánchez Grijalbas and the Grijalba Acostas (Román 1994). These two families are the most prominent pottery producers in San Vicente even now. Today the communal area is the soccer plaza, where meetings are held, fiestas celebrated, and religious ceremonies observed. The noticeable economic activity among the workshops confirms that the artisans of Guaitil enjoy a greater demand for their products than do the artisans of San Vicente. Large and small tour buses enter Guaitil; artisans conduct demonstrations of their craft several times a week to tourists who then purchase souvenirs; and groups of five to ten artisans gather in one workshop to complete pending orders from hotels or souvenir shops.

The more vibrant handicraft market in Guaitil can be explained largely by the interventions of state and nonstate actors in that community. The paved road linking Guaitil to the main Santa Cruz highway, which links the village to national and international tourism, was perceived as necessary for regional development because of the increasing volume of tourists visiting the women's cooperative, CoopeArte. The Santa Cruz government supported paving the road, and the local government saw its chance to promote itself as the center for folklore. Within its jurisdiction lay a valuable cultural resource, artisans crafting pottery that claimed a four-thousand-year-old tradition. Moreover, the artisans themselves were women, and their well-being appealed to national and international persons concerned with women's empowerment. Congresswoman Odete Héctor Marín from Guanacaste supported the bill to construct the road to the cooperative.[2] Although the villagers did not have traditional political connections, the cooperative's objective to empower women gave it a ready ally in the congresswoman. She intervened on behalf of the village to have the road construction approved by the central government. The first woman to be elected to congress from her district, Congresswoman Héctor Marín targeted the well-being of women and children in her legislation. She served during Alberto Monge's administration (1982-86); the road was built around 1983.

The new road gave the artisans access to tourist markets. A retired artisan in Guaitil recalls that the improved road changed the local economy by facilitating the entry of tour buses (informant interview, 15 February 2003, Guaitil). Moreover, buying agents for retail shops and resources more easily arrived in Guaitil, products more easily traveled outward, and more buyers returned. Some of the buyers offered the artisans assistance by providing start-up capital to establish their own workshops, and they also helped the villagers get their products to the beach souvenir shops and to the capital city. Even though some of these acts were meant as smart investments that would later have a higher payoff, the investments were considered generous gifts from newly found friends.

2. Congreso 1982-86; Una de las Diputados de Guanacaste, Odete Héctor Marín.

It was easier to find friends if one lived in a village with a paved road easing their entry.

The demand for the artisans' pottery first increased in the early 1970s after Peace Corps volunteers intervened in the local production practices of the women in the two villages. The volunteers encountered the two villages with women producing pottery for daily use but lacking many of the pre-Columbian designs that adorn that pottery today. The distinctive ceramics made by individual potters were typically piggy banks with figurines of country folks (Stone 1950: 271, 279), whereas it was the pre-Columbian designs that the inchoate tourist market would demand most. The pre-Columbian motifs had nearly disappeared among the pottery makers of Guaitil and San Vicente. Anthropologist Jim Weil reckons that these motifs and the physical forms of the pre-Columbian pots lay dormant for several centuries before being revived in the late 1960s (Weil 2001). The reappearance of these motifs and forms coincides with the entry of the Peace Corps volunteers.

These volunteers, Joy Danielson (who came to Guaitil in 1969) and Richard León (who came in 1970), worked with the women of Guaitil and San Vicente to establish the women's pottery cooperative, CoopeArte (Hernández and Marín 1975: 28). It seems that efficiency concerns drove the decision to locate the cooperate in Guaitil rather than San Vicente, given the proximity of the former to Santa Cruz and to the main road leading to the capital. By combining the talents of the women in the two villages, the cooperative would achieve economies of scale; the investment required to produce the first item is always high because of the cost of buying raw materials and any needed equipment. After the first unit is produced, however, the average cost of each additional unit falls because the benefits to large-scale production are realized. With economies of scale in mind, the cooperative required its members to work together under one roof instead of working in a decentralized way from their homes.

Luring the women out of their homes, the men argued, disrupted family life. When the women worked at home, they could also care for their children and their husbands. The cooperative required a more rigid time schedule for work and reduced the amount of time the women spent performing their domestic tasks, but the women had to obey the cooperative's rules. The artisans would pool their earnings and would make regular contributions to the group in the form of equipment or supplies. The cooperative's more rationalized work-system would make it easier for the cooperative's coordinating committee to monitor the quality of the artisans' works and to ensure that production volume remained adequately high. As the cooperative began to sell larger volumes of pottery, the women became the breadwinners in their families. Their husbands' incomes as plantation and small farm workers paled in comparison. In the late 1970s Doña Hortensia Briceño Villafuerte, the manager of CoopeArte, declared, "We really put the men in their places! [*Ahorita tenemos a todos los hombres sentados*]" (Hernández and Marín 1975: 10).

Eventually, the CoopeArte artisans became the victims of their own success. On the one hand, CoopeArte's success spilled over into the community. A road and other services came into Guaitil because it was the site of CoopeArte. Tourist came into the village in order to support the empowerment of women and to contribute to the preservation of local culture. On the other hand, CoopeArte's success attracted competitors. In particular, the men of the village who had been performing agricultural tasks as peons now saw a new opportunity to increase their earnings and to reclaim their "rightful" places as the heads of their households. The men felt that, as the heads of their households, they should earn more than their wives, so some of the men insisted that the village women step aside. The men changed their attitudes toward pottery production. Surely work well paid is not the task for a "faggot." Before the tourist boom, to dig their hands into clay too frequently would have marked the men as effeminate; after the boom, it marked them as breadwinners. Under pressure from the men, the women felt obliged to return to their homes to work, to teach their husbands the craft, and to pay more attention to their traditional tasks. With dissent at home, coordinating tasks became more difficult at work. Most of the members returned to their homes, and CoopeArte dissolved. But even after the cooperative collapsed, it brought to Guaitil a durable link to the tourist market.

San Vicente

Few tour buses take the unpaved road from Guaitil to San Vicente; the artisans do not conduct craftmaking demonstrations on a regular basis; the pending orders from hotels or souvenir shops do not result in large groups of artisans working together. Whirls of dust follow the vehicles that trek the mile and a half from Guaitil to San Vicente. In the center of the town, one sees little commercial activity. On the right-hand side of the road, a white cement building with Chorotega motifs is shut, its doors chained. To the right, a white building resembling the shut one is open, and occasionally a person can be seen walking in or out of it. The soccer field is empty, and the local bar has a few older men sitting outside in its shade. A few kiosks stocked with pottery are set just outside some of the larger homes.

The residents of San Vicente would like to have had tourists, buying agents, and materials moving freely from their village to the Santa Cruz highway. Unfortunately, the paved road that enters Guaitil stops two kilometers short of San Vicente. A number of residents commented on this handicap: If only they had a paved road, they could get their products out of the village more easily, especially at the end of the rainy season. One artisan remarked that tourists do not like walking in the mud, but his workshop is along a dirt road. At the end of the rainy season, his road takes a longer time to dry than do the other roads, so his sales suffer relative to other workshops in San Vicente. I did not ask the artisans about the importance of the road for their economic success; without being prompted, they lamented the absence.

I witnessed the importance of a paved road to this community over a three-day period as the locals eagerly awaited a visit by someone from the ministry of transportation. Reportedly, the government was planning to build a paved road to the village in order to promote rural economic development. On the morning of the planned visit, the shopkeeper at the corner *pulpería* wore makeup, earrings, and a Sunday dress. Several men in carefully ironed shirts and trousers sat in front of the corner shop waiting for someone from the government to come and tell them when the road and its attendant economic development would arrive.

They waited in vain. Mumbling erupted at the announcement that the visit would be postponed. About the ministry's planned visit little more was said. But the residents still had hope that even if the road might not be paved any time soon, they could eventually become a major tourist destination. Even though San Vicente lacks a good road, its relative disadvantage might change, if political promises can be believed. One informant predicted that a paved road would come to San Vicente in the next few years. He also anticipated that a museum on Chorotegan history, art, and culture would be built in San Vicente, drawing the tourist traffic away from Guaitil. *Almost fourteen years ago* the legislature approved the museum's construction. If the state backs up its plans with economic resources, "the last shall be first and the first last," one informant declared. "The tours will come here for the museum and to see the demonstrations of how the pottery is made. It will finally be *our* turn" (informant interview, 3 April 2003, San Vicente). How they will realize their goal, the informants could not say, especially since the Costa Rican state claims to lack the budget to support such local initiatives. The community must rely on the free market and the good-will of individuals. When I left the field site in 2003, a group of residents continued to meet and to lobby for a paved road and for a museum. In May 2007 the battle for the museum was finally won.

Different Starting Points

The differences in economic development at the village level are mirrored in the district level statistics. I use statistics from the 1970s and 1980s to show how different the economic and social situations were in my study sites. In 1973 the illiteracy rate for persons ten years old or older stood at 14.7 percent in the district of Nicoya (where San Vicente is located) compared with 8.1 percent in the Santa Cruz district (where Guaitil is located) (Costa Rican Census Bureau 1975). Nearly a decade later, the illiteracy rates fell in both districts, but the gap between the districts remained significant, at 9.6 versus 4.9 percent (Costa Rican Census Bureau 1987). Moreover, the infant mortality rate was 48.7 per 1,000 inhabitants in Nicoya in 1999 but only 39.1 per 1,000 in Santa Cruz (ibid. 48). The residents of Santa Cruz have also enjoyed more state services. In 1984 about 66 percent of the Santa Cruz district had access to a telephone compared with only 48 percent of the Nicoya residents. Trash collection was available for 27 percent of the Santa Cruz residents compared with 18 percent of the Nicoya inhabitants (MIDEPLAN 1991: 132). In 1999, Santa Cruz continued to outperform Nicoya in socioeconomic development (MIDEPLAN 2001). These statistics demonstrate that Guaitil is part of a district that enjoys a higher standard of living. Such factors as education, health, and infrastructure affect the capacity of local villages to enter the tourist market. In short, the more economically successful village has more material resources in its district upon which it could *potentially* draw. However, because I do not have data at the village level showing how evenly resources were distributed, I cannot conclude that being in a district with more resources helped Guaitil. Therefore, the district level data is only suggestive of the relative disadvantage that San Vicente may have suffered by virtue of its location when compared with its neighbor.

The Heat of Conflict, the Glow of Aura

Possessing the cultural heritage needed to attract international tourists and to enter the global markets for handicrafts is not sufficient for presenting one's village as a place that glows with the aura of authenticity. Villages find themselves caught up in a web of geopolitics, macroeconomic shifts, and shared understandings about what the country's cultural heritage is and how it should be represented. The viewpoints of the village artisans are seldom heard unless a conflict occurs that merits the attention of the entire province or the entire nation. With the conflict comes the salience of the artisans' cultural traditions as tools for constructing new opportunities in place of old threats.

Such a conflict has emerged in both Guaitil and San Vicente as the artisans confront their clay crisis. Left to the whims of the market, these indigenous artisans find the paths to economic opportunity blocked. An informant in Guaitil described the obstacles to upgrading his enterprise:

> [In the late 1990s] there were lots of tourists. Some of them wanted us to export our goods to the United States. So we started making an application to get an export code from the government over a year ago. . . . The application isn't difficult, and with the code we can get help from the government to export. . . . Then came the clay emergency. The place where we have always found our clay is owned by the Solorzano family. . . . The clay from other places is of lower quality. The price keeps going up, but we pay for it. Now the owner insists on selling us the entire mine. He wants 70 or 80 million for it. How can we afford that? So now we have to deal with the clay problem and have put the application for an export code on hold. What good is an export code if we don't have clay? (informant interview, Guaitil, Costa Rica, 15 March 2003)

Although other sources of clay are available, the pottery made with such lower-quality clay explodes in the kiln more often. The clay mine is located near the indigenous burial grounds, and so the mine is associated with those inputs that have always been used. Finding substitutes is more complex than the stated "quality" complaint suggests: the artisans have invested meaning into the clay mine because of its proximity to the ancient Chorotegan burial ground.

The clay seems to have always been a point of contention. Doris Stone's investigation in San Vicente in the late 1940s revealed that the locals complained about the price of the clay. Leonista Acosta owned the mine in the forties, and arguments would erupt because she allowed some families to extract clay for free while others had to pay. The villagers felt that extraction was a community right for all the artisans (Stone 1950: 272). Now everyone pays to extract from the mine. However, the present owner, don Marcos Solarzano, considers the price so low that it might as well be a gift.

A "gift" grudgingly given, the clay has not improved the economic well-being of the present landowner. His mother struggled to buy the land and has now passed the land to him. She is in her nineties and deserves something for her life of toil, don Marcos reasons. She and her descendants should benefit financially from owning the land, and since only the villagers of San Vicente and

Guaitil are using the mine, they should buy it. He owns little; more would be better: "They are the ones who benefit from the mine. Is it right that they benefit, and I get nothing? Is it right that we are poor [while some of those who use the mine are not]? It is not *just*. And I own this mine. I have a right to do with it as I please" (interview with don Marcos Solarzano, San Vicente, Costa Rica, 8 April 2003). The villagers have asked the government to purchase the mine as a gift to the artisans in both villages. They are willing to pay for the use of the mine, but they cannot afford to buy the mine. Even the government has declared the price too high. The villagers fear that they will lose this valuable resource, and they have embarked on a campaign to save the clay.

The campaign has taken the villagers to the capital city in protest. A group of sixty people took the four-and-a-half-hour trek to San José to meet the minister of culture on October 24, 2002. If this primary input is not protected, residents argued, Guaitil and San Vicente would be confronted with unemployment, large-scale emigration, and the associated problems of drug addiction, alcoholism, and prostitution. Moreover, in an area that perpetuates part of the national heritage, there is more at stake than a few unfortunate artisans (Hernández Cerdas 2002). On these artisans rests an integral part of the nation's cultural heritage. On the basis of cultural heritage, the newspapers and television stations have drawn attention to the clay emergency. In a televised interview, the president of Costa Rica declared the heritage of the Chorotegans a precious national resource. Like the natural environment that the nation holds so dear, Chorotegan culture requires national protection. While the government agrees that the village crafts are unique and merit special assistance, material assistance had not materialized at the time of this study. However, on May 27, 2007, the online *Nación* reported that the San Vicente Eco-Museum of Chorotega Crafts had finally opened after fifteen years of struggle, but that the clay supply remains at risk.

CHAPTER FOUR

The Flows of Production

If the community's reputation as an authentic site of cultural production (an evaluative frame) accounts for why the community's artisans receive a disproportionate amount of external attention and resources, artisans' social arrangements for facilitating production can increase the positive effect of the community's aura. Here we shift our attention from frames to flows: how the flow of people, money, and materials differs from one community to the next. By observing a number of artisans, each for a day or so, and by simply taking part in conversations over meals, without probing into their lives right away with intrusive survey questions, I came to understand how the artisans organize production and the importance of their social ties in mobilizing the expertise of other artisans for finishing designs, obtaining raw materials at affordable prices, and distributing their products within and outside of the country. During the same time period, I also conducted interviews with a nonrandom sample of artisans in the four study communities to ascertain whether gender, education, and age as well as property ownership might explain the economic performance of the workshops in conjunction with or to the exclusion of the artisan's social networks. The quantitative results cannot be used to compare the two villages, but they can be used to illustrate aspects of the craft businesses in both villages. Because I did not cast a broad net with a large number of random interviews, I do not pretend that my findings are representative of all handicraft artisans in any of my research sites; however, I can describe the processes of production, the social ties making those processes possible, and the shared understandings directing its course in the many workshops I did visit. (The appendix outlines my research strategy in more detail.)

The ethnographic method of direct observation, combined with the semistructured interviews of 123 artisans enabled me to address five questions: (1) How do social connections emerge? (2) How do those connections affect how the artisans produce? (3) How do they affect the way crafts are distributed? (4) Do the artisans' social ties account for the more dynamic economic performance found among artisans in Baan Thawai (Thailand) and in Guaitil (Costa Rica) compared with the economic performance of their neighbors? Finally, (5) do social ties to more powerful economic actors (buying agents, for example) place artisans and their traditions on a pedestal for protection or do these ties lead to the loss of authenticity as the artisans become bound to the whims of outsiders and to the urge for economic survival?

I expected to find a variety of reasons for the emergence of social connections (Portes and Mooney 2002). Most studies of social capital skip the question of how social connections emerge, focusing instead on the configuration of the network ties. However, Mark Granovetter ([1974] 1995) tells us that people build new ties by using their existing ones; in his study of how people get jobs, he finds that word of mouth and person-to-person contacts help match potential job seekers with employers on the hunt. Analogously, artisans making things the tourists do not want are willing to connect tourists in search of authentic crafts with friends of friends. Just as James Coleman (1993) noticed that merchants in Cairo would lead buyers to other shops by saying "I don't have it, but I know someone who does," the handicraft artisans in my study communities seemed to know a cousin or a friend in the neighborhood or region nearby who could accommodate a buyer's wish. Such connections proved especially useful for buyers who would come back for more. Buying agents also make discoveries, even while on holiday, through word of mouth passed through friends of friends (Little 2002; Causey 2003).

I began this study thinking that differences in social capital held by individual artisans and enjoyed by others in their village (the spillover effect) would account for the artisans' being able to mobilize labor and materials more cheaply and more effectively (Capecchi 1989; Putnam, Leonardi, and Nanetti 1993). I also expected that socially well-connected artisans would obtain more favorable trading terms from middlemen buyers compared with those lacking such friendly relations with their market brokers (Kyle 2000; Little 2002). This particular set of expectations presented a number of quandaries. When will networks make possible the things we like, and how do we figure out whether networks that provide bridges to opportunities outside of these communities are not themselves evidence of the success that they supposedly facilitate? Walter

Powell and Laurel Smith-Doerr (1994) raise this very question in their literature review suggesting that social connections might prevent artisans from mobilizing labor and materials, especially for innovative purposes. They cite
Glasmeirer's study in which a cluster of Swiss watch producers do not innovate
from traditional technology to digital processes because they are constrained by
their social networks; they also cite Grabher's study in which the steel industry
declines because of cognitive lock-in. Meanwhile, Juan Pablo Pérez-Sáinz and
his collaborators have encountered artisans who feel constrained by the expectations of their communities with regard to how each will engage in his or her
craft (Pérez-Sáinz and Cordero 1994). While such commitments to tradition and
instances of cognitive lock-in might protect the original production processes,
motifs, and forms from desecration, these commitments also might prevent talented artisans from reaping the financial benefits of the commercial market.
Worse, the research itself (never mind its implications) is susceptible to saying
nearly the same thing for the predictor as for the predicted: Traditional groups
of people produce traditional things (Portes and Landolt 2000).

The second quandary: If we do not know how connections emerge, we might
mistake advantageous connections to resources outside of the community as a
predictor for economic success when such connections are the outcomes of that
success. Robert Putnam's (2000) emphasis on "bridging social capital" makes
the important point that extra-community ties may enable communities to access resources that they themselves cannot obtain otherwise. While bridging social capital has been taken up by researchers at the World Bank as an elixir for
local economic development (Narayan and Pritchett 1999; Woolcock and
Narayan 2000), such bridges seem indistinguishable from the exporting of products abroad. The relationship is the export arrangement, and the exporting
arrangement is an integral component of the workshop's economic performance. In other words, the export relationship (bridging social capital) explains
the export relationship (a component of its economic performance). Keeping
this quandary in mind, I tried to learn how social connections emerged with
outsiders, especially with those who provided bridges to opportunities in the
global marketplace. In Thailand I found it difficult to extract information about
extra-community ties because the artisans viewed these ties as proprietary. But
they would allude to their extra-community ties whenever they talked about how
they found new clients or how outsiders convinced the artisan to "go global."
Therefore, a single method of direct interviews was not adequate for addressing this question. I had to wait for the artisans to tell me some of the more valuable stories after the formal interview had ended; some of the artisans had

decided to say (off the record) "a little something," as though they had thought about it intensely following the initial interview but were presenting the story as if it simply popped up in passing, "by the way."

Told either in passing or on point, anecdotes described situations in which social capital had affected the economic performance of the artisans' workshops. To guide my assessment of social capital and economic performance, I reviewed the theories, methods, and findings in Portes, Castell, and Benton's *The Informal Economy*, Portes, Dore-Cabral, and Landolt's, *The Urban Caribbean*, Kyle's *Transnational Peasants*, and Pérez-Sáinz and Andrade-Eekhoff's *Communities in Globalization*. I expected bounded solidarity and enforceable trust to be the types of social capital most relevant to the economic performance of each artisan's workshop, and I knew that these types of social capital would not always manifest themselves in the direct questions I had prepared to ask the heads of the workshops.

Bounded solidarity enables artisans to pass along their traditions from one generation to the next in a close-knit community because those traditions represent who they are as a group. These understandings of what makes each member of the group belong to the collective operates within particular circuits of exchange (Zelizer 2001; Zelizer 2005b) and can be assessed through careful observation. The artisans increase the economic value of their work and their own bargaining power as "real" (authentic) artisans by focusing on group values promoting their resistance to change. It would be a mistake, however, to view the expressed warm sentiments of group solidarity as its only indicator. In his work on ethnic business clusters, Alejandro Portes reminds us that Cuban shopkeepers in Miami seemed to the casual observer anything but tightly bound. They complained about each other's business practices and had a number of disagreements with their co-ethnic competitors in the community (Portes 1997). Likewise, entrepreneurs in New York's and San Francisco's Chinatowns demonstrated similar types of inter-business strife (Nee 1973; Zhou 1992).

In order to discern what is behind appearances, Portes calls for closely observing how agents behave over time. The complaints that business owners have about each other do not demonstrate whether solidarity and trust is at work. At this level of observation, such complaints tell us very little. Rather than focusing solely on what people *say*, Portes insists that we focus also on what they *do*: "Sources of social capital and their effects are not observable at this level [of disagreements and bickering among shopkeepers]; they manifest themselves instead over time and in aggregates of multiple individual transactions. Bounded solidarity emerges as an aggregate 'elective affinity' on the choice of business partners, employees, and customers, and in patterns of associational participation. Enforceable trust is reflected in the routine behavior of participants in business transactions, relative to how similar operations are conducted on the outside" (Portes 1997: 804). The social code of the community illuminates the patterns, giving them meaning. The elective affinity that shopkeepers display makes a statement about what it means to be an entrepreneur within a particular sociocultural milieu. Agents are constantly "taking account of others" (Weber, cited in Portes 1995: 4). An agent takes account of others, not only in her considerations of market transactions but also in the sense that she has formed a stable set of expectations as a result of market and non-market interactions over time. This stable set of expectations helps artisans fix problems more quickly because less negotiation is required in the heat of the moment.

Whatever the group's goals, agreements require enforcement in order to have the intended effect. In order to ensure that individuals will not act against the broader group's goal, the group must have the capacity to monitor and punish individual behavior. Hence, the paradox: "trust exists in economic transactions precisely because it is enforceable by means that transcend the individuals involved" (Portes and Sensenbrenner 1993: 1332). Rewards and information mechanisms are important determinants of enforceable trust: "The greater the ability of a community to confer unique rewards on its members, and the more developed its internal means of communication, then the greater the strength of enforceable trust and the higher the level of social capital stemming from it" (ibid. 1337). Therefore, artisans, suppliers, and distributors within the community are more likely to honor the expectations of the community for following through with their obligations to one another and for upholding traditional practices if informal sanctions are thought to be operative and reliable.

We are still left to wonder whether the goals of the artisans will stay fixed on protecting local traditions or whether the financial rewards found in global markets will trump local loyalties. Because traditions are passed from person to person, their longevity is amenable to sociological analysis, according to Edward Shils. We need not judge the aesthetic value of the traditions in order to see the networks of persons through which the traditions pass, the processes of their passing (ritual practices), and the media in which the traditions are preserved. Some media of transmission (oral traditions) are easier to modify from one generation to the next, while other media (written traditions) are harder to modify without leaving a recognizable trace. In some handicraft communities, some traditions have been revived because outsiders showed interest in their recovery. At the same time, the possibility always remains that outsiders might appropriate and modify local traditions to satisfy their profit considerations rather than respect the local concerns for cultural preservation.

VARIATIONS IN ECONOMIC PERFORMANCE IN THAILAND

I interviewed fifty-two heads of micro- and small-scale enterprises in Thawai and Sanpatong. The small handicraft workshops were micro-enterprises with fewer than ten people, usually employing family members or friends from the community. The economic well-being of these workshops differed dramatically from one community to another, as assessed according to three characteristics used by social scientists studying small-scale and informal enterprises (Benton 1989: 237): (1) the number of full-time, paid employees; (2) whether the workshop head owns the property where the workshop is located; and (3) the reported monthly sales. Micro-enterprises were prevalent in the more economically successful community of Baan Thawai (94 percent), compared with Sanpatong, where about two-thirds of the artisans interviewed had micro-enterprises but only one-third had the larger workshops employing ten or more workers. Of course, employing more people does not mean that an entrepreneur has obtained more economic success, but it does point to the capacity of that artisan to expand production without the help of other workshops. Moreover, the monthly sales question is a sensitive one, requiring me to visit many of the workshops a second time. Because many of the artisans operated their workshops out of their own homes, the question about owning the property where one works captures, however imperfectly, an indication that the artisan has some assets. Workshop heads in both villages reported exporting to foreign markets, but the percentage of enterprises in my convenience sample exporting from Baan Thawai (79 percent) was significantly higher than those exporting from Sanpatong (48 percent). Although I expected the number of years that the workshops have operated to be an indication of its economic health, the longevity of the workshops did not seem to differ significantly from one village to the next.

Just outside of the Sanpatong Wood Carving Handicraft Center I found a number of enterprises employing more than ten workers. However, among the artisans I interviewed in the Sanpatong area, I found a lower percentage of property owners compared with the artisans I interviewed in Baan Thawai. In Sanpatong most of the entrepreneurs worked from rental spaces; those operating from nonrental spaces accounted for 14 percent of the sample. The percentage of workshop ownerships is much greater in Thawai, at 77 percent. The reason for this difference is that many of the entrepreneurs in Sanpatong are participating in an income-generating project. They carve and sell from the same location, but some of their work is subcontracted to friends and kin in their village, away from the cooperative. The locus of work, however, occurs on the rental property. In Thawai much of the handicraft production occurs in front, beside, behind, or within people's homes. And these homes surround the market area where entrepreneurs rent retail shops.

The village with the greatest percentage of workshop ownership also reported higher monthly sales. Nearly three-fourths of the workshops in Thawai had monthly sales over US$1,250. (The average wage per month for employed persons in Chiang Mai was roughly $US150 in 1999 [National Statistics Office 2000].) Only about a third of the respondents in Sanpatong reported similar sales figures. Those with the lowest monthly sales were also concentrate in Sanpatong, where 42 percent earned less than US$500, compared with only 16 percent in Thawai reporting such low sales. (I use sales categories in the Thai communities rather than average sale amounts estimates for monthly sales, as explained in the appendix.) To facilitate interpretation, I transformed these three variables into a single index and categorized the economic performance as moderate to high for the top two quartiles of the index, and low for the first and second quartiles. Within the low category, six of the workshops are in Thawai and fourteen are in Sanpatong. Within the moderate to high economic performance category, sixteen are in Thawai and four in Sanpatong.

The difficulty with my estimates of monthly sales is the extent to which some artisans refused to answer the question. I was often asked if I was working for the taxation wing of the government. Sales reported "too" high might attract more official and unofficial fees, one businessman familiar with the industry confided. I obtained sales data on only forty artisans, but I interviewed another twelve workshops that did not disclose their monthly sales information. I also met with the owners of small handicraft factories just outside of Chiang Mai City and Thai exporters to obtain perspectives from outside of these communities on how these workshops and small factories operate.

Do the characteristics of the heads of these workshops explain how they organize production and how they fare in the marketplace, or should we look to the differences in social capital possessed by each to explain the differences in economic well-being? It is appropriate to think about the characteristics of the head of the workshop because these individuals often begin as self-employed artisans who add workers as the economic expansion of the workshop allows. Four characteristics are common among the entrepreneurs in the two convenience samples. (1) Most are over the age of forty, and (2) nearly everyone is married. (3) Schooling has not been extensive, with most having a primary level of education or less. And (4) most of the workshop managers are female. Because wood carving has been traditionally a male-dominated activity, the high presence of women may seem surprising. Direct observation qualifies this finding. The women often work in cooperation with their husbands, who do not function as enterprise heads. The division of labor is also such that most of the carving is done by men but most of the painting and finishing processes by women. If managers' education, age (a proxy for work experience), marital status, and gender do not differ significantly from one village to the next, these individual-level characteristics cannot be said to cause the different economic trajectories that the artisans I interviewed in the two communities have taken. While the individual characteristics of the workshop heads are similar, the nature of their business enterprises differs.

How Social Ties Emerge

Before turning to how the artisans use their social ties to facilitate production, it is helpful to look at how these social connections emerge. I distinguish between embedded and arm's-length ties, the former being more intimate (strong or integral ties), the latter more businesslike (weak or arm's-length ties) (Granovetter 1983). This distinction is important because, as Brian Uzzi has found, individuals who have a mix of these kinds of ties have more favorable market opportunities than those who have only embedded or only arm's-length ties. As I explored how social connections emerged, I saw clearly how a mix of both was much more likely for artisans in Thawai than for artisans in Sanpatong.

Some of the more successful artisans in Baan Thawai began their careers by seeking out arm's-length ties, leaving their villages in search of new market connections. Only in a few cases did they initially have buyers approaching them at home after seeing the artisan's work appear elsewhere, as in the case of Nopphadol, the wood carver in Baan Thawai who, as we have seen, was approached by outsiders in search of an authentic artisan. If Nopphadol had appeared to have too many arm's-length ties, he would have diminished his appeal as an artisan more concerned about his craft traditions than about "going global" for profit. His seeming lack of arm's-length ties made his acquisition of those ties more likely. On the other hand, consider Yuthana, a prime example of an artisan acting entrepreneurially. Before Baan Thawai had a reputation for its crafts, Yuthana traveled from Chiang Mai to Bangkok with pictures of his handiwork and a few samples strapped to his back. Accompanied by his son, he presented his work at shop after shop, and one shop decided to give Yuthana a chance. Yuthana's work brought swift sales, and the shop increased its orders and Yuthana's profits.

Yuthana's connection to Bangkok facilitated his first encounter with an American buying agent. Having encountered Yuthana's work in Bangkok, the agent wanted to establish an import-export arrangement directly with Yuthana. Knowing little about exporting or marketing, Yuthana was unsure how to proceed, but the buying agent agreed to teach him how to export and to provide him with start-up capital for the production and shipping costs. Yuthana could thereby begin exporting without incurring debt. Over time, he began to understand the expectations and requirements of the global market. He also obtained a reputation for excellence within the country and received visits from the royal family and the prime minister.

These artisans' success stories present a paradox. By virtue of their isolation, the artisans remain unmarred by too much market capitalism and thereby attract the interests of international buyers. Moreover, outsiders are more interested in the insiders who seem uninterested in what these outsiders have to offer. As the story of Nopphadol suggests, not wanting to go global makes the acquisition of global connections more likely. However, as these artisans establish more arm's-length ties, they lose the initial source of their attractiveness. Therefore, it is important to focus on the multiple sources of attraction that the artisans have at their disposal and how their capacity to selectively engage outsiders at different levels of intimacy maintains enough distance (and difference) within their arm's-length ties to maintain the barrier between the core rituals of the artisans and the discerning gaze of the outsider.

By contrast, the artisans in Sanpatong do not manage to attract attention from outsiders in the same way as their Thawai counterparts. Most of the villagers in Sanpatong could not rely on visits from international tourists or curious buying agents. Instead, these artisans embarked on trips to department stores and to small souvenir shops in Chiang Mai and Bangkok. Although artisans in Thawai used the same strategy to make new social and business connections, they had a mixed bag of contact strategies and could use information they obtained from visitors to find better matches for their goods in city shops and abroad. Thawai villagers now host foreign tourists interested in wood carving, and, as we have seen, the routes leading to Thawai are better marked and easier for international tourists and foreign buying agents to travel. With more frequent, casual visits to the village, outsiders are more likely to establish more friendly (embedded) ties with the artisans. As the previous chapter established, the key is to live within a village that attracts outsiders in search of a place where the locals themselves have struggled to revive and protect local traditions. The social mobilization within the Thawai community helped bring its talented artisans to the attention of other artisans within the province and eventually international buyers visiting the area. Unfortunately the lack of such a mobilization in Sanpatong renders the community unable to serve as an arm's-length tie attractor.

How Social Ties Affect Production

Thai wood carving workshops are organized vertically. The master carver oversees production and performs the most intricate carvings. Older artisans (usually men) carve subtle, intricate designs but remain under the supervision of the master carver. The youngest men and women of all ages occupy the lower rungs of the workshop hierarchy. They carve simple molds on which the more experienced artisans will carve the designs or paint the finished carvings.

The artisans use blades, handmade chisels, and handmade mallets, for the most part. With felt-tip pens they draw the coarse outlines of a figurine on pieces of wood more than three feet in length. With a pencil they draw intricate designs onto the wood. The artisans copy some of the designs from books on Thai mythology and art, and they make some modifications to the traditional motifs. Other designs they sketch from memory—things seen throughout childhood in their households, in the village temple, and at local festivals. The sound of their work is hypnotic—the chisel tapped and pounded by the mallet. The chisel or the blade sometimes enters the wood at a ninety-degree angle, at other times it enters slant. The flying wood chips are gathered and used for smaller carvings.

There are two ways in which workshops or small factories are organized in the Thawai village. Family workers or friends from the community usually operate the small workshops with fewer than ten people. The master carver, who is usually an older man, is revered for his skill and is expected to teach the more inexperienced carvers. However, the master carver does not make demands on the others. The pride of one's craftsmanship regulates the quality of the work, and the obligation to others in the workshop as well as the fear of shame among those outside of the workshop ensures that the workers complete their tasks with little formal supervision.

Social networks also offer job security. If one's business is having problems, one can ask for help from relatives and neighbors. Other workshops or small factories in the community can absorb artisans who must leave a bankrupt workshop. The scarcity of high-quality carvers means that these workers are highly valued. Finding work outside of the village is easy, though perhaps not desirable because work is also a highly social activity with a great deal of social rewards. The medium-sized workshops seem to operate using patron-client arrangements. I define medium-sized those workshops that resemble small factories, employing more than ten but fewer than fifty workers. The head of the enterprise has to create a sense of loyalty among his workforce. His workers are part of his "family" and must be made to feel that way. As one informant put it, "We have to listen to them and take care of them." The head of one such workshop laments that he must always be on site. No one does anything without getting his approval. Without his watchful eye, mistakes are likely to be made. The workers in these factories do not have the same informal job security as those in the smaller workshops; other small factories do not absorb the unemployed so readily. These workers find themselves neither obligated to others nor with others obligated to them. On the one hand, the heads of these larger business enterprises talk about how the people in the factory are part of a family, but at the same time the head talks about the businesslike character of the relationships. Differentiated ties exhibiting caring and commercial logics mix in these establishments.

We see these different logics brought to bear in cases of theft. Among the smaller workshops, the idea that workers would steal raw materials, supplies, or money is unthinkable. If a worker were to commit such an act, the worker would have to leave the workshop. In some cases, the worker would leave of his own accord without prodding from the owner: everyone in the community would know about it, and the shame would be too great for the worker to remain. "You see," one informant explained, "they all live together in the community, and the workers often see each other during the evening meals, where they gossip. If something happens during the day, it is recounted in the evening. Everyone knows." But just as a family member might make a mistake, so too might a worker who has made amends for a mistake be forgiven by the family.

In contrast, the medium-sized workshops are more accustomed to theft, since the workers come from a number of different places. Some of them will steal small amounts of raw materials or other supplies. So long as too much is not taken, the enterprise owner ignores the theft. If the culprit is known, then a warning is given and the guilty party is asked to return the stolen materials. If the theft continues even after the worker has been warned, then the worker is fired. The reason for the theft and the social identity of the person committing it affect the punishment meted out. To the extent that informal social control reduces theft, one would expect operating costs to be lower. Some of the medium-sized enterprises can count on these informal social controls and can remain competitive as a result.

In addition to social control, workshops benefit from informal cooperative arrangements. A number of enterprises in the Thawai village reported that they joined with other workshops to buy raw materials in bulk to lower production costs. These buying groups were several and were established primarily along kinship lines. Buying raw materials in bulk is especially important because wood is a scarce commodity. The largest exporters of wood to the Thawai village are in Malaysia, Burma, and Laos. Other suppliers are in Brazil, Cameroon, and New Zealand (Luechai and Siroros 2002: 23). Little trust is required in the transaction among the cooperative buying group because everyone pays for the shipment up front. If a workshop is having trouble paying for its share of the shipment, then it will be dropped from the buying group. I expected to hear stories about how workshops doing well would assist poorly performing workshops in the buying of raw materials, but no such stories were forthcoming. With fierce economic competition, some artisans told me, the workshops cannot afford to help a workshop that cannot cover its share of the supply shipment.

The workshops often establish relationships with subcontractors who provide unfinished goods that the workshop then paints, refines, or adds value to in some way. A common coordination problem is that of timing. Since the workshop has a deadline established by the customer, it needs its subcontractors to bring in the orders on time and in accordance with the correct specifications. There are two ways to deal with orders that do not arrive in a timely way. Either the workshop can dock the subcontractor's pay or the workshop leader can talk with the subcontractor and plead with him or her to deliver the materials in a more timely fashion. Most managers use the latter method, regardless of enterprise size. It is rare that a workshop will change its subcontractors when the subcontractor makes errors in production. Relational subcontracting (Dore 1992) binds the lead workshop to its subcontractors, and the lead workshop knows that the subcontractor will fix mistakes made on the product's specifications and that the subcontractor will be sincere in trying to meet the deadline.

Yuthana recognizes the importance of social relationships in his small "factory." He explains that his workers are members of his own family. If he does not express his interest in making sure that everyone feels good about coming to work and feels a part of a cohesive group, a bad feeling emerges among the workers, absenteeism increases, and the pace of work slows. (Several other small factory owners also acknowledged that sour "family" relations within the factory would affect production processes and the general sentiment within the workplace.) Yuthana's relationship with his workers helps him mobilize labor and resources more efficiently. If he subcontracts part of an order to a group of home workers, he is sure that they will follow the specifications he gives them. If they fail to do so, he talks to them and explains how the work should be corrected. He sees no need to find other subcontractors or to punish his subcontractors by decreasing their piece rates. He gives them some slack in return for their quick response to his needs. These relationships give Yuthana an advantage in the market because they help him maintain the high quality of his products while reducing the likelihood of having production disrupted (interview with author, 27 November 2002).

The social stigma of shame also exerts pressure on the workshop leaders to ensure that their products meet the specifications of their clients. Because the master carvers take such pride in their craft, any hint that their work is not up to par is shameful. The other villagers see the pickup trucks leave the workshops in the morning piled with goods for delivery. If the truck returns with the same shipment because the buyer has rejected it, the workshop leader is embarrassed. Likewise, if other villagers notice a change in the consumption patterns of a workshop owner, then the villagers infer that some products may have been rejected or that a client may have failed to pay. This situation reminded me of Malinowski's *Argonauts of the Western Pacific* (1961), describing travelers along the kula ring in Papua New Guinea who generate quite a spectacle in preparing for their trade journeys. These travelers move in a certain direction with one set of goods but return home with another. Not to follow the usual circuit is to announce failure and risk the loss of status. With these social pressures to maintain one's social status in the handicraft village, quality is ensured.

Social pressures from the community are not enough to promote efficient production when one's material resources are limited. Sometimes one simply needs a well-connected and well-resourced family on which one can depend. Consider Mr. A in the neighboring village of Sanpatong. He began his handicraft business around 1991, after he obtained a loan from the Agricultural Bank of Thailand to buy a small crane to lift logs of teak and an expensive anvil to split the logs. The Agricultural Bank has targeted small enterprise development for loans, and Mr. A was able to obtain his loan in part because he had property collateral and savings. In contrast to the success stories in Thawai, Mr. A did not report that foreign buyers helped him start his enterprise. In that he is a Thai of Chinese descent, it may be inferred that he had social and political connections through the Thai-Chinese community, which several studies of entrepreneurship in Thailand have pointed to as a source of support for entrepreneurial ventures (Phipatseritham and Yoshihara 1983; Skinner 1957; Unger 1998). However, in this case it cannot be confirmed that the respondent obtained resources from the Thai-Chinese community. Because Mr. A did not indicate having used such contacts, I could only establish that his main source of external assistance came from the Agricultural Bank of Thailand.

Mr. A employs six people regularly. When the orders increase, he hires up to fifteen more people on a temporary basis. He keeps his enterprise lean but flexible, able to respond to changes in the demand environment and to externalize the risk of sharp downturns. The part-time artisans do piece-rate work for Mr. A's enterprise. Some of them may work for other handicraft enterprises, may farm part-time, or may combine income-generating activities as opportunities present themselves. How the part-time workers fare when they are not working at Mr. A's factory does not seem to concern Mr. A. He can't give them work that he does not have, he explained.

Just down the road from Mr. A are a group of artisans struggling to sell their wood carvings through a local cooperative store. Remarkably, trust, solidarity, and reciprocity characterize their working arrangements, but economic dynamism does not characterize their business performance. For example, the artisans working in the Sanpatong Handicraft Center, in the front of the Kew Ler Noi village, exhibit high levels of cooperation. Their rotating savings and credit association (ROSCA) has about thirty members. Each member contributes US$2.40 to the revolving fund monthly. On the seventh of each month, all of the members meet together, share a meal, and count the contributions. The contributions total about US$70 in savings, and a separate fund remains in reserve to handle emergencies. If someone has an emergency, she or he must explain to the group what the problem is and they discuss whether the supplicant warrants assistance. There are three smaller meetings each month to socialize and discuss any problems that have emerged. Most of the members of the ROSCA are also members of the wood carving cooperative store. The cooperative requires all of its members to pay 3 percent of their sales to a central fund. The sellers have receipt pads on which to record sales. At the end of each day, the secretary of the cooperative registers those sales in her accounting book. The artisans trust one another enough to forgo more frequent accounting during the day, yet they are struggling to compete in global markets, their trust and cooperation notwithstanding.

There are some things that social capital cannot do directly. To upgrade production processes, to innovate in design, and to distribute the goods to more lucrative markets requires know-how and financial capital not readily available in most villages. One production process that has been critical for wood carvers is that of curing the wood. In the village handicraft centers, a makeshift shed of corrugated iron insulates the room where a wood-burning stove dries the wood. If the wood does not dry adequately, the change in the temperature during its passage by ship to a location with a different temperature and humidity will cause it to crack. The more advanced the curing process, the more confident the artisan can be that her or his products will arrive unharmed at far-away destinations. But without interventions from outside of the village, upgrading becomes a goal unlikely to be realized.

The social relationship of workshop owners with their workers, suppliers, distributors, neighbors, friends, and kin affects how their enterprises are organized and what goals they are likely to seek. These relationships also affect how workers are managed within the workshop, the types of cooperation possible among workshops, and how contracts are enforced with subcontractors or distributors. Enforceable trust enables entrepreneurs to make agreements without the constant fear of malfeasance. With all eyes in the community watching what the entrepreneurs and their providers do, the entrepreneurs could be assured that the providers would think twice before breaching an agreement. The shame of such a breach would be too great. To capture enforceable trust, I asked two question: (1) If there were a problem in the workshop, would others in the community know about it? (2) If a worker stole a little money or a small amount of material from you, what would you do? The first question offers an indication of the community's monitoring capacity with regard to agreements between workshops; the second, the informal means available for punishing or deterring malfeasance within the workshop itself.

In the more dynamic village, community monitoring was perceived by only half of the workshop heads. In Sanpatong, by contrast, everyone reported that the community would know about problems in their workshops. Because the local economy for crafts in the Sanpatong village cluster is less dynamic than that in Thawai, there seems to be less of a concern for secrecy. Secrecy hints that competition is fierce and that the entrepreneurs are trying to protect their innovations. Although the monitoring apparatus is strong, the rewards and punishments available to workshop heads may be few and far between. In the community where everyone feels that "word travels fast," less than half of the respondents reported that they could resort to informal sanctions for punishing wrongdoers, compared with 70 percent of the workshop heads I interviewed in the Thawai village.

Just as workshops heads punish wrongdoers, they also practice patience with artisans who simply make mistakes. To understand how these production norms differ from one village to the next, I asked how flexible workshop managers are with subcontractors. Unfortunately, asking respondents who their business partners are and how they know one another was not possible because of concerns among entrepreneurs about sharing important market information with outsiders. For this reason, I asked a more general question: "If a subcontractor did not follow the client's specifications or did not deliver goods on time to you regularly, what would you do?" If the entrepreneur chose to talk to the contractor or talk to a close friend of the contractor, the action would indicate that informal sanctions were strong and effective. If the entrepreneur chose to find a different subcontractor or to haggle over price or quantity, it would indicate that there were no informal sanctioning mechanisms in operation.

All of the economically dynamic workshops were flexible with subcontractors who were late in delivering orders, and 80 percent of these entrepreneurs would ask their subcontractors to fix an order that did not meet the specifications of the client. Of the intermediate and subsistence-level enterprises, 63 percent were flexible on the timeliness of delivery and 32 percent were flexible on the specifications. Therefore, I can conclude that the production norms in these handicraft workshops have a material basis. Wealthier enterprises can wait for artisans to learn how to perform up to par, but the poorer enterprises have to respond more quickly to market pressures, or such struggling business ventures do not survive.

Some entrepreneurs explained that subcontractors are late with deliveries for a number of reasons, including sickness, family problems, or the complexity of the job. If a subcontractor is perpetually late, then the entrepreneur sets fake deadlines, in order to make meeting the real deadline more likely. There are socially expected durations placing a margin of error around deadlines. A number of inquiries about progress are made just before and just after the deadline to ensure delivery. So long as these performances are enacted, delivery usually occurs along with an animated narrative explaining the cause of delay and how all the pieces of the puzzle came together in the nick of time. Disruptions in the performances bring about disruptions in the contracting relationship—stories that the artisans would rather not tell.

How Social Ties Affect Distribution

Just as artisans' social ties create marvelous stories of producing *just in time*, their ties to each other and to outsiders generate lively stories of how their goods traveled out of the village into local, national, and global markets. The artisans have cooperative arrangements with one another to share the costs of transportation so that they may more easily search for new marketplaces. In the interviews it seemed that a number of artisans in both study communities were trying to share the costs of transportation as a practical matter, especially when they were collaborating on a project. For example, the size of the order (volume) and the diversity of goods (scope) might require several workshops to bring their expertise to bear behind a lead workshop. Cooperative arrangements keep the movement of the handicrafts at a lower cost. However, the tit-for-tat exchange that enables cooperation in distributing the artisans' goods seems almost completely instrumental—a means to a material end without regard for interpersonal relations and the obligations they carry. If an artisan does not pay his or her portion for the transportation, that artisan gets dropped from the group.

Social connections also help regulate the distribution of goods. If a workshop is supplying its wares to a local dealer or souvenir shop in the city of Chiang Mai, other workshops in the neighborhood will try to avoid supplying to the same dealer. Otherwise, they would find themselves in a race to the bottom—undercutting each other's prices until the profits disappeared. Moreover, these workshop owners and workers live near one another, and the violation of another workshop's long-term trade relationship would create tension within the community. The workshops are willing to compete with one another on quality and price, but long-term trade relationships are off limits (Luechai & Siroros 2002: 30).

Long-term relationships, however thin, can make a big impact on the distribution of the artisan's goods abroad. Yuthana recalls fondly how someone he knows in the United States recommended him for an "emergency job." A handicraft distributor had received a large volume of broken goods from a producer in a different part of Thailand. He needed help in repairing the shipment to get the commodities to the market quickly because the sales season was upon him and a great deal of money was at stake. The distributor's buying agent was a Thai fellow who was studying for his master's degree in business. The agent knew of Yuthana's work and reputation (a weak tie), and with Yuthana's help he assembled a team of artisans to repair the damage. It seems that the Thai buying agent needed to lower the risk of having another failed outreach into the Thai countryside, from the point of view of the US distributor, so the broker called upon artisans whose quality would be self-monitored out of a sense of pride. Yuthana's successful intervention in this case provided a basis for establishing a longer-term relationship with the distributor, but at the same time Yuthana seems to have been sought out for this special case because of his ongoing relationships and the strength of his personal reputation.

Yuthana's story illustrates the economic benefits to be derived from having a mix of embedded and arm's-length ties. His arm's-length ties serve a matching function; those far away who are in search of the expertise and reliability that he represents may be more easily linked to him through weak social ties. Unlike the artisans we will encounter in Costa Rica, the artisans in Thailand have arm's-length ties to a number of foreign buyers. Over time, some of these arm's-length ties develop into embedded ones; the interactions are infrequent and the negotiations somewhat fierce, with each side getting as much as it can. A number of informants heading other workshops and small factories noted that they made distinctions between orders placed by their embedded clients and their arm's-length buyers. Embedded clients have to be satisfied first and foremost, but these same clients are willing to work around the artisan's schedule, especially when new economic opportunities present themselves. If a workshop has too many orders, the embedded client will negotiate with the artisan about what parts of the client's order are most lucrative and most timely. That way the artisan does not lose new clients because of a delay and the artisan still manages to keep the long-term client satisfied.

The leeway that long-term clients give these handicraft workshops is analogous to the situation of relational subcontracting between spinning companies and their suppliers. As Ronald Dore explains, when small merchants in the Japanese textile industry find that there are cheaper alternatives from other dyers, beamers, or weavers who have obtained more efficient technologies, these small merchants do not behave opportunistically to reduce their costs by simply switching suppliers and finishers (Portes 1995: 7). Instead, the merchants work with their suppliers to make their prices more competitive so that the relationship may continue: "The more common consequence is that other merchant-converters go to their finishers and say 'look how X has got his price down. We hope you can do the same because we really would have to reconsider our position if the price difference goes on for months. If you need bank finance to get the new type of vat we can probably help by guaranteeing the loan'" (Dore 1992: 163). So it is with the artisans' distribution channels. There has emerged what I call "relational distribution" between the artisans' workshops and the various distributors and other buyers. The distribution patterns do not make sense for isolated individuals concerned solely with maximizing profits and minimizing inefficiencies, but these patterns are understandable in the structural embeddedness of the finishers and the merchants in dense relations of exchange. Likewise, the distribution of finished goods takes place within particular circuits of exchange, replete with shared understandings about what will be done and how.

In Dore's metaphor, the difference in how an artisan behaves with embedded versus arm's-length ties is similar to that of an individual seeking a marriage rather than a one-night stand or a series of one-night stands (Dore 1992: 163). It is in these different social relations that we find correspondingly different methods of distribution. Most importantly, whether the artisan has arm's-length ties to the distributors, embedded ties with their distributors, or a mix of these tells us a great deal about how flexible those distribution channels will be with regard to the needs of the artisans and how lucrative the terms of trade will be for those artisans at the site of production rather than for the middlemen buyers.

How Social Ties Affect Economic Performance

When we consider how some distribution channels are more lucrative than others, and how some social arrangements lower the costs and increase the efficiency of production, we begin to see how social ties affect the economic performance of these handicraft workshops. The workshop heads could access skilled labor and raw materials based on their sense of solidarity with others in the community. The heads of the workshop managed to expand their enterprises and to export to lucrative markets abroad through the intervention of external actors, be they government agencies, nongovernmental organizations, middlemen, or buying agents. These factors—social solidarity and external assistance—had a greater effect on the workshops in the Thawai village cluster than in the Sanpatong village cluster, mainly because the overall demand for goods from Thawai was higher. I assessed demand anecdotally based on the number of tour buses and the number of packing trucks I saw. I confirmed this assessment of demand by obtaining self-reports from the artisans about their monthly sales in the high season.

Because my observations do not span a large number of years but rely on the recall of the artisans themselves, I cannot say whether the differences in social organization have caused or have been caused by the economic performance of the workshops. It seems that there is a two-way street between how social connections emerge practically and how the workshops perform economically. It may be that economic success in one situation leads the artisans to try to replicate the way they organized production in that particular situation to the exclusion of other arrangements. For artisans struggling economically to keep their workshops afloat, risk-taking is a bad idea, so potentially lucrative arrangements with foreigners may not be sought, and if such arrangements present themselves, such artisans may enter export arrangements that make their workshops vulnerable to the volatilities of the global market. In the worst-case scenarios, when the goods do not sell, the artisan must swallow the costs. Only where there is some goodwill between the buying agent arranging the export details and the artisans do we find that the artisans are given time to make mistakes and to learn from them. Otherwise, they remain in a position of dependence, and links to outsiders are merely chains of obligation and ties to greater vulnerability.

How Social Ties Affect Cultural Traditions

When we consider the effect of social connections within the community as well as between individual artisans and individuals outside of their communities, we see how sociability (sometimes) protects authenticity. First, bounded solidarity performs an important function in the training process. Wood carving artisans do not learn their trade from textbooks. The master carver has to be willing to transfer the skills to others. Those carvers who have learned the craft from family members were "born into" the craft. They have nonmonetary reasons for teaching their craft to others.

Second comes the question of how artisans learn to innovate, especially since it is difficult for them to understand what types of innovations in design might expand their market bases abroad. The object comes from somewhere else, the journey distances the object from the receiving society's traditions, and the production process defies replication (Appadurai 1986; Graburn 1976; Spooner 1986). To the extent that the innovation maintains or intensifies the conceptual distance between the receiving society's traditions and that of the site of production, the object's value increases. Because the artisans do not travel to those destination countries frequently, they depend on the reports of buying agents or those who travel abroad frequently to understand what sells best and what might be a lucrative innovation. How will the innovation be received? There is always the risk that the innovation veers too far from the buyer's expectations and thereby loses economic value. There is also the risk that the artisan receives so many orders for innovative work that he or she loses the rhythm (and the knowledge) of the original production processes. The question of what buyers want and what artisans are willing to do makes the artisans' social connections of paramount importance for the protection of local traditions. Ironically, having ties to global actors who recognize and affirm local cultural traditions sometimes protects the authenticity of the craft; however, the question is not whether being connected to global actors will diminish the authenticity of the craft. Instead, the question should focus on the dispositions of those global actors—the purpose for engaging these artisans in the first place.

I noticed that after an artisan had met with me on a few occasions, he or she would ask me about what Americans like most about Thailand and about what are the most popular items in the catalogs for furniture and home décor. I would try to remain neutral by saying that I'm not really a fashion expert, but some artisans would insist. Upon hearing that I was going back to the United States for a few weeks, one artisan asked that I bring back furniture and design catalogs. Although he could find some catalogs in Thailand, he wanted to get his hands on things that do not come so easily to Thailand. I suppose that this might give him a competitive edge in design, and this conversation alerted me to the small stacks of magazines that I would see but not notice (initially) in some artisans' workshops. When they used designs found in these magazines, one artisan told me, they did it the "Thai way." Presumably, local patterns and motifs mixed with designs found in the global marketplace. The artisans' social ties gave them access to these designs, especially for catalogs not readily available or, if available, expensive by local standards.

Artisans also use their social ties with outsiders to protect their authentic innovations. Keep in mind that an artisan has no legal recourse when others copy her or his innovation. Some artisans use their social ties to hide their innovations from local artisans while the trusted exporter moves quickly to get the product out of Thailand and into a boutique in a Western country. A British informant recalled how one of his handicraft suppliers beckoned him to a back room in her house and hushed her accessory to the covert operation. These are for our eyes only, she warned, and no one else in Thailand should see it. His mission was to get the product to his shop in Britain so that he could have something that looked out of the ordinary and she could have the pride and profit of her innovation, at least for a while. In time, the new product would lose its newness, but for now the artisan could reap the rewards of being a first mover in innovation.

Without denying that "money makes the world go 'round,'" I would advise against such a one-sided interpretation of cultural markets that presents participation in global markets as a threat to authenticity and to local innovation, because such an interpretation has only a tenuous relationship with the facts. In cultural markets, the profit motive may coexist with concerns for authenticity and cultural preservation: "To defend authenticity one must invest in economic and affective resources. The artisan, the broker and the consumer must 'desire to enter the game, identify with the characters' joys and sufferings, worry about their fate, and espouse their hopes and ideals' [Bourdieu]. This 'sense of investment' comprises the sometimes unstated and often misrecognized economic sense of maximizing profit as well as the affective sense of ingenuous commitment" (Wherry 2006b: 8). The affective resources emerge in the interaction of buyers, sellers, and others involved in the market. The involvement of the buyers and the artisans in the game of understanding what is and what is not authentic produces the market for authenticity.

THE TWO COSTA RICAN COMMUNITIES
Variations in Economic Performance in Costa Rica

When I moved to Costa Rica to compare how artisans used their social connections to organize production, I realized right away how much the economic context of the Costa Rican artisan differed from those of the Thai. To keep my comparisons roughly equal from one country context to the next, I tried using three indicators of economic performance for my convenience sample: (1) the reported monthly sales, (2) whether the workshop had intermediaries outside of its district to help distribute its goods, and (3) whether the workshop (knowingly) exported its products. The home-based workshops in Guaitil had three regular workers, but those in San Vicente had only two. This reflects the economic capacity of these workshops to employ more than a family-pair full time. The workshops in the two villages did not differ significantly in the ownership of the homes or in the number of full-time employees, so the indicators that had proved so useful in Thailand had to be discarded in Costa Rica. For these handicraft workshops, unlike the Thai workshops, exporting products was the exception rather than the rule, so I focused on monthly sales, which was easier to assess in Costa Rica because the artisans were so forthcoming.

I used reported monthly sales during the tourist season as my sole indicator of economic performance. Monthly sales ranged from a low of US$26 to a high of US$300. I tried to confirm the artisans' reported sales by comparing them with the reports offered by other workshops that appeared to have the same number of customers. For example, while living in Guaitil I observed a larger number of tour buses stopping in front of a particular set of workshops, and I observed groups of tourists buying products at those shops. I followed up with a second round of interviews and asked artisans what their monthly sales were in those cases where I suspected severe underreporting. I also reinterviewed workshops that I thought had reported more or less accurately. Those I suspected of underreporting their incomes (except in one case) responded more truthfully the second time. For the one case that did not correct his reported monthly sales, I asked someone from the neighboring workshop whether their neighbor earned as much as he did or less, and the neighbor confirmed that they earned about the same in monthly sales during the tourist season.

Admittedly, artisans' responses on monthly income are likely to be lower than their actual incomes because they do not wish to seem too successful for fear of inspiring envy or attracting loan seekers. However, through direct observation I could confirm that those who reported incomes in the higher range more or less had the same number of customers coming into their workshops. In one case, I adjusted the reported income because the neighbors confirmed that the workshop in question earned more or less the same amount of money in sales: "We make about the same per month." These income figures applied only to the high tourist season (late December through early April 2003). Although some of these artisans have achieved a moderate amount of success, it would be a gross overstatement to call them rich; yet among the poor they are doing pretty well.

Based on these performance indicators and direct observation, I categorized nearly 41 percent of the forty-nine workshops interviewed in the two communities as moderately successful, while the remaining 59 percent were low performers. I categorized workshops with reported monthly sales just below US$260 dollars but with links to intermediaries outside of the canton as moderate economic performers. I also observed these workshops—with low reported monthly sales but with links to intermediaries outside of the canton—receiving tour groups on a scheduled basis. I found a fairly even distribution between moderate and low economic performers in Guaitil (45 percent moderate and 55 percent low among twenty-nine workshops) but a skewed distribution in San Vicente, where the low economic performers dominated (35 percent moderate and 65 percent low among twenty workshops). The only significant difference in artisans in each village was the sex of the workshop head. In Guaitil nearly half of the workshop heads were women, but in San Vicente this number was cut to a quarter.

How Social Ties Emerge

Because international tourism accounts for a great deal of the artisans' incomes in these two communities, it made sense to ask how the artisans form the right social connections to attract these tourists. Through watching tour vans come into both Guaitil and San Vicente, always stopping in front of the same shops, it became apparent that the tour operators had specific relationships with specific artisans. When I tried to probe into how some artisans managed to have the tours stop but others did not, I noticed that artisans who had previously been offering a wealth of information closed themselves off with an uneasy silence. Some would simply say that a cousin works or used to work at a tourism agency at the beach or in town. One family had a son working in tourism who parked the minibus outside the family homes in the evenings. How much the artisans pay their friends and relatives for the exclusive rights to being in the tourism circuit, no one would say. It is clear, however, that the stronger, more intimate social ties were directing the flows of tourists into particular workshops of particular villages.

The paved road to the Santa Cruz highway facilitated the flow of buyers to Guaitil, while the gravel road connecting Guaitil to San Vicente made the entry of buyers as well as the movement of the artisans out of the community more difficult. As we have seen, when the government decides to build a new highway, even for reasons unrelated to the handicraft communities in question, not only does it affect the ease with which people and materials flow in and out but new social ties may be established after contact has been made between the artisans and potential buyers, business partners, designers, or distributors. Roads, telephone lines, and other communications infrastructure make those links possible.

Finally, international foreign aid groups such as the Peace Corps facilitate new social ties for the artisans. Although there are political considerations that go into where the Peace Corps will send its volunteers, luck also plays a role. Whatever the reason for the initial contact, Peace Corps volunteers tell their friends and other volunteers about their volunteer placements. Because the volunteers have no commercial incentives for speaking well of the handicraft village, their word carries a great deal of weight. Some tourists came to visit Guaitil because they had heard about a women's cooperative that Peace Corps volunteers helped establish there (see chapter 5).

How Social Ties Affect Production

In Guaitil and San Vicente, the process for producing pottery is articulated in seven steps. First, there are up-front investments in equipment. A local villager acquires old motorcycle wheels that serve as spinning pottery wheels. He buys these from friends who work as mechanics or acquires them by his own vigilance for dilapidated motorcycles. The artisans purchase paint brushes and small knives in the neighboring towns of Santa Cruz and Nicoya, but they find the remaining equipment in the village: a smooth quartz stone for polishing, a nail for etching, and either the curved, diamond-hewed hull of a calabash (jicaro) fruit or the corner of a plastic milk carton for smoothing the mouths of the jars.

On a regular basis the artisans gather raw materials, namely clay, sand, and curiol. Someone outside of the workshop performs this second step in the production process. A person (usually a man) on a bicycle delivers bags of clay sufficient for producing about eighty souvenir items. Someone in the workshop or a relative or friend in the village will use his own pickup truck to haul clay bought in bulk, averaging 1,000 colones (US$25) per bag. In addition to clay, the artisans also collect iguana sand—so called because iguanas favor such sand for laying eggs. Finally, the artisans gather curiol from the mountain. Curiol refers to the stones used to make paints: a white porous stone, a black volcanic-looking rock, and a red terracotta stone are separately crushed and mixed with water to make the paints. The red and white curiol are found on mountain summits; the black, in superficial clay beds. The villagers gather these paints as one would berries.

The artisans must prepare both the clay and the curiol. The clay arrives as gray stone and is pulverized in a three-foot-tall mortar by an equally long club. After the artisan mixes the pulverized clay with water, an adolescent youth stomps the mixture with bare feet, as one would a vat of grapes for wine. Adults also engage in the activity and sometimes parents do it with their children. Radio music keeps the stomping going at a good pace. The curiol also arrives as stones needing to be crushed. After they are mixed with the right proportion of water, they become paints.

To make a pot, the artisan slings a ball of clay onto the spinning wheel. She or he kneads the clay, then burrows a hole in its center. With four fingers, she molds the pot's walls. Spinning the pot on a motorcycle's rear wheel, she shapes its exterior, then smoothes it with a clay-stained corncob. An alternative method for shaping the pot is to use a standard mold as the base and to ring coils of clay, one atop the other. Spinning the stacked coils on the wheel, the artisan uses the corn cob and gravity's pull to merge the rings. The pot takes shape not because great care has been taken in measuring the length of the clay logs or the size of the clay balls. Once the potters begin the process, their hands mold and fingers curve by instinct. One artisan can produce about forty small pots over an eight-hour period.

Left outdoors to dry, the pot is ready for an application of white paint. After the base color is allowed to dry for about twenty minutes, the artisan paints the indigenous motifs onto the white base. These designs are not drawn onto the pot ahead of time. No measurements are taken to ensure that a band of duplicate images is equally spaced. The artisan measures the designs by sight and paints with great care. Other techniques are at her or his disposal. She may invigorate the pot's base by texturizing the paint: she may dip a toothbrush into the red terracotta paint and flick the brush's bristles, splattering the white base with red, or she may dab the pot's walls with a small, porous sponge—texturing the exterior, veined red on white. Painting requires the most time of any stage in the process, and not all artisans are equally talented in it.

After the painted pot has air dried, a smooth quartz stone or the fragment from the plastic milk carton polishes the exterior. The stone is the traditional instrument and resembles an arrowhead. The plastic is an adapted instrument allowing the artisans to shine the jars' curved mouths more easily. The very young or the very old usually polish the pots. Once the surface of the pot is smooth, the artisan etches the painted designs with a small nail. The etchings uncover the white base paint and give the pot texture. Numerous hatched marks fill in the circled motifs, revealing the white base. Elongated S-shaped motifs stretch across the bands. After etching, the artisan again polishes the pottery.

Finally, the trial by fire ensues. The artisan sets each piece of pottery inside the kiln. If the clay has not been well mixed or if stomping has not eliminated enough air bubbles, the pottery explodes. Since an exploding pot damages the pots around it, three days of work can be lost in an instant. The pots remain in the fire for about ten to fifteen minutes. The following day, the stock of pottery on the shelves professes the trial's outcome. I noticed that the way the artisans in the two communities organized these production tasks differed considerably. Enter a pottery workshop in Guaitil, Costa Rica. The mother, the father, or both sit at their own spinning wheels, the son or daughter prepares the paints, a grandparent rubs smooth the finished pot's exterior. When large orders need to be completed, others outside the family come to join the light banter and the laborious activity. A twenty-year-old man may be seen in one workshop during the morning hours, another workshop during the afternoon. Such workers keep their work arrangements flexible and revel in the demonstrations they perform for tourists on a regular basis.

At 7:30 in the morning one finds many of the Guaitil artisans already hard at work. By eight-thirty, movement has quickened. Bicycles, pickup trucks, and a few motorcycles whiz by the workshops, stopping here to deposit pottery, waiting there to borrow paint (as if asking the neighbor for a cup of sugar). In the late afternoon, a woman pushes a loaded barrow fifty feet to her competitor's workshop, where the kiln is already fired and ready to receive her pots. The kiln belongs to the Pilón Shop, but when the shop owner is not using his own kiln, the neighbors come.

At another workshop one finds four twenty-some-year-old men. They have come to help their friend with an order for sixty souvenirs due in eight days. Two are especially good at painting; the other two, adept at molding pots. They are usually found in their family's workshops, but when they have free time, they enjoy visiting their dreadlocked soccer companion. In the evenings they can be found together playing soccer, and when exhausted, gossiping beneath the tamarind tree. A man in his early thirties sometimes joins them in work and play, though he often works from home with his wife.

Nearby is Yolanda's workshop. She is the president of the pottery cooperative, CoopeGuaitil, but the cooperative members do not have a workshop where they all work together. They work from home and bring their pots to the cooperative shop located at the corner of the village square. Pictured on the wall of the shop are the group's members. Along with them is a 1970 newspaper clipping about Doña Lisa, who was one of the founders of the earlier cooperative, CoopeArte, and worked with a Peace Corps volunteer to transform pottery from its marginal status as a woman's hobby to the central source of the village's pride and income. Yolanda is quick to note how the women of the village got it connected to global tourism, and one of her sons now works as a tour guide. Doña Lisa remembered how the handicraft market boomed after the Peace Corps volunteers assisted with marketing and after the road was paved from the village to the main highway. The only external assistance she considered significant was the free supply of materials that artisans in both villages received to build their own kilns and set up their workshops at home. The governmental Institute for Social Assistance (IMAS) provided the assistance in the early 1990s. This early aid has contributed to Doña Lisa's success today.

Glimpse a workshop in San Vicente, just three miles away from Guaitil. The father or mother sits at the pottery wheel, and a part-time worker prepares the paints (if there is money to pay for this). On a good day, chairs are arranged for tourist demonstrations, but tour buses seldom come here. Instead, the buying agents or a few merchants from the neighboring Guaitil visit the villagers of San Vicente to collect otherwise stockpiled wares. In San Vicente, everyone works for him or herself, with few exceptions. Market competition is fierce because few buyers enter the village and those who come take advantage of the villagers' desperation. Many artisans in San Vicente report selling some of their ceramics at reduced prices to artisans in Guaitil, where the buyers are. Other artisans in San Vicente report competing in price to attract customers away from higher-priced producers in their own village: "I live further up the hill away from the main plaza where a few tour buses *do* stop. Just after the rainy season, the road leading to my house is muddy, so the tourists don't bother walking up here. To attract buyers I have to sell cheap. I don't care if others complain. I have to survive." From these introductory observations, it seems clear that the artisans in Guaitil are on sounder economic footing than are those in San Vicente and that their social connections may be facilitating their performance.

As I spent time among the residents of San Vicente, it became clear that the local artisans had no shortage of right norms or of good intentions. What they lacked were the opportunities to demonstrate the usefulness of applying these values and intentions for anything other than altruistic causes. Helping to repair a damaged school building or pooling resources to assist a destitute family were not unheard of activities, but such cooperative arrangements, my informants insisted, had nothing to do with business. What business means is survival in the best way one knows how, and historically cooperation has not been one of those ways. The artisans I interviewed in San Vicente were less likely to have flexible, cooperative work arrangements, yet many of them expressed high regard for cooperation in business. In an interview, the contradiction between what the artisans regard highly and what they pursue was set in stark relief.

> *Interviewer:* I will read statements made by two people. Please tell me who you think is right.
>
> Estela says that in the past the artisans tried to cooperate, but the competition among them was too great, and their economic situation worsened as a result; but Adriana says that in the past the artisans tried to cooperate, and as a result, their economic situation improved.

Who is right? Estela, the first person; or Adriana, the second.

Respondent: What do you mean? Working together? Forming a cooperative?

Interviewer: Yes.

Respondent: Well then, it would be the second, because it is better to work together.
. . . Just like the old adage goes, "In unity there is strength."

Interviewer: Do you think that there is much unity or cooperation in the village?

Respondent: No. It is individualistic.

(Informant interview, 3 April 2003, San Vicente)

The respondent added that the villagers do not give one another loans of money because almost everyone is broke. The little that they do have is pooled reluctantly, if at all. Is the lack of cooperation among them the cause of the depressed local economy in San Vicente?

The inability of the artisans to work cooperatively does not cause their low economic performance. In the past they *did* work together because they realized that cooperation would increase their productive capacity and lower price competition. However, the market did not respond favorably to their efforts. As one artisan sees it, cooperation does not work well in resource-poor environments because the markets do not respond to local initiative alone. If people come together because they believe it is in their interests to do so, and if they pay the costs of coordination while reaping none of the benefits, then they will not be able to sustain their cooperation.

To demonstrate the limits of cooperation in poorly resourced environments lacking a strong client base, I offer the story of a failed cooperative. About ten years ago, one of San Vicente's cooperatives fell apart. There were no warning signs that it would. Each member contributed his or her particular talents as well as money for materials to the group. Those not contributing their share would be excluded from the group. Therefore, members of the group could trust that others would not shirk their responsibilities. With few outside options available to an outcast, the group could credibly enforce its rules. When one of the group's leaders could not contribute money for materials because of his obligation to support a family member living abroad, he was banished from the group. Without him, the group was unable to complete its orders for a generous patron in the United States. The rules were enforced but the main goal was not realized. By the time a third shipment either arrived incomplete or not at all, their patron lost her patience. With few tourists coming into the village, there were not enough alternatives for selling their increased stocks of pottery. The group had too much unity, too few markets. Without the market's vindication, the members began to desert the group. Cooperation and solidarity had run their course (informant interview, 3 April 2003, San Vicente).

How Social Ties Affect Distribution

As we saw in the Thai cases, social ties also affect the distribution channels available to artisans, and distribution channels determine how much power the artisans have to negotiate their prices and their terms of trade. The most disadvantageous situation for artisans in Costa Rica is having only arm's-length ties with outsiders. The micro-enterprises in our two Costa Rican villages found themselves easily substituted for other workshops offering cheaper goods. Artisans with only arm's-length ties distribute their goods by traveling themselves to souvenir markets or waiting for individual tourists and the occasional buying agent to visit their workshops in the village, in search of a good buy. Artisans with only arm's-length ties with individual tourists and occasional buying agents are more likely to compete on price and will find that they have less negotiating power compared with artisans who have long-term business and personal relationships with their buyers. This lack of negotiating power tends to dampen the profits realized through distribution channels that are characterized as arm's-length only.

Embedded ties move us out of the realm of dyadic negotiations into that of relational distribution. Rather than learning by doing in a dyad, artisans engaged in relational distribution can appeal to overarching social structures to facilitate the flow of their goods and of their reputations. The tourism operators who bring van loads of buyers to the workshops are sometimes the children or close kin of the workshop heads, or friends of friends. Although the operators are paid for delivering buyers to the workshops, they must choose who will benefit from organized tourism. Other embedded ties have emerge when volunteers from such religious organizations as the Mennonites have lived in the village with a family and returned to the United States with pictures of their host families and of their pottery-making techniques. In some cases, a volunteer's parents have returned with their children to purchase large volumes of pottery from the host family. I met a gentleman on the bus from Santa Cruz to Guaitil who was doing just that; he wanted to show his thanks to his son's host family and seemed especially pleased that he could do so without a patronizing handout. By coming to the village to buy from the host family, as well as a few others, he would help these artisans, as the saying goes, help themselves.

This sense of goodwill does not pervade all embedded ties. In some exchange circuits, the artisans' low social status as peasants (however talented) gets in the way of their status as authentic purveyors of an indigenous tradition. There are some buyers who have known the artisans for a long time but who, because they come from the higher economic classes of Costa Rican society, call the shots in their hierarchical relations with the artisans. It is as if the buyer is doing the artisan a favor through patronage and considers prices that cover the artisan's costs of operation as more than adequate. By contrast, buyers who come into contact with these artisans with an attitude of respect have evaluated the work as beyond the logic of costs-of-operation or cost-per-unit-of-time principles. Though embedded in terms of how long the artisan has known the buyer and how much the artisan interacts with the buyer in social as well as economic situations, the circuits of exchange are imbued with different meanings and different implicit understandings (Zelizer 2005a). The shared understandings carried in these circuits of exchange affect how economically beneficial the distribution channel will be for the artisan.

Having a mix of both arm's-length and embedded ties to outsiders offers a mixed set of distribution channels that the artisans may utilize strategically. In other words, the embedded ties that the artisans have give them a sense of stability when negotiating with arm's-length buyers. If the embedded relationship has instilled in the artisan a sense of importance and pride, the artisan cannot become too subject to the whims of arm's-length ties without jeopardizing her or his relationship with dependable (embedded) ties. These embedded ties affect how businesslike the artisans may appear when negotiating with new buyers. In general, the economic effect is positive by virtue of the diversity of distribution options at the artisan's disposal.

How Social Ties Affect Economic Performance

Production and distribution dynamics combine to explain the supply side of economic performance. Community solidarity and external assistance for starting up the enterprise best predict the economic performance of the workshops in the Costa Rican cases because these factors account for how the more successful artisans may engage in relational distribution in the first place. To assess the effect of outside interventions on enterprise performance, I asked whether the entrepreneur received help from individuals or agencies outside of the village to build a kiln or to establish the workshop. Such help came largely from a nongovernmental agency partnered with the state to provide the artisans with building materials gratis. Among the artisans receiving start-up assistance from outside the community, 62 percent were in Guaitil compared with

38 percent in San Vicente. Among the artisans not receiving start-up assistance, 42 percent were in Guaitil and 58 percent were in San Vicente. The difference is not statistically significant, but the figures begin to matter when we simultaneously consider how much social solidarity there is among the workshops in each community.

Between those who have and those who have not received help from outside of the community to start up their enterprises, there is roughly a US$21.69 difference in reported monthly sales income. This difference in sales applies to those workshop heads at the median in terms of how much solidarity they felt existed within their community. As the feeling of belonging to a unified community with a unique tradition increases, community solidarity increases and the artisans are able to derive greater benefits from external interventions (such as the start-up funds that some of them received to establish their workshops and to build their kilns). Among those who have received no assistance from outside the community at the start-up stage, community solidarity had a smaller effect on monthly sales, highlighting the limits of social solidarity to generate material resources that no one in the community possessed in the first place.

How Social Ties Affect Cultural Traditions

In the two Costa Rican communities social connections within the village helped protect local cultural traditions. Artisans recognized that the crafts in their villages differed from the crafts in other villages, and they reported feeling social pressure to produce their pottery in a particular way. Paradoxically, connections with people outside the community also helped protect local cultural traditions. As outsiders asked artisans about the origins of their local cultural traditions, the artisans found themselves needing to research their local histories and needing to ad-lib where the narratives of what was original did not emerge with clarity. Some of these local traditions may be old, others new, and still others indeterminate, but the need to define production processes as traditional makes them so, for all intents and purposes. On the flip side of having to answer outsiders' questions about authenticity is having no one to answer to: Artisans who had felt most estranged from international tourism had less motivation to present themselves and their work as authentic. With no audience for the performance of authenticity and few rewards available from fellow villagers, such artisans responded to economic hardship by turning their craft into piecework, accepting whatever specifications the buyers had in order to survive.

Just as we saw in Thailand, social ties are the conduit for the intergenerational transfer of these local craft traditions. During my interviews with artisans,
I asked, "How did you learn your craft?" Those who had learned the craft from
other family members would sometimes express their sense of being "born into"
the craft tradition. Because sixteen artisans in Guaitil and thirteen in San Vicente learned the craft from family members, the differences in the intergenerational transfer of the craft did not differ significantly from one village to the
next. Likewise, the social pressure that the artisans felt to do their work the same
way as it had "always" (in the imagined history of the past) been done seemed
to be a source of frustration for some of the younger artisans, exposed to images on television and able to access the Internet in the nearby town of Santa
Cruz. While they took pride in being able to do what other artisans in other
places could not, they bemoaned being tied to the tethering post of tradition
(e.g., Herzfeld 2004). This lack of freedom enables cultural traditions to survive. Also enabling the survival of the craft traditions was the network closure
of these villages. Without a great deal of commercial traffic and without the possibility of leaving and returning with great ease, these artisans relied a great deal
on their home communities for affirmation and for help in times of trouble. As
James Coleman observed, when network closure is high, social control is also
high. In these villages, social control leans in favor of protecting cultural traditions, and those who try to stray from that goal find themselves talked about,
annoyed, and otherwise socially punished.

CONCLUSION

As much as these analyses tell us, they leave much unsaid. Does solidarity
promote higher incomes or do higher incomes make solidarity easier to achieve?
It is impossible to measure the levels of solidarity five to ten years ago. Respondents are likely to remember trusting relations in the past if they currently
enjoy higher levels of economic success, even if the past was riddled with conflict (Sabel 1993). It is also possible that the solidarity felt among the artisans
is also related to where the artisans live. Noticeably, along the perimeter of San
Vicente, questions regarding social cohesion received less enthusiastic responses
compared with the respondents in the center of the village. It was the perimeter where those dispossessed of land settled and the center where the landholders made their homes. These structural features might go further in
explaining the economic conditions these artisans now face as well as their outlooks on solidarity. The evidence gathered here cannot determine whether sol-

idarity led to higher levels of economic success or whether the causal arrow ran in the opposite direction, but the ethnographic data certainly suggest that positive market experiences have contributed to the social solidarity of the artisans.

Cooperation notwithstanding, village artisans require outside interventions if they are to enjoy the fruits of globalization. Economic globalization can create opportunities for local economic development and cultural revival through international tourism and the thriving crafts market. However, these benefits do not emerge naturally from the interactions of supply with demand. Agents from within and from outside the community must act with particular goals in mind. Most significantly, the outside interventions affect (1) the prices that the artisans negotiate, (2) the way they mobilize labor and capital, and (3) the monthly incomes they derive from sales. The interventions can turn the tide from a globalization of destruction to a globalization of creation.

Artisans do not negotiate the prices of their crafts in a vacuum. The artisan and the buyer have different stories each tells her- or himself and each other. These stories create distance between the traditions of the buyer and seller and make the act of purchase a singular experience. The buyer will remember and recount the act each time he or she responds to someone else praising the object. Were the state to inform tourists that these handicraft vendors are not to be trusted, the tourists would approach the act of sale with distrust and without regard for the producer's or the seller's "authenticity." What would be most important would be the price and the brevity of the exchange. However, in an environment in which the state and the tourist agents praise the local cultures and traditions, the tourists approach the act of buying with enthusiasm.

Moreover, as we learned in the story of the cooperative in San Vicente that failed, the way in which artisans perceive solidarity depends on the benefits they reap from cooperation. To promote solidarity and economic development, the state or other external agencies must pay attention to the networks of artisans as they enter new markets and must provide the kinds of support that would make success more likely. Just as the protection of infant industries benefits noncultural industries, it also benefits the cultural industries. In the arena of global markets, there are some things that local communities cannot do. Paving roads, validating the local cultural traditions in international forums, and improving information flows from the global to the local marketplace are some of those things. The local and national government, nongovernmental organizations, and buyers who establish partnerships with the village artisans affect how these artisans will distribute their goods. In the previous chapter we saw how the state changed the travel patterns to two provincial cities with the construction of a road. We also saw how the Peace Corps volunteers assisted the women's cooperative in Guaitil with organizing production and marketing their goods. Later marketing assistance occurred as shop owners from the United States and elsewhere came into contact with these artisans while on vacation. In other words, the location of the workshops and the lure of the village for outsiders are key factors explaining local economic development. The local histories and ethnographic evidence point to the importance of the village, the interventions therein, and the village's embodied cultural capital for the economic livelihood of the artisans.

The findings in these four communities across two countries and world regions show how the concept of social capital helps us understand the dynamics of local production in global markets. As we explore the limits of social capital in the context of globalization, we find that the capacity of social connections to facilitate local economic development is greatly affected by the history of these communities, the ways their social ties to outsiders have emerged, how their social ties to each other affect the production process, how their relationships to outsiders promote the relational distribution of their goods, and how their relationships within and outside of their communities affect the cultural traditions on which their crafts are based. The case studies suggest five key propositions to explain the flow of production and its consequences:

1. Participation in the global economy is a heterogeneous phenomenon for small enterprises. Dynamic economic activities are rare among micro- and small enterprises. More common are the moderate economic performers dependent on a limited number of buying agents (middlemen) and the workshops operating at the level of subsistence, barely covering the costs of production and able to tap only a limited flow of tourist spending. Each type is empirically identifiable (e.g., Portes and Itzigsohn 1997).

2. Structural (e.g., paved roads), political (e.g., small enterprise assistance and export promotion), and cultural (e.g., elective affinities) conditions promote the emergence of social ties to outsiders. The first two factors are amenable to government manipulation, suggesting a role for policy to play in promoting local cultural industries, but the third factor warns against pat solutions for complex processes. When distributors evaluate artisans from different cultural traditions, the distributors already have a definite idea about which cultural traditions are most worthy of reverence, whatever the product quality is.

3. The quality, efficiency, and cost of production will vary from one circuit of exchange to another. The notion of circuits of commerce stands in strong contrast to the input-output model of social capital (input) and economic development (output) so popular at places such as the World Bank. The ties themselves come with roles, protocols, rights, and obligations (Zelizer 2005a, 2005b) inculcated in the network members (Portes and Sensenbrenner 1993).

4. Distributors and other outsider actors enable some artisans to engage in relational distribution, whereby their concerns for the long-term relationship with distributors are based on extraeconomic concerns such as what people will think of them in their home community (not to mention what they might think of themselves). How these distribution channels work depends to a great extent on overarching social structures, rather than solely on the power that the distributor has to punish the artisan economically.

5. Moreover, overarching social structures may provide some protections for the authenticity of local cultural practices. Commercial markets remind the artisans of the distinction between the sacred and the profane, and the artisans' ties to one another—their own material and political resources—as well as their ties to sympathetic outsiders help them to protect those traditions they hold to be sacred.

These findings further suggest that it is not enough for artisans to have the "right" social ties; they must also have the "right" understandings about what is appropriate to ask of those ties. This logic of appropriateness frames how artisans use their social ties in the flow of production (March and Olson 2004).

The Thawai Village Market, Thailand

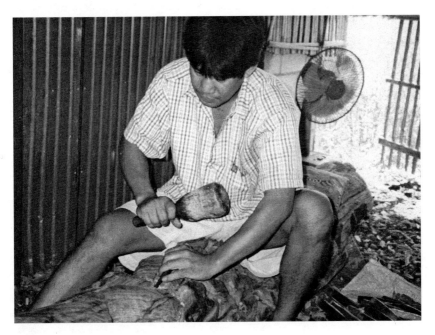

A wood carver in Sanpatong, Thailand

Typical house in Guaitil, Costa Rica

A woman in Guaitil transporting clay

Coope-Guaitil, a Costa Rican cooperative in Guaitil

A kiln in the backyard of an artisan's home in Costa Rica

CHAPTER 5

Framing Authenticity

In the last chapter, we focused on how people and things move, in part motivated by the symbols that cling to the work the artisans do. We saw how artisans use their relationships with other artisans and with buyers to mobilize labor
and materials and to obtain more favorable financial conditions for exporting
their products. To have social ties that act as bridges to opportunity, the artisan
needs to live in a community that attracts people to the supposed site of authentic cultural production. The outsides who are motivated by the importance
of authenticity for handicrafts are those who help protect the artisans' claims to
authenticity by paying higher prices for goods and by respecting the rights of
artisans to refuse to change some crafts according to the preferences of the Western consumers. The artisan may demand better prices and better trading terms
and may refuse vulgar alternations to authentic forms and processes when outsiders consider those artisans and their communities worthy of special attention. Therefore, the key question is how some artisans and their communities
become more attractive to outsiders and thereby more worthy of special attention while others do not. Randall Collins might explain this inequality thus:
"[The sum of] privilege and power is not simply a result of unequal material
and cultural resources. It is a flow of emotional energy across situations that
makes some individuals more impressive, more attractive or dominant; the same
situational flow puts other persons in their shadow, narrowing their sources of
EE [emotional energy] to the alternatives as participating as followers or being
relegated passively to the sidelines" (Collins 2004: xiii). I will draw upon my
fieldwork in Thailand and Costa Rica to demonstrate that the emotional

energy—defined as "a strong steady emotion, lasting over a period of time . . . [that] gives the ability to act with initiative and resolve, to set the direction of social situations rather than to be dominated by others in the micro-details of interaction . . . [and] to be self-directed when alone" (ibid. 134)—varies from one community and one buying situation to another. The vignettes in this chapter point to the ritual ingredients of the market interactions and their outcomes for price and for authenticity.

Since the civilizations of antiquity, the marketplace has been the privileged locus for exchange, where the communal actions of observing, bargaining, buying, and selling incessantly occur and reoccur. Along with the products, feelings, emotions, and information are also changing hands. In short, culture is part of what gets exchanged; culture *is* the exchange. At the same time, cultural markets erect barriers to outsiders, because the artisans possess a tacit knowledge not easily transmitted, especially when the buyer speaks a different language. Nevertheless, as personal narratives about the artisans and historical tales about local traditions focus the attentions of the buyers and sellers on a common theme, a shared mood becomes perceivable, intensifying the mutual focus of attention. For example, as buyers touch the pots, feel the tickling roughness of the clay, feel it as the producers do, the buyers and sellers create an emotional energy that permeates the scene. The collective effervescence—defined as "a process of intensification of shared experience" (Collins 2004: 35)—emanating from the interaction ritual empowers the symbols of membership (sacred objects) and activates the sense of solidarity in the artisans who defend those membership symbols. The resulting emotional energy leads to the buyer's respect for the authenticity inherent in the objects (ibid. 48).

Taking my cue from Collins, I show how the artisans in my study communities sometimes succeed and sometimes fail to frame themselves and their objects as authentic. The performance falls flat when factors unrelated to the authentic performance disperse the buyer's attention or when the buyer does not engage bodily and face to face with the artisans and their objects. The performance seems forced when the artisan offers too much detail about how authentic the objects and processes really are (Collins 2004: 50-53). Truth becomes "obvious" in the interaction with artisans who have nothing to prove. The authentic frame takes shape insofar as the interactions feel natural, somehow raw, at times improvised. As important as price negotiations are for how well handicraft artisans fare in global markets, we know too little about the processes that generate more favorable terms of trade for artisans. The preliminary framework offered here moves toward addressing the question of how artisans can make the market work to their own advantage and how these market interactions affect the authenticity now for sale.

FRAMING AUTHENTICITY AS INTERACTION RITUAL

As we have considered how authenticity gets framed in various situations, we have seen the basic process of the interaction ritual in operation. The four ritual ingredients of the interaction manifest themselves as follows:

1. The artisans gather in a site where tourists and other buyers have been invited (explicitly or implicitly) to observe the artisans at work, to interact physically with the objects and with the artisans, and to see and be seen by other buyers and tourists (*"group assembly with bodily co-presence"* [emphasis added, Collins 2004: 48]).

2. Outsiders notice the barriers to producing these crafts and the scarcity of these objects in their home communities. The tacit knowledge possessed by master craftspeople cannot be found in textbooks and the designs refer to specific cultural traditions (history). Moreover, the language that the artisans use often differs from that used by the tourists and other global buyers. The barrier to outsiders attracts them to the artisans in the first place (*barrier to outsiders*).

3. The outsiders focus their attention on how the artisans produce their crafts, and the artisans at times seem so caught up in their work that the presence of outsiders seems to go unnoticed, until the artisan invites the outsider to feel the texture of wood made smooth or pottery still in the rough (*mutual focus of attention*).

4. This mutual focus of attention generates what seems to be a shared mood of awe among the observers and a sense of pride among those observed. For the artisans, the repetition of this interaction draws them more into their stage roles as they intensify their beliefs in the parts they are playing and their pride in playing their parts well (*shared mood*).

Collins writes: "As the persons become more tightly focused on their common activity, more aware of what each other is doing and feeling, and more aware of each other's awareness, they experience their shared emotion more intensely, as it comes to dominate their awareness" (2004: 48). The artisans get caught up in the rhythm of working and of showing their work. Engrossment increases with each explanation, each attempt to communicate something not obvious, each invitation to touch the thing in the process of creation.

The interactions whereby artisans attempt to frame themselves and their works as authentic have five key outcomes with important implications for the cultural integrity of their craft.

1. The artisans become acutely aware of belonging to a group whose traditions are rare and respected by economically powerful outsiders.
2. Some of the artisans feel great pride in the work that they do and boast about how they became involved in exporting their crafts by accident. They derive emotional energy from the recognition they receive and from the rhythmic entrainment of working in front of an appreciating audience. At times the artisan's hands seem to have a mind of their own.
3. The locale of operation seems to emit a glow (aura), enveloping the persons, practices, and things contained therein.
4. The artisans continue to produce objects that represent their cultural traditions. They treat these symbols with respect in much the same way as religious believers treat sacred objects.
5. Standards of morality emerge: The artisans find themselves ready to defend against the desecration of the objects by disrespectful outsiders and maverick insiders alike. Artisans who veer too far from acceptable norms of the craft become the subject of gossip and may find themselves ostracized.

These ritual outcomes result in the artisans' deciding that some things, such as the real spirit house, cannot be put on sale, and these restrictions about what can and cannot be commercialized increase the social and economic value of the artisans' works. Figure 5.1 depicts the framing of authenticity as an interaction ritual and helps us see the process whereby different circuits of exchange gather the emotional energy needed to bathe the artisans in their aura of authenticity.

The vignettes that follow have been articulated into seven interaction situations: (1) the works in progress. (2) the backstage rounds, (3) a staged play, (4) a staged transcendence, (5) awkward play, (6) child's play, and (7) common play. In the first, I describe my initial visits to the Thawai village in northern Thailand and the emotional energy derived from seeing half-finished carvings in process (*works in progress*). In the second, I recount the excitement of going behind the scenes in the village by the invitation of a local artisan. These backstage rounds intensify the witnessing of authentic craftspeople at work and affirm the exclusivity of being chosen to go on such special visits through a behind-the-scenes circuit (*backstage rounds*). I then highlight the possibility of staging these authentic processes without losing the emotional energy gener-

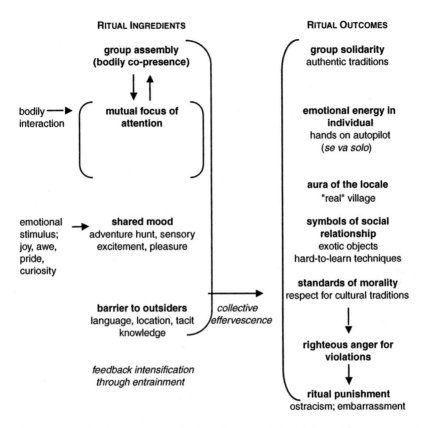

RITUAL INGREDIENTS

**group assembly
(bodily co-presence)**

bodily ──▶
interaction

**mutual focus of
attention**

emotional
stimulus;
joy, awe,
pride,
curiosity

──▶

shared mood
adventure hunt, sensory
excitement, pleasure

barrier to outsiders
language, location, tacit
knowledge

*collective
effervescence*

*feedback intensification
through entrainment*

RITUAL OUTCOMES

group solidarity
authentic traditions

**emotional energy in
individual**
hands on autopilot
(*se va solo*)

aura of the locale
"real" village

**symbols of social
relationship**
exotic objects
hard-to-learn techniques

standards of morality
respect for cultural traditions

**righteous anger for
violations**

ritual punishment
ostracism; embarrassment

Figure 5.1. Authenticity as Interaction Ritual. *Source:* Adapted from Collins 2004: 231.

ated by the backstage rounds through illustrations from Costa Rica, where staged demonstrations of pottery making are standard fare for tourist groups (*a staged play*). I return to Thailand, where a struggle over transcendental values ensues as a foreign buyer asks an artisan to make a sacred object (a spirit house) for a profane purpose (to serve as a bird cage). As a result of the contestation over what is sacred and what profane, the artisan (operating just outside of the geographic confines of Thawai) replicates a different version of the spirit house using a different production process to differentiate it from "the real one." The buyer markets the spirit house by playing on its transcendental values and on its practical worth (*a staged transcendence*).

I also use a vignette depicting a small factory owner in Thailand who sources some of his products from the Thawai village to show how awkward staging authenticity can be (*awkward play*). The buyer's affection for adorable children also works into how buyers assess prices in vignettes from Costa Rica and Thailand (*child's play*), especially when those children seem to be so incorporated into the life-worlds of their artisan parents that the children themselves confirm that their community is transmitting these craft traditions "naturally" from one generation to the next. The final situation I describe is the highly competitive market scenario in which the buyer is trying to get the lowest possible price for the greatest volume and quality combination available. The *common play* typical of this scenario dooms the artisans and their communities to lower prices and to an unfavorable position in the marketplace. As ideal types, these situations do not exhaust all possible types of encounters in which sellers are trying to frame their products and their locales as authentic sites of production or as simply worthy of a higher price, yet the situation types explored in this chapter capture the crucial elements that give or fail to provide advantages for artisans framing their production as cultural and somehow special.

Staging a Work in Progress

Artisans who present themselves, their crafts, and their producers in the raw give the buyer a sense that he or she is observing a work in progress. The improvised presentation comes with its interruptions; misplaced props slow down the pace of maneuver; but the seller does not invite the buyer for a tour "behind the scenes," because however improvised the show is, it nonetheless must go on. The work in progress becomes a totalizing market experience, each moment stitched into a motley quilt of memories and rationalizations. Not from making the rags uniform to ease comparison but from making a grab bag of misfit bits and pieces does the buyer stitch together an account of what is being sold, how sincere the seller is, how sincere the artisans are, and how much the buyer should be willing to pay for the object and for the experience of buying and later displaying it.

The Thawai village handicraft market offers an excellent space for buyers to walk into a performance *in medias res*. I recall walking down the main street of the village market along the canal. On the two wooden platforms astride the canal groups of women sit cross-legged putting finishing touches on bowls and wooden figurines using small tools (a skinny paint brush, a small brush, a small etching nail). On both sides of the canal, I notice the variety of activities going on as they would have with or without me present. Artisans are talking about food, television programs, the foreigner passing by: "Look, he's so black!" They assume that I can't understand what they are saying, and for now, it is better so. Their assumption that language acts as a barrier to my understanding comments that might damage a potential commercial transaction relies on a simple fact: A language with five tones does not attract the casual learner on holiday.

I slow my step before an open-front shop and immediately become nervous about how the interaction will progress, and what kind of game this person might play and I might engage in. A man in his thirties peers at the details of a small wood panel, etches onto a fold of the wood, blows from parted lips to remove the debris to get a better look. He seems to be "caught up" in performing his work, and I am carried along with him as I hesitantly take one long step toward him for a closer look. "Hello," he begins, in English, spoken as if it too were a tonal language, the "o" arched upward in pitch before careening down. He introduces himself as Mr. Nui, mispronounces my name as Fresh, until reminded of Fred Flintstone, and offers the usual inquiries: Where are you from? Are you on holiday? Can you eat spicy food? You like the Thai people? Do you have a girlfriend? The perfunctory introductions come from textbooks aimed at Thais learning English; perhaps Mr. Nui is unaware that these introductory phrases provide the grist for the humor mill among Western tourists mimicking Thai speakers of *Tinglish;* perhaps the joke is on me as I assume that Mr. Nui is like any other Thai guy in the countryside rather than a shrewd businessman performing authenticity. Mr. Nui did not talk immediately about his carving and about the crafts in his shop. Remarkable to me as a potential buyer, Mr. Nui did not try to rope me into buying his crafts because of their cultural significance but tried instead to express the personal investment he had in each piece.

His shop is a place of personal memories. Not only does he contrast how long it takes (over a month for that one over there) to carve some of these objects, but he also talks of his physical travails: His eyes strain when he tries to make the proper etch marks, and his car accident left him hobbled, so heavy lifting and learning to carve larger pieces is not an option. He offers me a glass of water and insists that I find comfort in the shade of his shop, for he has more stories to tell. His brother painted the watercolor on the wall, he tells me. His cousin, who lives in the Isaan (northeastern) region, painted the oil beside the watercolor. Because his cousin studied design at the university, Mr. Nui says, the quality of the design is superior to what one might find among the village artisans who paint similar pictures. Most of what he has to sell is wood carvings, hewn by his uncles.

In the shade of Mr. Nui's open-front shop, I have found superficial intimacy through his stories about his relatives and through the detail he provides about

the social origins of each craft on display. The shop space protects me somewhat from the distractions in the full marketplace and helps me focus on what
Mr. Nui is telling me (group assembly with bodily co-presence). After all, Mr.
Nui's personal narrative shields me from having to figure out what is happen-
ing in the totality of the market. After Mr. Nui offers me a glass of water, I become aware of my thirst and of my physical exhaustion from the heat and from
walking. I wonder about the physical exertion required to carve carefully and
beautifully.

The three small guitars on display provide an opportunity for Mr. Nui to explain his love for traditional Thai folk songs. He plucks the strings, and en-
courages me to stroke the wood, to feel the taunt line, to flick it with my
fingernail. "You could learn how to play. I could help you." I express interest in
learning to play and in buying the guitar. I begin to feel some unease with how
focused we have become on each other, so I transform myself into a researcher
by announcing in Thai that I am here to shop but also to start my research project. This delights Mr. Nui. "Good. You speak Thai. Good. But do you speak the
northern dialect?" Before I can express my interest in learning it, he offers, "I
can teach you. This will be fun." Without missing a beat, he returns to the subject of selling. "You don't have to buy the guitar today. I'll see you around. And
if you come back tomorrow, I can show you something. This woman is coming
to buy some of these instruments. You will want to be here for that, and I can
introduce her to my new American friend." Before I can leave him that day, he
insists on giving me a gift, a wooden coaster with a silver inlay of an elephant
in the forest. "I carved it myself." Mr. Nui reminds me that Thais love their fun
(*sanuk sanaan*) and implies that so long as I am willing to go on an occasional
drinking spree (*bpai thiaw*), I may ask of him whatever I wish.

Backstage Rounds

I return at 9:30 the next morning to begin the backstage rounds. In contrast
to seeing the work in progress, I now leave my role as a member of the audience and become an informal inspector of the stage props, producers, stage-
hands, and the stage itself. I have been invited to meet Mr. Nui's uncle, cousins,
and friends. The contrast between the carving that I may see as a casual tourist
and the activities I may see while being escorted by an insider highlights for me
the *barriers to outsiders*. I could not have understood this backstage world without the help of an insider, and the insider's help generates in me fondness for
my escort. Mr. Nui's selection of me as someone worthy of escorting into the

backstage focused my attention on how special my encounters would be. Even knowing that I am not the first nor the last to be taken backstage does not diminish my sense of moving past a barrier and the pleasure I derive from Mr. Nui's invitation.

Mr. Nui and I spend nearly two hours on the rounds. First he takes me to the neighboring shop that his older sister manages. In the back of the shop, she is painting and applying black resin to a pot. To her left, nearly out of sight, is an old man carving a mystical animal onto a piece of wood about three and a half feet long. He is in no hurry, because the work requires great attention to detail, but he does not lose too much time because he understands that the customer's patience is not unlimited. Mister Nui and I walk away from his uncle into a slightly wooded area, where we find a small open-sided work station: a rectangular board nailed to trees to create a roof, wooden planks assembled into benches, and enough space on the dirt floor for four men to sit comfortably. A calendar (featuring a topless Thai woman) and an old television and cassette player are set against a pole where an electrical outlet offers the only source of electricity. In the center of the work station, there is a man carving. Along the benches, three men watch, another swings lazily in a hammock, and another lies flat on his back along a bench, sleeping. The man carving works on the face of a Buddha. Beside his foot is a glossy magazine picture of the Buddha's face designed in the Sukhothai style, with the Buddha's hair represented by symmetric rows of small knots. There are several rough-hewn pieces of wood with the outlines of a head lying about the floor, waiting to be transformed into faces of the Buddha.

Our inspection done and introductory remarks made, Mr. Nui and I jump a small ravine and approach a house. At home in his kitchen, a man sits on the floor working on a flat piece of wood. It is probably five feet long and two and a half feet wide. He is carving a face into it—another Buddha! He etches the motif along black lines made by a magic marker. We leave him after a few minutes for another outdoor shop nearby, where a man is carving scenes from Thai folklore onto a large panel of wood. I am becoming overwhelmed by the repetition of motifs and by the reproduction of Buddhist images from one site to the next. I know that there are many temples needing to be supplied with Buddhist images and that such images are prevalent in hotels, restaurants, and shops. To have all these images (fragmented in my memory across multiple sites) come together in one place is to intensify the images through repetition. I breathe a sigh of relief when Mr. Nui asks me if I am hungry.

Over lunch and over the course of the next five months, I learn that backstage rounds are not uncommon, especially for buyers expected to purchase in bulk. Even those who have seen it all expect the backstage rounds and the adventure through the village it entails. The rounds regenerate their interest in the lives of the artisans and reconfirm the ongoing integrity of the performance. After lunch, on our way back to the shop, we find three Thai women waiting at Mr. Nui's shop, wanting to buy the types of instruments that I had almost purchased the previous day. Their requirements are more specific than mine, and Mr. Nui doesn't have exactly what they need, so he asks for their patience as he initiates several phone calls. Within ten minutes, he reaches for my mobile phone, asking only, "No problem, right?" With two phone calls, he has located the instrument. We all pile into Ms. Oi's car and travel less than ten minutes to a nearby village. We walk down a narrow lane of tall shrubs that opens onto a small yard and a tall house. On the side of the house is a workshop with walls. There are several large power tools and four men in the shop. In the anteroom where Mr. Nui leads us, an older gentleman and a teenage boy sit as the older man tunes a traditional Thai instrument, similar to a guitar. We are all focused on the instruments, how they look, feel, and sound. The women select an instrument from those assembled by the feet of the older gentleman. Looking down on the scene from the wall is a picture of a Thai princess with the older gentleman. He seems not to pay attention to what the women say they are looking for. His mind is fixed on the music; he blows into what looks to be a recorder as the teenage boy plucks a traditional folk song on the forty-two copper-colored strings of the instrument. As we listen to the music and observe the performance, a shared mood of delightful respect becomes perceivable. I become aware that the artisans here are considered authentic purveyors of local knowledge, gleaning this not only from the picture of Thai royalty patronizing the business but also from the identity of this house with the production of these difficult to produce and hard to find instruments. The instruments themselves and the process for producing them function as indicators of who the real artisans are and how buyers should behave when assembling in special places of production.

What I see in the raw, behind the scenes, and through other paths not marked to provide easy access of tourists helps me understand how some commercial transactions feed back into the sense of authenticity held by the artisans. Mr. Nui's invitation to me seemed personal, not staged. As much as he played the host and guide, I felt that my journey had been worthwhile. The sense of adventure that gathers from moment to moment cannot be replicated in a single themed locale but must unfold with question marks rather than full stops. Indeed, while writing this book I heard about how a less nuanced understanding of authenticity led to unintended outcomes.

The Tourism Authority of Thailand has tried to formalize authenticity in the Ban Thawai market by encouraging the artisans to perform all of their work in front of the businesses in full view of the tourists. The government support comes as part of the One Tambon, One Product (OTOP) project, which provides loans and marketing assistance for locally produced goods. The government supported the construction of storefronts, where the artisans were asked to display themselves at work. In other words, the artisans were expected to make the backstage more fully visible. They did not refuse the assistance, but many of the storefronts go unused. The artisans prefer having the option of closing the backstage to some but not other passers-by. They artisans understand intuitively that barriers to outsiders are important elements of authenticity. The observer has to be let "in" for a tour backstage or for a viewing of works in progress to confirm the agency and kindness of the artisan and to validate the experience of authenticity as exclusive. As we have seen, when artisans appear reluctant to engage in global markets, they become more "real" and more worthy of going global, from the point of view of buyers.

A Staged Play

I do not mean to suggest that the attempt to stage authenticity always fails. Cultural practices can remain special even as they are predictably performed for the market. One sees how the demonstration of the production process as a staged event helps artisans in Guaitil. Grand Circle Travel offers a tour to the village, where tourists can witness the four-thousand-year-old pre-Columbian artisanal tradition of pottery making. The artisans are descended from the Chorotega, who escaped from the Olmec, who descended from the Mayans. The lineage signals cultural heritage, and as the tourists consider the value of the crafts, they also chat about what objects such as these must have looked like at a much earlier time among a more isolated people. The vague lineage of the Chorotega alerts the tourist to the subordinate status of the indigenous group, not important enough for an exhibit at the Metropolitan Museum but not so minor as to be undocumented by researchers.

A tour bus stops, at approximately ten thirty in the morning, a kilometer short of the village square. About two dozen people disembark and are met by two men in their twenties. Gustavo leads half of the group to his family's workshop, while Edwin takes the other half to his own. The bus then carries the rest of the tourists a kilometer farther, to a workshop facing the village square. The working area behind the demonstration is more important than the area where the demonstration actually occurs. It resembles an outdoor garage with white cement walls rising three feet, met by five feet of steel bars. A wooden A-frame supports a tin roof. Behind the bars, a seated elderly gentleman shines the pot in his lap with a smooth quartz stone. A young man rolls cylindrical logs and rings them atop his spinning wheel. A teenage boy paints half-man-half-animal figures onto the bodies of the waiting pots. The artisans work as if alone, ignoring the tourists who point toward, photograph, and film them.

The tourists sit in a semicircle on mix-matched furniture—three plastic lawn chairs, four kitchen-table chairs, two logs upturned to function as stools, three metal, plastic-cushioned rocking chairs. A weather-worn wooden demonstration table faces them. On it are the artisans' tools: a quartz stone the size of a man's palm, a spoon made from the hull of the calabash (jicaro) plant, a small strip of leather, a corn cob, a small piece of sponge, a cutting file, an etching nail, three paint brushes, a base mold; a small mound of clay; three cups filled with white, red, and black paints; three small saucers with a white porous rock, a red terracotta stone, and a volcanic black rock; a small saucer of gray iguana sand; and finally the spinning wheel (formerly a motorcycle tire wheel).

To the left and farther upstage is the sales table covered with ceramics. These three sites—the working area, the demonstration table, and the sales table— form the points of a broad-based triangle. About fifteen meters behind the demonstration table is a kiln: a white cement dome on a rectangular base of roughly hewn stone. To the right of the kiln is Edwin's two-bedroom house, cement walls supporting a tin roof.

Clad in a loose-fitting sports T-shirt, nylon shorts, and sandals, Edwin welcomes the tourists to the demonstration. A few chickens strut behind him. A ripe mango crashes against the workshop roof and rumbles heavily for its second fall, to the ground. A teenage boy veers into view on his bicycle, transporting a fruit bowl. He sets down the bowl on the sales table, then crouches to observe Edwin's heavily accented English presentation. As Edwin begins to explain that everything is done by hand, that all of the colors are made by pulverizing the white, red, and black stones, and that electricity is not even used for the spinning wheel, he is interrupted.

"I thought the women started this," an elderly woman asks.

"That was in the beginning. Now it is the whole family."

"But where are the women?"

The elderly woman had read her travel guide. She remembered the Peace Corps volunteer and the cooperative that empowered the village women. That was why she had come. "My mom is resting, but she'll be out here later in the afternoon." Edwin flashes a smile. His interrogator smiles in response. Families, after all, are good things. And certainly hard-working mothers (devoted to their families and communities) deserve rest.

These demonstrations take place four times each week, if the tourism agency can fill the bus. The neighbor, Rigo, paints an indigenous motif as a band around the pot's base. Then half the surface of an unfinished pot is shined with quartz stone so that the tourists can touch its surface and feel the difference between the smoothness of the shined and the roughness of the raw. It is the rough that invokes the object's cultural biography (Kopytoff 1986). As an unfinished product, the pot puts the buyer in touch with the premechanized era of production. As a newly transformed surface from the rough to the smooth, the texture may remind the tourist that she or he has observed the product "backstage," under production (Goffman 1961). The emotional energy produced in the production process overwhelms the senses and insists on the power of the ancestors and their embodiment in their ancestor artisans as well as in the products themselves.

Inviting discernment, Edwin warns: "Because we use these stones to make our paints, we cannot make the color green. Red, white, and black do not make green. So when you see a pot painted bright green, it is not from here. It is not of the Chorotega tradition." For the skeptical, he has given them a way to check for authenticity. Colors serve as indications of membership in the Chorotegan tradition, and the tradition itself inspires pride in the artisan who tells the story as well as awe in those listening. The production process itself invites the buyer and the seller to focus on the "original" conditions and forms of production.

The demonstration concludes with the tourists checking the bottoms of the pottery for the names of the producers. Pots lacking names are quickly inscribed upon request, to clinch the sale. Noticeable is the reluctance of the tourists to ask for discounts. "After all," one woman reasons, "it takes so much time and talent to create this type of pottery. They deserve every cent and more." On another occasion, a woman chides her husband for asking how much money these artisans make per hour: "How can you ask such a question? This isn't manual work. It takes special skills." To reduce the artisan's work of culture to the production-and-pricing logic of any old thing evokes righteous anger and a punishing tone. It is the recognition of the special character of the ceramics that keeps the prices afloat and that protects the traditions themselves through shared respect.

In Guaitil one artisan recalled with laughter how a retailer from the United States had failed to understand the importance of the artisan's emotional energy for complying with the retailer's orders. The buying agent for the retailer had come to the workshop and asked that lots of small pots be produced, spec-ifying that they be of a uniform color and design. The artisan tried to comply but was bored by the concept. Her heart, as is commonly said, just was not in it. The artisan terminated the deal. She had enough other work to do, and the price of alienation was too high.

In the 1970s two anthropologists studied this village and recognized that emotional energy becomes embodied in pottery's production. They described how one of the village artisans invited the on-looking anthropologist to touch the clay and to feel the energy that flows from it, explaining how the rhythmic energy of the activity takes over her hands and her body. Her hands mold the pot without conscience direction from her mind, as if operating on autopilot or being directed by a force outside of her body. *Se va solo,* the artisan explained; it happens of its own accord. The artisan's invitation to engage in the activity is sensual: "Once I put a little clay in my hands, I make whatever the clay leads me to make. I let my hands do whatever they do. They operate on their own. Then I take a peek to see what has been made. Sometimes it is a large vase or a little jar. It happens on its own. I don't guide the process. . . . Touch it. Here. Try it for yourself" (Hernández and Marín 1975: 16). That emotional energy has remained in the production process even today. As I sat in workshops and ob-served the artisans at work, they tried to lure me into the ritual. "You can do it. Just put some in your hands. Let your hands feel the clay. Feel it. Here it is. Feel it." The similarities between how artisans talked about production in the 1970s, when there was less commercialization, and the way they talk about pro-duction now are remarkable. The production process unleashes emotional en-ergy and creates significance in the crushing of small stones, the coiling and spinning of clay, the rubbing of the stone, the stroking of the brushes.

Most remarkably, the interaction ritual shields the sellers from the most com-petitive pressures of the market. Because the seller and the buyer are not likely to have repeated transactions, it would seem that the buyer has an incentive to bargain for the lowest price possible, yet the buyer is more reserved and talks much less about the price than about the techniques and the importance of maintaining those traditions. The buyer and seller have arm's-length ties, but the narrative of the artisans' long-held tradition as well as the presence of wit-nesses (other buyers) and the unscripted entry of seemingly irrelevant infor-mation restrict opportunism among the buyers by emphasizing the "natural" rhythms of village life and the legitimacy of the artisans. The buyer learns that if he tries to negotiate prices too low, his companions will scold him. We also see the buyer sending messages to himself, his companions, and to the seller about what the buyer knows about these traditions, how widely he has traveled in similar commodity contexts, and how learned he is about these cultural traditions. Such a scenario is what Goffman calls a multifocused gathering in which "persons ostensibly engaged in one encounter can simultaneously sustain an additional 'subordinated' one. In the last instance the 'subordinated' encounter is sustained through covert expressions or by deferential restriction of the second encounter so that it does not get in the way of the officially dominating one" (Goffman 1961: 18-19).

The pricing negotiations observed during staged play push economic sociologists to go beyond the concept of embedded ties. While relational subcontracting explains how trust deepens through long-term, tit-for-tat exchanges, interpersonal relationships do not provide an overarching facility to constrain malfeasance or to ensure that expectations remain stable and met (Portes 1995). The sensory cues within the market and the unscripted events punctuating the experience create the emotional energy for enforcing the collective's expectations.

A Staged Transcendence

The collective expectations found in religious communities sometimes enable market actors to transcend the material constraints of the marketplace. In fact, it is the strong, sustained beliefs found in religion that protect some authentic cultural forms from becoming victims of vulgar commercialization. In the analysis of conventional social reality conducted by Harold Garfinkel and the analysis of the sacred conducted by Emile Durkheim, shared understandings about social reality are functionally equivalent to sacred objects, and their violation is equivalent to a ritual taboo (Collins 2004: 104). Similarly, in the market for cultural commodities, authentic forms are sacred and the desecration of these forms calls forth anxiety and intense reactions to punish and amend the violation. Studying handicraft objects that are considered to be sacred objects help us understand how different actors frame their traditions as authentic and thereby appear more worthy of time and money.

Matters of the spirit alter the buyer's frame of mind. Take the example of the Thai spirit house. The spirit house does not require comparison with a museum-certified object to verify its authenticity because the proof of the object's authenticity lies within its use-value and within the ceremonial enactments that enable its utility. In the sacred domain, the spirit house shelters ghosts and spirits displaced from the land by the arrival of humans who chop down the trees that host the spirits. In return for the displacement, the human occupants of the land build a miniature house, the size of a Western bird cage, ranging from about one foot by one foot by one and a half feet to a much larger structure that could be three feet in height or more. The size of the spirit house depends on the ages and the types of trees removed. It is believed that older trees host more formidable spirits.

Traditionally, each day a representative of the household would pay homage to the displaced spirits in return for the peace and tranquility that come with having one's guardian spirits appeased. At both homes and business establishments, the human occupants of the land set out offerings to the spirits and whisper prayers while holding lit joss sticks. The offering consists of fermented rice wrapped in a banana leaf, a garland of flowers, lit candles, and red joss sticks. The supplicant recognizes the power of the spirits to grant peace and tranquility (Anuman Rajadhon 1988). With regard to the supplicant's personal life, the prayer acknowledges that life is uncertain and that accidents happen; with regard to the supplicant's professional life, the prayer suggests that market forces create instability and great dangers to survival. With so much change wrought by life's natural cycle and by the global market's incursion into all corners of the world, the supplicant seeks protection wherever it may be found. Those selling the spirit houses in the West extract this sacred narrative of peace, protection, and spiritual balance and transfer it from its sacred context to a profane market context. Instead of advertising the merits of spirituality, some Western marketers have used the form of the spirit house as a design for ornate birdcages.

In the market transaction for spirit houses, the Thai producers and sellers have had to think about the distinction between the sacred and the profane. One informant constantly used the English phrase "the real one" (*khong ching*) to distinguish the spirit house from the bird cage as he discussed the dilemma that he faced. According to the informant, everyone in Thailand knows about the sacred significance of the spirit house. Its Thai name translates as "the house in which the spirits are invited." For the spirits to feel welcomed in the house, the human occupant of the land invites the Buddhist monks to the property to hold a special ceremony welcoming the spirits to their new home. As the spirit house ages, the person becomes concerned about where the spirits will reside, because the spirits do not exit the dilapidated house without a proper ceremony that invites them into a new home. The old spirit houses, in fact, have to rest beneath the old *Bo* tree, which holds sacred significance as the place where the Buddha was enlightened. For this reason, one will see lots of old, broken spirit houses discarded beneath these gnarled trees.

Because the Western buyer proposed that he had customers willing to pay up to $1,000 for very old teak spirit houses, the informant agreed to furnish these items under a set of specific conditions. If the buyer wanted an antique spirit house for artistic purposes, the Thai seller would provide it, but it would take some time to have the monks come and decommission it properly. However, if the buyer only wanted a birdcage that looked like a spirit house, the Thai seller would instruct the artisans to build a new spirit house and to set the object out of doors during the rainy season to make it look old. For inauthentic uses of the object, the Thai would use inauthentic processes. The informant stressed, "We can't treat a real spirit house as if it's just any old kind of thing." Explaining what the object *is not* makes more salient what the object *is*. This explanation also requires that the pricing negotiation change course. The buyer can purchase a sacred object, but she has to understand that the object is sacred and she has to pay an appropriate sum to honor the object's special powers.

Awkward Play

My interaction with one entrepreneur highlights how awkward the playing up of authenticity can be. While attending the Small and Medium Enterprise Day Fair at Chiang Mai University, I encountered Rick (a fictional name). Rick speaks English fluently, is well-read, and insists on using his English nickname. As we discussed the items on display at his booth, one of his managers handed me a business card. I noticed right away that "Collection" of "The Collection" was misspelled. "What's missing?" Rick asked, pointing to his associate's card. With unease, I responded, "c." His lips broaden into a smile. Strange, I thought, he seems pleased that there is a misspelling on the business card and that I noticed it right away but did not point it out. Before I could conjure a cultural explanation about how the smile might be his way of concealing embarrassment, he flipped the card over to reveal a bold message: "The C that is lost is *Culture*." I became immediately aware of and uncomfortable with the assumptions I had made in an instant. Had I, a politically liberal and multicultural omnivore, taken a patronizing attitude toward Rick? If I had seen him as an "equal," I would have lost no time in telling him that there was a minor mistake on his business card. As soon as he flipped over the card, my mood changed. I felt immediately relieved. Rick reminded me that the lost "c" of authentic culture alluded to the forgotten history of the Lanna Kingdom, which Rick hoped to revive interest in by playing up local traditions under a brand name referring to the kingdom that ruled the area around Chiang Mai from the thirteenth through the sixteenth century (interview with author, 12 October 2002).

By disarming the potential buyer through staging an awkward situation, Rick had created an opportunity for focusing attention on the question of culture, but the awkwardness of the interaction did not create a shared mood. Instead, it highlighted the barrier that I faced as an outsider in understanding where I stood socially in relation to this creative entrepreneur and his team of artisans. This particular interaction did not lead to group solidarity for Rick or the artisans accompanying him, nor did emotional energy arise from our discussion of how Rick was using culture strategically to market his products; however, the market interaction did bring to the fore how much of the "c" in culture I missed upon my first glance into the situation and it made me question how much more I was missing. My capacity for a quick riposte had been taken away in an instant, and I began to perceive more clearly how important sociability is for marketplaces in which cultural commodities change hands.

Awkward or smooth, social interactions are responsible for the creation of markets. It is well known among economic sociologists that markets do not create sociability; instead, sociability creates markets and becomes part of the taken-for-granted fabric holding markets together. In order for financial transactions to take place, the buyer and seller must establish some kind of mutual understanding. This shared understanding, however imperfect and affected, depends on the practices and understandings coming from other areas of social life. Georg Simmel likens economic transactions to romantic exchanges: "Competition compels the wooer who has a co-wooer . . . to go out to the wooed, come close to him, establish ties with him, find his strengths and weaknesses and adjust to them, find all bridges, or cast new ones, which might connect the competitor's own being and doing with his" (Simmel 1955: 61). Sellers do not necessarily learn to intuit the predilections of their customers as a result of market participation; rather, this is a spillover from their participation in intimate (non-economic) relationships (e.g., Zelizer 2005a, 2005b). Sellers must learn how to sell their products within a range of expectation sets. Participation in a variety of social institutions provides individuals with the tacit knowledge they need for understanding these expectation sets. Often, these expectations are breached, intensifying the emotional energy in the situation and highlighting the tacit knowledge and taken-for-granted practices of the group. Actual and anticipated breaches require the moral standards of the group to be considered, its righteous outrage to be expressed, and its ritual punishments to be exacted.

Child's Play

Just as buyers respond to the traditions of the dead, they also are moved by the children of the living as they see them at play, reenacting sacred and authentic processes. Goffman notes that examples abound from the Pueblo Indians of New Mexico; likewise, black African children make dolls that replicate the sacred ones used in special ceremonies, just as Catholic children play games to imitate Mass, confirmation, and funeral rituals (Goffman 1961: 73). Though child's play, these games have rather adult consequences.

Consider a small handcrafted object purchased from an artisan's child, which carries the memory of the encounter with the adorable child. In villages such as Guaitil, one sees the artisans' children setting up small kiosks on the edge of the village plaza in view of their parents' kiosks. The children reproduce the working world of their parents in their afternoon games, much as children in American families set up lemonade stands in the neighborhood to earn spending money. The children chat eagerly with tourists and explain how the older sister molded the drinking vessel from clay and how the younger brother made the paints from natural sources. For the visitor, the children's games unfailingly attest to the fact that the villagers are born into their craft, that they carry these special skills "in their blood."

The tourists who purchase goods from these children do so under the watchful eye of an adult. The children seldom have small currency denominations to make change and speak very little English. Mimicking English-speaking television personalities, the children welcome guests with "Hello!" They alter their tone to sound like the American tourists who enter the village with cameras and commentary. "Adorable," a tourist proclaims, referring not to the artwork but to the children. For the children's sake, this tourist is eager to purchase a small piece of pottery. She does not haggle with the children over the price because she fears that she would take advantage of an innocent child. By the time money changes hands, an adult has entered the scene to ensure that the price is fair. From a child, the tourist is willing to buy smaller, less spectacular items. The emotional energy that emerges in this transaction creates a small price bonus for these artisans-in-training.

In the Thai study communities, the nature of wood carving precluded the involvement of children in the production process itself, but they served as scenery props. A visitor to Chiang Mai's night market would see women carrying babies on their backs and baskets of hand-crafted items around their necks. In the calm of the wood carving communities, as the parents cut, paint, and sell, the children make a mess of their coloring books, some tracing Roman letters and others tracing Thai characters. The sight of children sometimes touches the heart, causing the harshness of one-on-one bargaining to soften. The presence of children makes the buyer see the purchase as both an economic and a sentimental engagement. To bargain too nastily would set a bad example for the children and it might degrade their parents, who ought to remain always in their children's highest esteem. In the face of the child's wonderment, pricing negotiations change track.

However, the social context can determine how adorable an artisan's children are, as Walter Little demonstrates in his description of the handicraft street market of Antigua, Guatemala. A group of Mayan handicraft vendors had been trying to sell their crafts to a group of tourists who happened to disembark a bus nearby. The vendors hawked, "*Compre* [buy]. Good price, mister. Cheap." Then a little Mayan girl, the four-year-old daughter of one of the vendors, tugged at the dress of a woman tourist. In response, the woman pushed the little girl and shrieked, "Don't touch me. Leave me alone." When later asked why she had responded so violently to the child, the woman explained that the girl might have been a pickpocket. Even the tour guide had warned about the number of pickpockets preying on tourists in the city. Perhaps embarrassed that she would consider a little "dark" child so badly intentioned, the woman added that she, indeed, had wanted to make contact with some indigenous peoples but could not easily discern the real Indians from the fake ones (Little 2002: 78-79). Had the woman encountered the child in a different context and with a different preconception of what little dark children did in the city, the failed sales initiation might have been otherwise. Having denied a child the benefit of the doubt, the woman felt the need to justify herself to her peers. On the one hand, her curiosity attracted her to the exotic. On the other, she feared the unpredictability and the devious wiles of the potentially "fake" *indio*.

Why are some indigenous artisans and their children marked as devious coloreds rather than angelic ethnics? The children of artisans, no doubt, want to be regarded as adorable, yet they cannot control the impressions that others have of them. The artisan's child is framed by representations that are taken as true by faith and by convenience. "We automatically pursue, prefer, and remember 'evidence' that supports our stereotypes (including untrue 'evidence') and ignore, discount, and forget facts that challenge them" (Reskin 2002: 223). These collective representations of a group prime the buyer to give the benefit of the doubt to some and to exercise extreme caution with others.

Common Play

In the absence of highly ritualized spaces where production processes are demonstrated and buyers and sellers share special moments, profane principles of pricing are more easily sustained. The buyers justifies their more aggressive negotiating tactics as appropriate, given that they have left a special site of authentic production. Aggressive pursuit of the best price acts as a foil to the more tempered pursuit of the appropriate price conducted within the space aglow with aura. The cultural commodity detached from the special moment in which the buyer discovers it anew offers a less mediated view of the transaction. Though less mediated, these social forces still influence the goals pursued and the manner of pursuit.

The buyer seeks the lowest price possible and searches for this price in two ways. The buyer makes an extensive search, scanning the sellers and negotiating with them in order to compare and average the prices for particular items; or the buyer makes an intensive search, negotiating with only one seller until agreeing upon a sufficiently low price. In contrast, the extensive strategy is more animated. Each has to anticipate the breakpoint of the other. When will the buyer walk away in search of something or someone else? Usually both the buyer and the seller have exit options, and by virtue of these options, the buyer seeks to understand the average prices offered in the market by trying to bargain as hard as one might to minimize the negative effects of information asymmetry but not too hard as to offend the seller, who might refuse to enter into an exchange with a person so nastily disposed. Among these various actor sets, information about prices and quality as well as a stable set of expectations about comportment emerge and enforce the informal terms of exchange.

Take, as an example, the intensive strategy: The seller usually has no exit option. If the seller cannot make an agreement with the one buyer who comes, the seller cannot sell. Sellers who are isolated from the center of the physical market in their communities often find this strategy deployed. One informant in Costa Rica explained how buyers for retail and souvenir shops sometimes come at the end of the rainy season, when the muddied road to his house and workshop discourages more benign travelers. Away from the crowds, the buyer tries to deflate the prices according to the perceived desperation of the seller. The buyer offers a very low price, the seller responds with a much higher one, and in turn they step upward and downward until they reach an agreement. The buyers and sellers mostly talk about price, not tradition, not technique, not quality. And there exist no witnesses to the buyer's shamelessness. Buying cheap and selling dear is the name of the game. Long-term relationships between the buyer and the seller, however, tend to reduce the level of opportunism on the part of the buyer.

The buyer is not always too far from the crowd, since even in a remote trans-action, the larger world seems to stand in judgment. As one older lady put it, she looked at this one *gringo* as if to say, "You ought to be ashamed of yourself. You know better." And know better the buyer did. Although the buyer had the artisan cornered literally, she did not persist in pushing the price lower than it had already fallen. An artisan in San Vicente also noted the way that culture works for him with international, but not local, buyers. A woman from abroad wanted to buy some pottery, and instead of seeing a commodity, she saw a piece of art. She found the prices fair. By contrast, the local buying agents wanted the lowest price possible: "There was a woman who would come here from the states and she was a good customer. She would look at the art and you could tell her, 'It costs this much.' And she would say, 'Very well. That's fine.' By contrast, this buying agent from here comes and we tell him how much it costs and he says, 'Oh no. That's way too much.' And we tell him that these things are hard to make and it takes lots of people to make them. He wants us to give our work away. But not me, no way. I don't give away my work because its value is too great" (informant interview, 3 April 2003). Presumably the artisans' contact with the global market has reinforced their sense of value. Outsiders tell them that their work is valuable, marvel at the skill of their craft, and pay them what they are worth. In one circuit of exchange, the artisan's worth is higher (in financial terms) than in another. The difference in value does not come from the arti-san's skill at framing himself or his work as authentic but rather from the mean-ingful relationships the artisan has with the network of buyers. The buyer's understanding of the marvelous and of the common gets imbued in the com-mercial relationship, and the buyer acts accordingly.

THE WAY FORWARD FOR ECONOMIC SOCIOLOGY

An artisan and her or his objects do not generate economic value independ-ently of the circuit of other individuals, objects, and histories in which she or he is embedded (e.g., Velthuis 2003; Zelizer 2005a, 2005b). In his astute analy-sis of handicraft merchants in Otavalo, David Kyle observed that the deference that tourists gave to artisans presumed to be authentic depended not on an as-sessment of historical accuracy but rather on the social accumulation of cultural cachet afforded to some groups but not others. Although the artisans in Azuay create authentic crafts while some of the handicraft merchants in Otavalo sell inventory from other Latin American groups, the artisans in Azuay have failed to convince foreigners of the authenticity of their crafts. Attempts in the 1980s by the Ecuadorian government to correct the false notion that the products from Azuay are not authentic were rationalized away by international tourists and other buyers who objected that such announcements denied what everyone knows to be true (Garfinkel 1967). Confronted with the discrepancy between how an individual expects another to behave in a given situation and how the other behaves, the individual tries to "fix" the problem (the non-sense) through polite conversational redirections meant to spare all involved the embarrassment of exposed ignorance or manifest abnormality. International tourists treated the "corrections" being made by the Ecuadorian government as breaches requiring a quick fix so that they would not be embarrassed as cultural dupes. The Otavalans are given the benefit of the doubt as being authentic: "Nearly anything they [the Otavalans] sell is considered by foreigners as socially noble and culturally 'authentic'" (Kyle 2000: 192). Any evidence to the contrary is regarded with skepticism. Given this tendency in observers, it should come as no surprise when we visit a group of tourist buying handicrafts in Guaitil, Costa Rica, that the wife of an American buyer put an end to her husband's breach of strongly felt social expectations as he tried to assess how much the artisans earn per hour. Can't he see that their *cultural work* does not merit the same economic evaluation as *regular work*? More significantly, artisans, communities, and nation-states cannot simply become branded for authenticity by virtue of the fact that they possess cultural riches and that they have remained true to original production processes and local motifs.

The performances that an actor (e.g., an artisan) can enact come from a prior accumulation of socially significant moments. The templates for action are finite and cannot be enacted by anyone simply by virtue of the person's needs and desires. The history of the group and the way that group has come into contact with others over time creates a set of believable performances and a set of legitimate-looking actor types. This dynamic can be summed by looking at the way Goffman takes on the well-known dictum attributed to W. I. Thomas that "if men define situations as real, they are real in their consequences." The dictum, Goffman warns, is "true as it reads but false as it is taken." He continues: "Defining situations as real certainly has consequences, but . . . [a]ll the world is not a stage. . . . Presumably, a 'definition of the situation' is almost always to be found, but those who are in the situation ordinarily do not *create* this definition, even though their society often can be said to do so; ordinarily, all they do is to assess correctly what the situation ought to be for them and then act accordingly" (cited in Goffman [1974] 1997: 149).

The buyers receive collective stereotypes and process them before ever entering the handicraft market. When they enter the market, these messages are either reinforced or challenged. The market's scenery and props further inform the buyer's assessment of the appropriate pricing logics to bring to bear and the types of seller-explanations to be believed. The importance of stories, myths, and the pricing accounts they enable cannot be overstated (Fine 2003). The buyer enters the market looking for a "good deal." But what constitutes a good deal depends on the buyer's concept of what the market, its objects, and its human occupants are. These accounts act as "switchmen on the tracks" (Weber [1922-23] 1978: 280), directing the buyers and sellers to pursue multifarious goals by indicating the direction of those pursuits and limiting the means of pursuit. Understanding how some communities of artisans and some nation-states have more successfully framed their cultural riches as real helps us understand the economic track their cultural industries have traveled.

CHAPTER SIX

Conclusion

The Three Fs of Globalization

Global Markets and Local Crafts responds to a new cultural, social, and economic reality occurring in developing and developed countries. Some artisans have gone global, either exporting their crafts abroad or selling directly to international tourists, if not both. With low- and middle-income countries struggling to compete in low-wage manufacturing, national governments and regional bodies have awakened to the prospects that their material culture might work to their benefit. The economic development of handicraft communities are emblematic of what Joseph Schumpeter called "creative destruction." The global capitalist system mutates without ceasing, as capitalism "incessantly revolutionizes the economic structure *from within*, incessantly destroying the old one, incessantly creating a new one" (Schumpeter 1976: 82). In 2006 a group of industry representatives, government export agents, and academics gathered for an Asia-Pacific Economic Cooperation (APEC) Meeting on local cultural industry, sharing lessons on how to make these industries more competitive. In Latin America, the Organization of American States has adopted the "artisans as entrepreneurs" slogan. In Africa, images of earthy black women and authentic African traditions have fueled the sale of "indigenous" cosmetics such as shea butter lotion (Chalfin 2004) and other handmade products. Local traditions have been placed in the service of local, regional, and national economic development.

In my four community sites, two in Thailand and two in Costa Rica, I have asked how participation in global markets has affected the cultural traditions of the artisans, the social relations among artisans and between the artisans and outsiders, and the prospects for local economic development. The emergence of handicrafts as a means to earn income and as a source of local economic development has generated more speculation than understanding. Local people have transformed their handicraft practices from a hobby, transmitted as cultural know-how from one generation to the next, into a highly coveted and productive skill that enables the artisans to find work and generate income. Indeed, Dean MacCannell (1976) argues that modernity's rise has increased the fragmentation and alienation in Western societies to such an extent as to compel its inhabitants to seek the immediacy and presence of an authentic (shorthand for unspoiled, original, and tradition-grounded) other. "Authenticity" gets staged, in MacCannell's view, merely for the sake of the outsider's needs and in response to the global capitalist system. Meanwhile, David Harvey (2001) has recognized cultural sectors of the global economy as a paradox in that their uniqueness serves the aims of capitalism by generating scarcity (and its attendant economic values) but the very quality of collective symbolic resources provides a basis for resistance against otherwise overwhelmingly powerful economic actors. From a different theoretical perch, George Ritzer (2003) has acknowledged the possibility that artisans might escape the trend toward eradicating the meaningful content and the local control out of all global commerce. With the global demand for ethnic crafts on the rise, do handicrafts offer a new alternative for local economic development? Do the artisans who make the wall hangings, the candles, the tables, and the gift boxes sold in the United States, for example, earn only enough money to survive or does the handicraft sector offer opportunities for better remuneration, upgrading, and economic dynamism among micro- and small-scale artisans? Are local traditions revived, polluted, or transformed (García Canclini 1990)? What leads to each of these outcomes?

To address the local economic and cultural consequences of globalization using close-range observations and middle-range theory, I employed a comparative research strategy that reaches into regions from two very different areas of the world and, while transcending regional boundaries, my analysis offers insight into the role that culture plays in shaping the economic strategies of nation-states, local communities, and individuals, with attention to the contexts in which social ties facilitate the response of local actors to global forces.

I have described the small-N maximum differences research design and the importance of choosing case studies from vastly different national and cultural contexts, reemphasizing these differences to remind the reader that my findings hold across widely different contexts. The similarities and differences between these country contexts make them appropriate terms of comparison for the examination of local economic development as well as social and cultural change. Sociologists concerned with economic development, however, have been slow to seize on the experiences of countries in Southeast Asia and have focused on East Asian and Latin American experiences. But in order to understand globalization, I would argue, we have to move beyond the intense study of one region of the world at a time. Indeed, we cannot understand the plurality of global forces, the liveliness of global flows, and the ways in which cultural commodities have been framed in the global community unless we dare to transcend the habitual geographic boundaries in our analyses.

This is why my analysis focuses on three general factors or processes that characterize globalization across my two study regions: (1) economic and political forces, (2) flows of people and materials, and (3) frames that differentially define cultural and market situations. These three factors or processes recast Michael Burawoy (2000) and his collaborators' ethnographic investigations of forces, imaginations, and connections. The first factor, the economic and political forces, refers to the large-scale economic processes to which artisans, community leaders, and nation-states respond. Macroeconomic changes in the economy spur reactions from the nation-states, private industry, and private citizens in their efforts to fend off threats and to take advantage of opportunities. The second factor, flows of people and materials, emphasizes the interactions among actors and institutions as well as their exchanges of information, goods, money, and status. The circumspect investigation of these flows unveils the third dimension of globalization, the frames that differentially define cultural and market situations—how actors and institutions define their (Goffmanian) situations, frame their traditions, and perform their own sense of authenticity. These definitional frames and on-site performances have important economic, social, and political consequences that previous studies have not fully understood.

FORCES

Global economic forces operate beyond the control of the individual artisans and even of the body politic of the nation-state. Yet these forces do not necessarily determine how individuals and nations will respond to macroeconomic change or how states and communities might empower themselves to create opportunities in place of threats. After the severe economic crises of the 1980s, countries around the globe reoriented their manufacturing apparatuses in an effort to export their way out of debt. Political economists rightly predicted that the global hierarchy within the world-system would reproduce itself (for the most part) because those with comparative advantages in manufacturing would be able to react quickly and well to the new economic opportunities. International tourism and handicraft sales have complicated and somehow unsettled these predictions.

A number of countries receive large flows of foreign currency from international tourism. As international travel became more accessible to the masses in Western countries and as the disposable incomes of the middle class grew, a new class of consumers emerged who increased the demand for tourism goods and services. At the same time, declining incomes in agriculture and the higher cost of credit to obtain agricultural technology made farming increasingly less appealing for a growing number of workers, who then shifted their labor from farming to artisan craft production and sales and thus created a new class of workers to meet the demands of international tourism (Little 2002; Nash 1993). With agricultural employment drying up in the countryside, individuals in communities with some history of craft production have turned to their pastime as a mean for generating badly needed income. With some agricultural workers choosing to remain in the countryside rather than migrate into overcrowded cities, the national governments have applauded the emergence of capitalism and ever-larger farming and husbandry estates in the countryside.

As national governments began to see the flows of international tourists as a significant source of foreign currency, government tourism agencies became more engaged in marketing their tourist attractions, and the government's labor economists and urban planners saw in tourism an answer to the problem of rural-to-urban migration. As countries such as Thailand and Costa Rica achieved middle-income status, they could no longer compete with the cheap labor offered by countries like China. While manufacturers left countries with higher labor costs, government economists turned toward tourism services, high technology exports, and their creative industries for new sources of comparative advantage. Global economic forces acted as catalysts for large-scale social change but had not determined the direction of those changes.

I have stressed that while global economic forces pivot the direction of a country's economic history, shared understandings angle their pivot and weave the texture of their flows. The public culture of the nation-state comes to be represented in the policy choices made and the options forgone. The ways in which the nation-state becomes economically integrated into the world-system, and the resulting socioeconomic meanings of such an integration, affect the kinds of industries that the nation-state supports and the activities that generate a positive self-image in the eyes of in-country capitalists. When presented with the option of making money from a high-status versus a low-status enterprise, most entrepreneurs will choose the high-status venture, all other things being equal. The shared understandings among policy makers, capitalists, and artisans about what constitutes a high- versus a low-status product functions as a social force that conditions individual and institutional responses to global economic forces. The way in which these understandings emerge, the places where they travel, and the force with which they can be sustained are factors that depend on the flows among various social and institutional actors.

Political economy explanations have long argued that structural forces preclude economic dynamism among micro- and small-scale entrepreneurs. For the most part, the political economy explains failure. Take, for instance, the case of the Nigerian pottery artisans in the community of Tsugugi, just outside of the town of Zaria. Anthropologist Rob Allen (1983) describes the life histories of four potters in the Tsugugi community in order to show how the political economy of the region forced the potters to seek cash incomes from their craft and why these potters have not been able to break out of the poverty trap. In the 1950s the government required people who had formerly existed in a non-cash economy to pay their taxes in cash. In order to fulfill their new obligations to the state, a number of people had to migrate to urban centers where cash incomes could be found. Those who remained in the village had to turn their crop cultivation into cash (Allen 1983; Portes and Walton 1981).

The political economy in which these potters operate has doomed them to subsistence. First, the urban expansion in Zaria has pushed up the cost of food, space rental, and raw materials (mud and grass). Second, the seasonal migration patterns of the potters prevent them from holding onto their products and waiting for better sales offers. Instead, they sell to traders at a fixed rate and try to maximize the number of objects they sell. This market glut depresses the prices they can demand for their products. Because they will migrate back home, cannot be on-site to sell the products year round, and lack other avenues to enter the market, the artisans are stuck in subsistence production. Allen sees no hope for economic dynamism among these artisans: "The potter is thus caught in a circular trap in which he cannot win. He must achieve high productivity, in which case he must forgo the retail profits, or he must reduce his level of output. In both cases, he is left with little more than the ability to keep on going as he is" (1983: 166). As the capitalist economy expands in the nearby city, the market for the artisans' pottery increases, but the artisans capture none of the surplus value. Unable to remove the middleman from the negotiations, they sell cheap and suffer dearly.

Try as hard as they might, handicraft artisans cannot escape these structural constraints even when they have strong community ties. In Santo Domingo,

Wilfredo Lozano (1997) studies a group of amber jewelry artisans. These artisans sell their products to a few gift shops and have no direct access to the end-buyers. They buy their primary input, amber, from a small number of large landowners who control access. The gift shops and the landowners agree on the price of amber so that they can keep their own profitability high, with no regard for the market conditions faced by the artisan suppliers. In a weak tourist season, the market risks are largely borne by the artisan producers. And in a strong season, the market gains are largely reaped by the landowners and the gift shops. The experiences of these artisans are especially important because they have strong cooperative relationships and a strong sense of solidarity. Their inability to overcome the structural conditions in the market demonstrates the limitations of social capital for dynamic economic development. Squeezed on both ends, the jewelry artisans fail to realize dynamic development, their solidarity notwithstanding.

High levels of social inequality within a society are reflected in the village craft economy. For example, those who own sources of raw materials or the machines used by artisans are generally the same people who have always been in the landowning classes (Carruthers 2001: 359). And the middlemen who market the products capture the surplus value of the artisans' labor, so the artisans become trapped in a low-level equilibrium of subsistence production. These forces are not the only factors or processes at play, however.

FLOWS

Global forces have unleashed global flows of people, information, understandings, and money. These flows are global in the sense that they transcend the jurisdiction of nation-states but rely on nation-states to ignite, in some cases, their flows and to maintain, in many cases, their velocity. National tourism agencies and national cultural institutions (museums, historical societies, and research institutes) have provided international tourists with the kind of specialized information that facilitates the encounters between the tourists and the producers of local tradition. These government agencies attract the flows of international tourists to specific locales within the nation-state, but the government's criteria for selecting these locales do not depend solely on either the authenticity of the community or the political connections of its residents. Historically contingent events and the artisans' capability to nurture their sense of their own culture affect the likelihood that the community will be crowned as a special place of production—a place where they can make their local culture work globally.

If the national certifying agencies (such as the national tourism board) are unwilling to consider a community as a special place of production because the community's traditions seem "too ethnic" for a country with high aspirations, the flows of international tourists and retailers might alter such considerations. In other words, everyone loves a winner, so if an influential set of outsiders (brokers for retail stores, cultural critics, international cultural organizations) or a large group of international consumers indicate that the country has a set of market winners in its midst, the national government often responds as if it had always known this to be so. [Local communities of handicraft producers appeal to economic actors who lie beyond the nation-state, and these actors, who are or represent buyers of handicraft products, enable the handicraft producers to insert themselves into the vibrant dynamic of local-to-global exchange.]

I use Gary Gereffi's (1989) global commodity chains concept to sketch how local artisans get linked to global markets. In his typology of buyer-driven chains, Gereffi discerns three levels of linkage. At the first level in the chain, the export assembly producers receive their design specifications from the customer or from the middleman sourcing handicrafts out of the local handicraft villages, but the village artisans do not complete every phase of production from within their communities. The finishing touches happen elsewhere. At this first, bottom level of the commodity chain, therefore, the handicraft artisans are less able to advance the economic performance of their local enterprises because their control of the shape and design of the final product is relatively limited.

At the intermediate level of the commodity chain, the handicraft workshops can produce the object and send it fully finished to the intermediary or directly to the customer. This means that the community's workshops are able to use and promote their design expertise in shaping the final product, but they are still depending on intermediaries when it comes to distributing their products to the consumers. The artisans have the factories, their workshops, but their "brands" do not exist because they lack the autonomy and power of a firm. And the buying agents for such firms as Pier-1 Imports, World Market, Eziba, and Ten Thousand Villages have firms without factories. Those in the intermediate level of the commodity chain are able to capture some of the surplus value from their talents. However, their products find their way to retail shops across the globe carrying the retailer's label. Under these circumstances, a finished product from the developing world does not bear the name of the village in which it was produced or the artisans who produced it; instead, the customer knows that the object comes from Thailand and is a "Pier-1 Exclusive."

Third and last we find the own brand manufacturers (OBM) at the top of the commodity chain. These handicraft artisans sign their personal names or the names of their enterprises to the finished products. The customer comes to know about the artisan's reputation and the artisan eventually can charge a higher price because the name carries with it the guarantee of fine quality and innovative designs. This most advanced stage of the global commodity chain requires a great deal of investment on the part of the artisan, because everything, including design and marketing, occurs in-house. With the exception of a few superstars in the handicraft sector, OBM handicraft workshops also engage in original equipment manufacturing (OEM). In the latter case, the bulk of their export orders carry someone else's brands, but a few of their choice crafts carry their own label. Among these handicraft workshops lies the greatest potential for dynamic, autonomous economic growth.

With new opportunities come old threats. In *Behind the Label* (2000), Edna Bonacich and Richard P. Appelbaum have identified how buyer-driven global commodity chains, based on retailers responding to demand conditions, are encroaching on producer-driven ones. In the older system, the marketer focuses on selling whatever the producer is manufacturing (pushing out) anyway. In the new system, the retailer focuses on identifying consumer demands and pulling in those goods through flexible, decentralized networks. This new system diminishes the power of workers to strike collectively as they would in a producer-driven chain. In the buyer-driven chain, the power of the workers (artisans) depends on fads and identity. If an artisan's work is trendy and difficult to imitate, it gets pulled into the buyer-driven chain. For niche markets, the artisan's identity and that of his or her place of work (if it is a village well known for its craft specialty) become part of the object's brand. If the brand encompasses at least implicitly the notions of fair trade, cultural preservation, and individual dignity, the artisan will have some bargaining power with the more powerful economic actors. The buyer purchases and markets an image, an identity, and a set of relationships along with a well-crafted object. In short, cultural symbols and expectations modify the workings of the global commodity chain.

Understanding how they are linked in the chain, some artisans have used their social ties to protect their innovations. A British man who purchases handicrafts in Thailand to sell them in England reports that artisans use their connection with him to patent their new designs informally. On his visit to a woman in a handicraft village in the Chiang Mai area, he recalls, she stage-whispered, "Come this way. I have something for you to take back to England." Before showing him her new craft design, she made him promise that he would sell the object only in England and not in Thailand. She feared that as soon as it would appear in a shop in Chiang Mai, it would be copied and she would lose her edge in the market. These two had known each another for some time, and she knew that if her sample design sold well in the market test, the British fellow would return with requests for more, and she would be able to command a higher price. Moreover, if she restricted her new designs to the export market, she would buy herself time to benefit from her innovation.

Beyond offering certain forms of protection, social ties have also facilitated learning by doing. As we have seen, some artisans have been interested in entering global export markets but have feared its pitfalls. How does one go from carving wood or making pottery to exporting? These types of expertise differ, and the likelihood of being duped is high. It is therefore important that artisans and potential market mentors encounter one another frequently in spaces of interaction that encourage interpersonal, meaningful exchanges. The market mentors become friends who are bound not only to making a profit but also to furthering the career development of their friends. These cross-cultural exchanges and the socially meaningful partnerships they facilitate are the results of the global flows of people, understandings, and emotionally charged energy.

FRAMES

Enmeshed in global flows and buffeted by global forces, handicraft communities have learned to empower themselves through framing their communities and themselves as the repositories and purveyors of authentic culture. The concept of framing refers to how actors define their situations, how they manage the impressions of themselves that arise in dialogue, and how those impressions affect the response others have to the actors. When individuals come to believe that the situation corresponds to a certain frame, their behavior makes the situation conform to their expectations. The definition of the situation becomes, in Robert K. Merton's formulation, a self-fulfilling prophecy (Merton 1957).

Sometimes the definition of the situation occurs by accident. For example, if a group of buyers thinks that an artisan's designs are authentic, they are willing to pay more. As the artisan receives more money for the supposed authentic designs, the artisan begins to pay more attention to these objects and begins to learn more about their supposed origins. The artisan may free up time spent making other objects to improve the handiwork on these higher-priced goods. Over time, the buyers' belief in the authenticity and superior handiwork of an artisan's goods increases and the buyers' actions affirm those beliefs by creating a set of incentives to encourage the artisan to adhere to the buyers' beliefs.

At other times, artisans hone narratives of cultural distinction in order to frame their situations. In Thailand, the Thawai villagers were used to hosting, informally, a wood carving festival on municipal lands years before the festival was recognized by the national tourism authority as legitimate. The villagers benefited from the inflow of international tourists and from the interest of Thai people themselves in celebrating the local knowledge and cultural traditions represented by the wood carvers and their work. As a special place populated by special people, the Thawai village could request government assistance in marketing its festival and in improving the roads that carry tourists as well as cargo trucks in and out. The villagers did not need to have special political connections or their own stocks of financial capital to gain entry into the global market. What they required was the right frame for negotiating more favorable terms of trade.

Artisans cannot develop such frames in any way they please. The definition of the situation is simultaneously created and found. On the one hand, the artisans come to understand how, through their interactions with international tourists, they obtain a felt, unarticulated sense of the hierarchy of value in the global economy. At the same time, they manage themselves and their communities in such a way as to fulfill the roles they have been assigned. The artisans understand that while the whole world may be a stage, not all actors are deemed fit to play all roles. The templates for action are finite and cannot be enacted by anyone merely by virtue of one's needs and desires. The history of the group and the way that group has come into contact with others over time creates a set of believable performances and legitimate-looking actor types. Thus those who try to enact performances not deemed appropriate for their age, gender, country of origin, language group, or ethnicity find themselves rebuffed as lacking legitimacy.

FORCES, FLOWS, AND FRAMES

In response to these large inflows of tourists looking for a scene of authenticity, communities around the globe have begun to highlight their own craft traditions. With agricultural employment drying up in the countryside, individuals in communities with some history of craft production have turned their crafts into a means for generating badly needed income, rather than migrating into overcrowded cities, and the national governments have applauded the emergence of capitalism in the countryside. Moreover, as the artisans have stressed the importance of their local cultures in their attempts to market their products as unique, they have generated pride for their communities and have won the endorsement of their national governments. Without strong connections to politicians in the relevant government agencies, these artisans have used their individual cultural capital and the aura of their communities to attract state resources and the goodwill of some private-sector buyers. Guided by economic sociology and the sociology of culture, I summarize the study's inductive findings:

1. Local cultural industries in general and handicraft workshops in particular have become one of the main sources of economic livelihood for the communities examined in this study, yet not all of the communities have benefited equally from the economic opportunities generated in global markets. Those communities or artisans thought to glow with the aura of authenticity have engaged global merchants (buying agents for global retailers) and international tourists on more favorable trading terms than those communities and artisans thought to be "real" (authentic) and good (quality) but not special.

2. The concept of cultural capital helps us understand how local cultural industries have found a niche in the global economy (Kyle 2000; Meisch 2002; Pérez-Sáinz and Andrade-Eekhoff 2003). The tacit knowledge of the craft and the inimitable character of the work defy wage labor logics that help buyers evaluate how much the artisans would be paid by the hour. Instead, the marketplace honors the traditions that the artisans preserve by paying an appropriate sum for cultural works.

3. When cultural capital presumably exists equally among artisans in nearby communities, the collective concept of aura, as developed in the present study, proves useful for understanding how artisans in one community enjoy more market advantages than do artisans in another community by virtue of operating in a geographic location known as and felt to be authentic.

4. These feelings of authenticity result in part from the interaction rituals in the marketplace where the bodily co-presence of actors, the expectations created before assembly, and the mutual focus of attention among the actors generate a collective effervescence, symbols of membership, and sanctions against their defilement (Collins 2004). Felt authenticity is also framed by the history of the locale, the struggles that have generated social capital through reactive identity (Portes and Sensenbrenner 1993), and

the stored emotional energy (Collins 2004; Hirschman 1984) that the artisans may place at their disposal for their future interactions with tourists, buying agents, nonprofit representatives, and government officials.

5. How a community becomes framed (authentic or not; special or not) and how different frames influence the terms of negotiation in the marketplace depend on social processes at the workshop, village, national, and international levels. The social processes of concern here have been the forces and flows that respond to and generate the frames whereby outsiders, along with the artisans themselves, evaluate the crafts as reflections of culture (a favorable framing) or as the only work available (an unfavorable framing).

6. The forces of the global economy have rendered low-cost manufacturing an outmoded strategy for economic development for the countries under study. With a labor force enjoying more social protection and human rights, the cost of doing business in middle-income countries has risen and the motivation for operating in these countries has dropped. Losses in manufacturing have made local cultural industries an attractive alternative for economic development, but not all countries (and within each country, not all capable communities) have seized on these opportunities with enthusiasm or success.

7. As we examine the flows of people, material resources, and ideas in and out of artisans' workshops, we see the importance of local dynamics for shaping what gets produced and how. These flows of production enable some communities (but not others) to protect their local traditions and to mobilize the needed resources to compete in quality as well as price. While social capital has referred to the capacity to mobilize resources within the artisans' networks, I have focused on the circuits of exchange (Zelizer 2005a; Zelizer 2005b) that have influenced how these social connections will be put to use, what will flow through them, in what direction and with what media of exchange. In this sense, the distribution of goods becomes a relational process (relational distribution).

My findings have benefited from studies in economic sociology, the sociology of culture, and comparative development. While thinking about how well theoretical concepts travel to inform my research in the various sites, I have also assessed the physical difficulty with which I moved from one region to another. My own physical and economic limitations did not permit me to cast a wider empirical net, but doing so would greatly enhance our understanding of local cultural industries and of the concepts enabling our examination of cultural work.

A RESEARCH AGENDA FOR ECONOMIC SOCIOLOGY: LOCAL CULTURAL INDUSTRIES AND COMPARATIVE DEVELOPMENT

The study of cultural industries responds to the current gaps in economic sociology and in comparative development. Richard Swedberg points out that economic sociology needs more ideas, lacks innovation, and approaches the subject in too piecemeal a fashion. Recalling Weber's model for an interpretive sociology, Swedberg paraphrases the first paragraph of *Economy and Society*: "Economic sociology is a science concerning itself with the interpretive understanding of social economic action and thereby with a causal explanation of its course and consequences. We shall speak of 'economic action' insofar as the acting individual attaches a subjective meaning . . . to his behavior—be it overt or covert, omission or acquiescence. Economic action is 'social' insofar as its subjective meaning takes account of the behavior of others and is thereby oriented in its course" (Swedberg 2005: 2-3). When an artisan carves or molds an object, the artisan may be entertaining himself or herself, preparing an object for a religious/spiritual purpose (e.g., a spirit house), preparing an object according to the specifications of a buyer, or engaging in a household chore. When buyers encounter these artisans, they themselves may be engaging in a leisure activity primarily or may have sought out the artisan for specific commercial purposes, for specific sizes, volumes, quality levels, and styles. What the actors think they are doing affects what they bargain about and how much emotional intensity the bargaining generates. With so much meaningful content and with so much controversy over questions of quality, authenticity, and cultural heritage, handicrafts enable economic sociologists to study culture and markets with as much clarity as nuance.

I focus on how market actors involve themselves in what Michel Callon, Cécile Méadel, and Vololona Rabeharisoa call "hybrid forums." Reaffirming the ancient function of the market space as the privileged locus for all types of exchange, be it economic, political, social, or cultural, the handicraft markets are forums because, as in the agora in ancient Athens, the buying and selling occurs in a space meant for public meetings as well as for other economic, social, and political exchanges. The markets are hybrid in that the actors and institutions involved originate from different species and sources: Tour buses from different parts of the country unload visitors from different parts of Thailand

and different parts of the world into a market square where all meet. There one finds the Thai tourism authority and the police as well as the vendors and the packing and shipping businesses, as the market teems with people and their children, their pets, and stray pets, and the scene is set by exotic fruit, the smell of spices, the flash of shiny cloth, the knock-knock of carved wood. There also, interviews take place, conducted by people from the International Labor Organization (ILO) and other supra-national organizations as well as sociologists, anthropologists, economists, demographers, and journalists. The hybridity in the types of people and institutions gathered is matched by the diversity of the issues that emerge from participating in the market (Callon, Méadel, and Rabeharisoa 2002: 195). Is the object somehow authentic, or is the object kitsch; is the experience a lie? Is the buyer promoting local economic development and cultural preservation or economic exploitation and cultural emasculation? Is consumption a positive social force in the lives of these artisans and their community or does the history of exploitation repeat itself in miniature?

These questions bear upon the activities in the marketplace, where "all the world's a stage" and different social scripts are featured. Charles Smith's study of auctions highlights the various scripts for strategic play in marketplaces, emphasizing the hodgepodge of instrumentally rational, affective, and conventional logics that shape the course of bids made and taken. No single logic dominates the public negotiations. Instead, "human behavior . . . [in the auction setting is] contextual . . . [It] reflect[s] and constrain . . . social expectations, [and is] governed more by expressive aims than instrumental tasks . . . [It is] more emotional than rational, and more interactive than self-directed" (Smith 1989: 108). The actors conceive of themselves as thespians, engaged in a drama. Unlike a fully scripted play, however, here the thespians carry partial scripts onto the stage and improvise the rest.

These scripts cross different spaces to generate what Viviana Zelizer calls "connected lives." What happens in one set of social relationships may spill over into another set of seemingly nonsocial (business) transactions. Zelizer reminds us that the hybridity and differentiation, emphasized by Michel Callon, are part and parcel of the market experience, and she proposes that social analysts chart a course between the structures of play, the meaningful relationships among the players, and the meanings of play for the individuals caught up in different types of exchange. In their acts of buying and selling (among other things), Zelizer writes, "people create connected lives by differentiating their multiple social ties from each other, marking boundaries between those different ties by means of everyday practices, and sustaining those ties through joint activities

. . . but constantly negotiating the exact content of important social ties" (Zelizer 2005b: 32). A handicraft seller may differentiate customers by whether they are given a back-stage tour as well as by other acts of feigned or sincere intimacy. In the hours when the sellers are selling and the buyers are not looking to buy, both buyers and sellers are constantly swapping stories among themselves and with the other group. In these stories, they make sense of how important or trivial different products and relationships are. The pricing negotiations manifest what Clifford Geertz has called "deep" and "shallow" plays (Geertz 1973), with the former associated with tradition and status and the latter intent on maximizing the economic profit of the game. Buyers and sellers engage in a myriad of practices that mark the boundaries of their social ties (Geertz 1979) along with the difficulty with which authenticity may be trespassed. For example, in their display of handicraft objects for sale in their shops, vendors may arrange the objects that represent the vendor's relationships with socially significant others: some of the objects come from family members, neighbors, good friends, or friends of friends; others, from the vendor himself. If the buyer asks about the characteristics or the cost of an object, the vendor may allude to or somehow emphasize the social relationships that resulted in the object's production and its distribution to this site of sale. At times, the person(s) evoked can be seen, spoken to, touched, or in some other way perceived and made real. The buyer then purchases a story, a direct experience, and an object that has use value, exchange value, and, most importantly, a symbolic value resulting from its relationship to its place of production. This symbolic value, in other words, depends on or *is* the object's aura.

My analysis brings culture and symbolic interaction back into the sociology of development in ways that enable us better to understand the processes of social change. The structural models offered by the dependency and world systems theorists as well as the social systems theories of the neofunctionalists have failed to capture the processes whereby collectivities and the individuals within them construct definitions of the global market situation and how these very definitions effect change. To keep myself out of the tautology of industrious, culturally rich countries doing industrious, culturally rich things, I focus on specific interactions in which old definitions of the situation are recognized, ignored, contested, and/or transformed. I stress that social interactions in particular contexts might have led to different outcomes—that the social system influences and routes, but does not determine, destiny. The framework I offer and the research strategy I pursue offer an empirical approach for understanding the thorny problems of development, globalization, and social transformation.

The ways in which the nation-state defines its situation in the world community affect the likelihood that the government agencies will promote and the capitalists will pursue opportunities in the global handicraft market. In other words, it is not enough to possess stocks of symbolic capital to convert this into economic capital (through export promotion); the nation-state and its capitalists inherit a collective understanding (orientation) of the uses (appropriation) to which different types of symbolic capital ought to be put. It is not only that former agricultural workers are being pushed out of farm and factory, and that protected government employment is being pulled into handicraft production and tourist services, but it is also that both the workers and the capitalists "see" (sometimes subconsciously) the production of some types of cultural commodities as a means to protect cultural traditions and to validate a favorable cultural identity for the nation-state.

There is a deep structure of inequality in the social statuses of different nation-states. These relative statuses come from the inter-state comparison of prestige and stigma symbols accumulated during periods of war, economic struggle, and political wrangling. This enduring set of status perceptions orients the course of the country's economic development, sometimes diverting economic development energies away from those stocks of symbolic capital easily appropriated but socially stigmatized. For example, countries willing to import the world's trash might choose not to do so because they do not want the associated stigma of the dumpster; likewise, a country fighting outsiders' perceptions that the country is backward might want to curtail the images that the country exports confirming such negative perceptions. On the flip side, prestige symbols assist the country in portraying a positive image of itself. It stands to reason that some national governments will be motivated to support the production and export of material cultural that both promotes economic development and presents a favorable image of the nation-state and its polity.

IMPLICATIONS FOR PUBLIC POLICY

The most important actions that a government can take in the interest of handicraft enterprises are enacting reasonable cultural roles in global arenas and creating a market interface. In both of these, however, public policies may bring about unanticipated outcomes unrelated to the original goals or (in the worst-case scenario) may lead to the very outcomes that the policies were meant to prevent. For example, governments' attempts to engage in impression management so as to promote local cultural industries may lead to buyers' perceiving authentic practices as somehow inauthentic, and market interfaces meant to promote local economic development may lead to gentrification, making the artisans victims of their own success. How this happens and how it might be avoided are the most important issues that have emerged in my study.

When a government has helped create a market interface for the villagers by officially recognizing the handicraft communities and by advertising their festivals, the official tourism authority can give the cultural claims of the villagers' legitimacy and help artisans reach potential clients. Because the state-sponsored tourism agency can improve the information that tourists have about the handicraft traditions and the locations of these communities, the handicraft entrepreneurs incur lower costs in searching for new client pools. The client pools come to them. Also, official festivals have been effective in conveying the cultural authenticity of handicraft producers because these formalized rituals generate categorical identities (Collins 2004). However, tourism promotions that come out of the blue, as it were, draw a blank, since the identities associated with them do not have a store of emotional energy on which to draw or an accumulated legitimacy from other, noncommercial activities. So long as the buyers can see that the rituals have taken place long before the market for the objects emerged, the government's attempt to engage in impression management works well.

Sometimes, impression management works all too well. Recognized as an authentic site of production, the village may find itself inundated with business. With more commercial success come higher costs of operation, especially for those who do not own the market spaces in which they encounter tourists. Recall how the Thai government supported the initial construction of the Baan Thawai Handicraft Center. As business soared, so too did the rents. Although the rents in the first handicraft center eventually became too expensive for its intended beneficiaries, the government's initiative gave the villagers the impetus they needed to establish their own handicraft market in the middle of their village. Were it not for the capacity of the villagers to mobilize and the unwillingness of the government to quash the mobilization, the new handicraft market would have made the economic situation of these villagers worse, not better. The commercial success of the first handicraft center has also had spillover benefits in the village because of the number of packing and shipping services available there and because of the heterogeneity of the shop types to be found in the first handicraft center. The outcome of the ordeal chronicles a course not foretold.

From the case studies we have learned, however, that the state is not the only important actor for creating markets. In some cases, the private sector has been

more important in helping the artisans upgrade their designs and in identifying new markets abroad. Public policies that complement and encourage such
private initiatives are likely to lead to dynamism among handicraft enterprises.
More importantly, by also providing the artisans with a "way out"—the ability
to decline exporting assistance from those who act with both opportunism and
guile—the state and the private sector expand the menu of choices for handicraft entrepreneurs and reduce the likelihood of rampant exploitation in the
villages.

CONCLUSION

The fate of small businesses has captured the attention of social scientists
and policy makers alike. Sociologists studying the informal sector have identified dynamic clusters of small businesses defined by their capacity to accumu-
late capital, upgrade their equipment, and adapt new technologies. The clusters
of micro- and small businesses that "take off" do so because they have successfully inserted themselves into the global economy. Those that remain stag-
nant suffer from a lack of capital, information, reliable institutions, and trust.
These fates are complicated, in the present cases, by the things the artisans
create and the authentic traditions their work represents. It is not enough to be
a good businessperson; one must also be "real." The authenticity of the products and of their production processes matter as much as, if not more than, the
prices of the handicrafts. As the mass market for handicrafts grows, opportunities open up for specialized producers. International brokers can enter a country and can distinguish between the handicraft workers whose quickly produced
work will help the brokers meet profit expectations and the handicraft artisans
whose careful work need not generate mass sales. The personal satisfaction the
broker receives from supporting authentic cultural producers helps the broker
account for the prices paid and the time taken for production.

The proposition that some small businesses may benefit from the global economy has fostered hope on the political right and skepticism on the left. For the
right, the increased flow of labor and capital are the natural outcomes of the
free market. Savvy entrepreneurs who dedicate themselves to working hard will
succeed, bringing jobs and pride to their local communities. Referring to small-
and medium-scale enterprises, James Wolfensohn, president of the World Bank
from 1995 to 2005, quipped, "People don't want charity; they want a chance"
(International Financial Corporation 2001: ii). Rugged individualism is alive and

well. On the other hand, for the political left the global economy is a menace that quashes small producers and homogenizes cultural practices. Small businesses either yield to homogenizing pressures or depend entirely on subcontracts from large firms. Small and informal businesses are the "reserve" producers who glean crumbs in times of plenty and bear the brunt of low demand during times of economic recession.

Both sides of the debate remain vexed by the dialectics of globalization. Neither the neoliberal prescriptions for laissez-faire nor Marxist predictions of the market's overwhelming force can explain how some of the small businesses in this study become dynamic while others operate at the level of mere subsistence. In this way, the handicraft sector may be considered a strategic research site, "an area where processes of more general import are manifested with unusual clarity" (Portes 1995: 2). Looking at how these micro- and small enterprises operate, one can see the economic, social, and cultural effects of globalization at close range.

Communities, social networks, government agencies, private citizens, and businesspeople outside the nation-state interconnect with global markets, overlapping one another like roof tiles. To protect the inhabitants from rain, the builder pays attention to how each tile is placed. The interconnection of the tiles relies on a fragile equilibrium. As the past imbricates the present, handicraft entrepreneurs devise new layers of protection, keeping out the market's metaphorical rain but limiting what may be placed beneath the roof. Forces imbricate flows and frames. How easily and how well the artisan communities can frame themselves as unique depends on the macroeconomic forces that have increased or decreased international tourism and disposable incomes, as well as the national economic response to global markets that might generate a flood of handicraft producers who have entered the sector as a career of last resort. Similarly, the flows of people, knowledge, and objects in and out of artisan communities provide stimuli for revising local frames and opportunities for establishing more favorable distribution channels for their goods. As a result of these various factors and their interdependences, facile accounts of globalization will not do. The Three Fs of globalization should enable social scientists to develop general rules of thumb for approaching empirical reality, but nothing can substitute for the direct observation of global processes at close range. Such has been the approach of this book—a direct engagement with artisans and their communities as the individuals make culture and generate works in global markets.

Appendix:
Study Design

The first methodological task I faced in my research on Thailand and Costa Rica was defining community development and specifying why I chose the economic performance of micro- and small-scale handicraft enterprises as a proxy for community development. Human development refers to the increased capabilities of individuals to improve their socioeconomic conditions, such as education, health, and life expectancy. To the extent that economically successful enterprises emerge in the community and employ the residents therein, these enterprises increase the capabilities of the owners and some of the workers to improve their socioeconomic conditions. And if most of the community's residents find employment in the local micro- and small-scale enterprises, the economic performance of these enterprises approximates the socioeconomic capabilities of the residents. This study assumes that in communities where such enterprises agglomerate into clusters of high economic performers, socioeconomic development is high. Hence, the handicraft workshops in communities where most families earn their livelihood from handicraft production and/or sales are the appropriate units of analysis for understanding community development.

COMMUNITY DEVELOPMENT AND CONTEXT

Community development occurs under vastly different circumstances and in vastly differently political contexts. There are differences in nation-states and in the extent to which the states support micro- and small-scale enterprises in the handicraft and tourism sectors. There are also differences in the material resources available at the provincial or district level. Some districts have enjoyed better socioeconomic conditions before their residents decided to leave agricultural work for handicrafts. These conditions might contribute to the ease with which the community's enterprises access tourism and export markets.

Finally, there are differences in the types and efficacy of external interventions in the different communities that contribute to the economic success of the artisans' enterprises. In Costa Rica, one community benefited from having a paved road from their pottery cooperative to the main highway, while the comparison community depended on a gravel road. In Thailand, one community benefited from having a state-recognized handicraft center and yearly wood carving festival, while the comparison community had only recently tried to imitate the success of the other's handicraft center. These external interventions probably affect the demand for the community's product. This study demonstrates to what extent social capital and external interventions remain powerful predictors of the economic success of the handicraft workshops even after taking into account the differences in the country-, district-, and community-level contexts.

COUNTRY SELECTION

I chose to study communities in countries enmeshed in global tourism. However, to implement the maximum-differences research design, I also needed to select countries that differ dramatically from one another. I chose Costa Rica and Thailand for their similarities in how important tourism is for the national economy, for their socioeconomic similarities that make them comparable, and for the many characteristics that distinguish these cases. Why would anyone compare a small (in terms of population size) Catholic country in Central America with a medium-sized Buddhist one in Southeast Asia? This frequently asked question confirms the appropriateness of these countries as comparators in the maximum-differences research design.

The maximum-differences research design requires me to compare community case studies from widely different country contexts. Costa Rica and Thailand fulfill this criterion. Both Costa Rica and Thailand share the rank of the number one recipient of tourist expenditures in their respective regions. This makes them appropriate countries for studying communities linked to the global economy through tourist craft sales and handicraft exports. Even in tourism and handicrafts, Costa Rica differs from Thailand, since there is much greater support from the national government in Thailand.

COMMUNITY SELECTION

Selecting the study communities in Costa Rica and Thailand posed a number of challenges. There was no comprehensive roster from which to select at random communities engaged in handicraft production. I took a three-pronged approach. First, I reviewed the official tourism ministry's website for each country in search of artisan communities. The Costa Rican Tourism Board has mapped the country's hand-

icraft centers. In the Nicoya Peninsula, the board recognizes only Guaitil as a center for handicrafts. The tourism board's map designates the remaining handicraft
centers in the greater metropolitan area of San José: North Sarchí, South Sarchí,
Escazu, San Vicente de Moravia, and Turrialba. Guaitil's neighboring rival, San
Vicente, is not designated as a handicraft center on the map. Newspaper reports,
however, and discussion with the artisans indicate that the villages of Guaitil and
San Vicente share the same traditions and produce the same types of pottery.

In Thailand, the tourism authority has provided a list of twelve handicraft villages
well known for their craft traditions in Chiang Mai. The village names and their spe-
cialties are the following: (1) Si Pan Khrua (known for bamboo works and laquer
ware); (2) Wua Lai (known for silverware and lacquer ware); (3) Mueang Kung (known
for earthenware); (4) Roi Chan (known for basketry); (5) Thawai (known for imita-
tion antiques and wood carving); (6) Kuan Thahan Kaeo (known for earthenware);
(7) Nong Ap Chang (known for handmade natural-dye cotton); (8) Don Kaeo (known
for bucket weaving); (9) Pa Bong (known for woven products); (10) Bo Sang (known
for umbrellas, fans, and wood carving); (11) Ton Pao (known for mulberry paper
products); and (12) Ton Phung (known for umbrella making and wood carving).
From these featured villages, I selected the fifth, the Thawai village.[1]

Armed with the lists of handicraft communities in each country, I consulted with
social scientists in each country who had studied such communities. In Costa Rica,
my primary contact was Juan Pablo Pérez-Sáinz, who had studied a wood carving
and furniture making town in Costa Rica and other artisan communities throughout Central America. In Thailand, my primary contact was Luechai Chulasai, a sen-
ior economist at Chiang Mai University who had close ties with the leadership of
the Northern Organization of Handicraft Manufacturers and Exporters (NOHMEX).
Because NOHMEX represents a dynamic network of handicraft exporters from the
north of Thailand and because their network resembles the dynamism described by
Vittorio Capecchi for Emilia-Romagna, Dr. Luechai and some of the leaders of
NOHMEX were able to give me important information about the key sourcing communities for handicraft exports.

Finally, I asked the handicraft artisans themselves (in Guaitil for Costa Rica and
Baan Thawai for Thailand) about the other villages producing handicrafts similar to
their own. I also inquired casually with souvenir shops in San José, the capital of
Costa Rica, and with handicraft boutique stores in Chiang Mai City, the capital of
the Chiang Mai province. I wanted the second handicraft community to be similar
to the first, but I also wanted it to be less successful economically. I did not ask about

1. The Tourism Authority of Thailand, www.tourismthailand.org/about_thailand/provincial_
guides/north/index.php?province=CHIANG%20M AI&data=toshop, accessed 8 March 2004.

characteristics of the other handicraft communities, though the artisans in the first community would add that the second community of artisans did not perform as well as their community did. I especially did not want to select the second community based on how much social capital might be there or how many links the second community might have had to external sources of support. In this way, I tried to diminish the bias of selecting handicraft communities nonrandomly. In the end, my selection of the study communities depended on whether I thought those communities represented the set of villages where most of the households receive a significant proportion of their incomes from handicraft production or sales.

After I selected the study communities, I inquired about their corresponding districts. Each of my four study communities is located in a different district. In Costa Rica, the community of Guaitil is located in the Santa Cruz district, while San Vicente is located in Nicoya. In Thailand, Baan Thawai is located in the Hang Dong district, while the Sanpatong handicraft villages are located in the Sanpatong district. Bureaucratic activism from the central government has been crucial for creating the marketplaces in one of the Costa Rican study communities (Guaitil) and in both of the Thai study communities.

QUANTITATIVE DATA

For the most part, I used quantitative data to establish trends in socioeconomic development at the national and district levels. Most of this data came from the national census bureaus, but a few key statistics came from other published studies. To examine my hypotheses about how social capital affects the economic performance of the community's handicraft enterprises, I fielded a survey of forty-three enterprises in Costa Rica and forty in Thailand. The field survey confirmed my hypotheses, namely that social capital has a positive effect on the economic performance of the handicraft workshops and that the effect of social capital becomes more potent if the artisans have received assistance from external sources to start up their enterprises.

Census Data

In Costa Rica and Thailand, the census data at the national and provincial levels are far more complete than those at the district level. The census data enable me to establish trends in socioeconomic development, such as adult illiteracy, infant mortality (for children under the age of five), and life expectancy. The data also enabled me to follow trends in national income growth. However, the data do not consistently measure the percentage of the working-age population who are artisans. Nor do the data say much about inequality in land-ownership, especially at the district level. Because census data on labor force participation used different definitions for artisans from one year to the next, we lack reliable information on how large the population of artisans is and on the types of work in which these artisans engage. From the tourist expenditure data by country and from the size of global trade flows generated in the crafts industry (see the introduction), we can surmise that the population of artisans is large enough and economically significant enough to merit further investigation.

Published Studies

To the extent possible, I have tried to find the published reports of other researchers who have investigated my study communities. In Costa Rica, the anthropological works of Doris Stone, Mireya Hernández and Flora Marín, and Jim Weil offer insight into Guaitil and San Vicente. In Thailand, the economic analysis of the Thawai village (Luechai and Siroros 2002) and the anthropological analysis of the Sanpatong villages (Jamaree 1996) offer points for comparison.

The Field Survey of Handicraft Enterprises

I used a field survey to measure the economic performance of the community's handicraft workshops and to assess how much social capital the workshop's leader had at her or his disposal and to what extent the workshop leader obtained start-up capital, working capital, or other sources of support to upgrade the business enterprise. The survey also asks about the age, sex, and education of the entrepreneur as well as other details about the business enterprise, such as the number of full-time, paid employees, whether the enterprise exports its products, and approximately how much the workshop earns per month during the season when tourists are more likely to visit the village.

Unfortunately, there were no rosters available of the village workshops. Many operate from the artisan's home.[2] The workshops with more than five full-time, paid employees were easier to find because of the movement of people in and out of the house and the things they carried. In Thailand, I walked through the village sites listening for the sound of saws and chisels. Sometimes I would be alerted by the smell of paint or I would see a pickup truck being loaded with wood carvings. In Costa Rica, the sight of fresh clay clinging to the individual's garments and the location of the outdoor kilns helped me determine the most likely candidates for the

2. Frequently, Thai houses are raised on stilts, and beneath the house a number of household-related projects occur. Cooking, washing, and craft activities are commonly witnessed beneath these houses. The space beneath the house is also a common area for socializing.

survey. I sketched a map of the communities and tentatively marked the houses most likely to be functioning as handicraft workshops.

I befriended some of the village artisans and explained my research project. They were happy to confirm where most of the workshops were located, and one informant walked me into some of the "hidden" spaces between homes or along inconspicuous dirt paths to outdoor workshops. Unsure how large the population of workshops was for each village, I tried to maximize the number of workshops I interviewed. I had to make a number of return trips to the workshops when the leaders were absent or when their work prevented them from granting me an interview right away. In Thailand, only two workshops refused to grant me an interview. In Costa Rica there were no refusals in the two study communities. I interviewed roughly three-quarters of the identifiable handicraft workshops in the study communities.

In Thailand I usually traveled with four advanced undergraduate students from Chiang Mai University's economics department. A fifth student served as a substitute whenever one of the others could not attend the weekend interview days. At least one of the students had grown up in northern Thailand and understood the dialect. I myself speak central Thai, but during the course of my fieldwork I learned some key northern Thai question words and phrases to facilitate my work.

I usually went into the village for four to five hours at a time with the students, and we would divide into two teams. I would alternate which team I accompanied to ensure that I observed the dynamics of the survey interviews. I also selected some of the questionnaires at random from interviews that I myself had not observed and revisited these workshops to see if some of the key questions (age, number of years in business, sources of support, and cooperation among the artisans) would elicit the same responses from a different interviewer.

Since the artisans in Baan Thawai usually would not consent to the use of a tape recorder, having the students with me to take copious notes proved crucial for the success of the project. In Costa Rica, the artisans in the pottery villages did not object to my recording the interviews, so I conducted these interviews without assistance. I would listen to the tapes as a way to check the accuracy of my questionnaires. I also sent a number of tapes to an advanced undergraduate anthropology student at the University of Costa Rica in San José to transcribe the tapes. With the transcriptions and the tapes, I could cross-check my notes for accuracy.

ASSESSING ECONOMIC PERFORMANCE

The set of responses that concerned me most were those meant to measure the economic performance of the handicraft workshops. In Thailand I quickly discovered that the artisans did not want to give me an estimate of their monthly revenue.

After consulting with a Thai linguist at Chulalongkorn University (Ajarn Janpanit) and with my primary contact at Chiang Mai University (Ajarn Luechai), I created income categories which most of the artisans would freely select. I noticed that the likelihood that the artisans would answer my monthly income question increased with the amount of time I spent in the research site. The artisans would say, "Oh, you're back." The frequency of my visits demonstrated my seriousness, increased my trustworthiness, and made the respondents more willing to give me information on their monthly sales revenue. In my last month in the field, I reinterviewed the first set of handicraft workshops (about fifteen) to confirm the reported monthly revenue. Among those workshops I suspected of underreporting, higher monthly revenues were reported the second time I interviewed them.

I also used the number of full-time, paid employees, and whether the enterprise exported globally, to create an index of economic performance. These indicators of economic performance have been used by the contributors to *The Informal Economy*. They also provide a more robust way to measure economic performance, especially if the respondents are likely to underreport their monthly incomes. In the Costa Rican communities, where the handicraft markets were less dynamic than in Thailand, most of the artisans would give me an estimate of their monthly sales income for the tourist season. From these responses, I randomly selected fifteen workshops and used an abridged version of the survey for a second interview. Most of the respondents gave the same monthly sales figures in the second as in the first interview. I used direct observation of transactions in the workshops to confirm whether those sales figures were more or less accurate. My sole indicator for economic performance in Costa Rica was monthly sales income. Few workshops export their products with any frequency, and few reported having full-time, paid workers. Most of their workshops are family based or peopled by friends or kin, appearing when the workload requires them.

MEASURING SOCIAL CAPITAL

To measure social capital, I developed a set of questions that capture how social capital might manifest itself in the handicraft community. To assess community solidarity, the source of social capital most likely to influence the economic performance, I referred to the Social Capital Integrated Questionnaire (SC-IQ) developed by Christian Grootaert, Deepa Narayan, Veronica Nyhan Jones, and Michael Woolcock (2004) at the World Bank. I used an earlier draft of this questionnaire as my touchstone. Other useful measurement tools are the Social Capital Assessment Tool (SCAT) developed by Anirudh Krishna and Elizabeth Shraeder (1999) and the Social Capital Assessment Tool (SOCAT) developed by Christiaan Grootaert and

Thierry van Bastelaer (2002). I developed my survey instrument keeping in mind the questionnaire items used in these tools, but adapting them to fit the characteristics of the handicraft villages and of the survey respondents. I focused on the kind of behaviors that would occur within or between handicraft workshops as well as the perspective of the workshop's leader on community relations.

The Social Capital Integrated Questionnaire (SC-IQ) has a core set of twenty-seven questions meant to assess the six dimensions of social capital at the individual level of analysis: (1) groups and networks, (2) trust and solidarity, (3) collective action and cooperation, (4) information and communication, (5) social cohesion and inclusion; and (6) empowerment and political action. I address the relevance of these categories and questionnaire items for analyzing the effect of social capital on economic performance in the handicraft communities studied in Costa Rica and Thailand.

Groups and Networks. The SC-IQ asks about "the groups or organizations, networks, associations to which [the respondent] or any member of [the respondent's] household belong[s]." I asked the respondents in Costa Rica if they belonged to voluntary associations and if they received any help for their businesses from any associations. In Thailand I asked if the respondents received any help from community groups. In neither country do voluntary associations correlate with any of my outcome variables.

The SC-IQ also asks if the respondent's voluntary associations work with or interact with groups outside the village or neighborhood. In Costa Rica I asked about the workshop's ties to tourist agencies, souvenir shops, or other governmental or nongovernmental organizations. I also asked whether the workshop received start-up or working capital, information, or other resources from groups outside the village. In Thailand, I asked whether the workshop received start-up or working capital, help with new designs, or any other forms of assistance from outside the community. In both countries, receiving start-up capital from outside the community correlates positively with the higher economic performance of the workshops.

Finally, the section on groups and networks asks about the number of close friends that individuals have with whom they can talk about private matters or can call upon for help. I chose not ask this question in the context of the handicraft workshops because the phrase "close friends" (*peuen sanit*) carries more intimate connotations in the Thai than in the English language and emphasizes reciprocal obligations. The artisans used the phrase "people I know" (*khon rujak*) loosely to refer to subcontractors or to regular customers. In the Costa Rican context the phrase "close friends" follows the meaning given to it in English more closely.

Trust and Solidarity. In the first chapter's discussion of social capital theory, I describe solidarity and social cohesion in the same way. As far as trust is con-

cerned, the sentiment that people can be trusted did not withstand the construct
validity criterion. By construct validity, I refer to the likelihood that the respondent will interpret the question in the manner the question was meant to be in-
terpreted. When I fielded my survey in Thailand, any reference I made to
whether people in the village could be trusted was countered with an explanation of the Buddha's teachings. The Thais, especially those in the north, I was
told, value social harmony and trust. To suggest otherwise (whether or not it
was true) was blasphemous.

Collective Action and Cooperation. In Thailand I asked whether the artisans in
the community cooperated with one another, and if so, how. I asked a similar
question in Costa Rica, but I also included a number of questions about the different types of cooperation (loans of materials or tools, exchanging work for
work, and small money loans). To assess collective action in Costa Rica, I asked
whether people in the community would come together to repair public property, such as a school damaged after a flood. To this question, nearly everyone
responded yes. The respondents qualified their replies: "Working together to
help someone who is really poor or to make sure that the children's school is
okay is one thing. Who wouldn't? But when it comes to money, business relationships, buying and selling things, and giving discounts, that's something entirely different. You don't do that with just anybody" (paraphrase, field notes).
Asking the Thai informants about the benevolence of the Thais toward one another elicited the predictable Yes. I hold little confidence in the response's content. To respond otherwise, the respondent would "break the face" (*thaek naa*)
of the entire community. Why shame one's whole community in front of an
outsider?

Information and Communication. I did not ask my informants about how
many phone calls they made or received. However, I developed a question on
how households obtain information about government projects (agricultural ex-
tensions, workforce, family planning, etc.). Likewise, I asked about the artisans'
most important sources of information regarding marketing outlets, new designs, and new client pools. For the more successful artisans, this question
proved to be too sensitive, and understandably so. The artisans guard their privileged ties to information; I could only obtain superficial and unreliable information about these sources.

Social Cohesion and Inclusion. The questions in the SC-IQ do not capture the
essence of social cohesion and inclusion in a handicraft village. I wanted to know
how the artisans learned their craft, because I assumed that if the craft has been
passed down from one generation to the next, those artisans feel bound to one
another by their traditions. By sharing the craft tradition, the artisans may be

willing to engage in acts of altruism to keep the workshops of other artisans thriving for the sake of keeping the tradition alive. These acts of altruism, such as cooperating with other workshops or showing leniency toward one's workers, even when one has nothing to gain materially from doing so, manifests the presence of social capital. In particular, the altruistic source of social capital is the community solidarity that results from having a common tradition and from seeing oneself and the other community artisans as a distinct group, facing common external pressures, and protecting the integrity of a common craft tradition.

Empowerment and Political Action.   Based on Peter Evans's (1995) discussion of collective action in Kerala, India, I wanted to know whether past attempts to organize the village artisans had negative or positive economic outcomes. I assumed that if past attempts to organize collectively led to negative economic outcome, social cohesion and community solidarity would be lower. In Thailand I encountered the NIMV (not-in-my-village) response. Therefore, I did not include it as an item on my final survey instrument for Thailand. By contrast, the Costa Rican survey used a paired-phrase question to assess the sense of empowerment that comes from having won collective battles as a community: either past attempts to organize collectively had resulted in a better economic conditions for most artisans or had failed to do so as a result of the intense competition among the artisans. I did not find significant differences in response between the communities or between the more and the less economically successful workshops.

Phenomenal Identity and Conceptual Equivalence

A common problem in cross-national research is that words translated from English only seem to share the same characteristics out of context (phenomenal identity); if one digs into the meanings the respondents assign to the words, one sometimes finds that the same word in two different national contexts refer to different concepts. In short, phenomenal identity does not ensure conceptual equivalence. To ensure that the questionnaire items measured roughly the same concepts in the different contexts, I discussed my survey questionnaire with social scientists and linguists from Costa Rica and Thailand. I also discussed the survey instrument with the artisans in both countries to see how they perceived the questions, which questions they thought were odd (or comical), which ones they had trouble understanding.

Developing the questionnaire was an iterative process, and it meant that the questions used in each country do not translate the same into English. I also had to pay attention to questions that the informants thought inappropriate or that might have brought shame on the respondent. Finally, with the respondent's permission, I used a tape recorder while administering the survey. Most of the recording occurred in

Costa Rica, where the respondents felt more comfortable with the tape recorder. I enlisted the help of bilingual university students in the countries of study to transcribe selected tapes, and with the transcriptions I discussed the transcribers' and my own perceptions about what the respondents meant by their responses.

Sampling on the Dependent Variable

Regrettably, I interviewed only the heads of the handicraft workshops but did not have the resources to interview the heads of other economic enterprises in the community (the corner store, for example), nor did I interview those people who led no economic enterprises. As a result, I cannot say whether these entrepreneurs differ from entrepreneurs engaged in other types of work, nor can I confirm that these entrepreneurs differ from those who do not become entrepreneurs. These questions, however, are not central to my exploration of how social capital and external sources of support promote community development.

My methodology does not enable me to rule out the possibility that social capital and external sources of support might also be present among entrepreneurs in other fields of work who do not achieve a high level of economic performance. It may also be that those who do not manage a micro- or small business may also have access to social capital, but without the resources to establish an enterprise, they remain entrepreneurs without enterprises. However, because I have a diversity of economic outcomes among my handicraft artisans, my sample does address the population of existing handicraft workshops in these communities. And my predictors only tell me the likelihood that the economic performance improves in the handicraft workshop compared with the economic performance of other handicraft workshops in the same two neighborhoods. Collecting data on workshops that have gone out of business proved too difficult, so I was also limited by my censored sample.

Emblematic Samples

What makes my sample of handicraft workshops valuable is the extent to which these enterprises represent a new form of work and a new pathway for economic development at the community level. A growing number of studies confirm that handicraft communities have emerged as a type of collective actor tied to the global economy through international tourism and craft exports. The authors of these studies include Rob Allen (1983), Jeffrey H. Cohen (1998), Rudi Colloredo-Mansfeld (2002), Tyler Cowen (2002), David V. Carruthers (2001), Michael Chibnik (2000), David Kyle (2000), and Juan Pablo Pérez-Sáinz and Katharine E. Andrade-Eekhoff (2003).

QUALITATIVE DATA

As seen in the previous section, the quantitative data have a number of weaknesses that the qualitative data need to address, since the quantitative data do not tell us how the handicraft markets emerge or the particularities of how different artisans achieve remarkable economic success. At the same time, the quantitative data reinforce the qualitative findings by establishing whether social capital and external sources of support (prominent in the qualitative reports) are also statistically significant factors within the sample of workshops.

Interviews

I interviewed key informants for two reasons. First, I needed to gather information about the history of the handicraft communities and how external interventions might have given some artisans the impetus for economic success in the tourist crafts or the global crafts market. Second, because no rosters of village handicraft workshops existed, I needed to talk with informants knowledgeable about the other enterprises within their community.

Selection Bias

A multiple-entry-point strategy enabled me to select expert informants who would provide a range of perspectives on the community. By randomly selecting artisans and other informants, I freed myself from any one informant's circle of reference. This strategy offered me a diverse set of views on how the handicraft communities have emerged and where the community's workshops can be found. In this way, I attenuated the bias in my selection of key informants. By contrast, snowball sampling would have exacerbated selection bias because the researcher would have been led to see some networks of artisans but not others. And each subsequent contact (a unit of observation) would have been heavily dependent on the prior contact (another unit of observation).

Ethnographic Fallacy

Although I used a multiple-entry-point strategy to select the key informants, I found it difficult to know when to take the views of the informants at face value and to what extent I could attribute transformations in these particular handicraft communities to large-scale changes in the structure of the national economy. These difficulties exemplify the ethnographic fallacy. I tried to confirm the reports of the informants by triangulating different reports or by searching for confirmation of the informants' stories in old newspapers, pamphlets, or memoranda from planned community events. These safeguards notwithstanding, the ethnographic fallacy remains inescapable. To the extent that the quantitative data confirm the ethnographic impressions, the explanatory power of the interviews increases.

Archives

Archival data on my Costa Rican study communities came from the University of Costa Rica's Ethnography Library and from the library of the National Museum of Costa Rica. In Thailand the major source of my archival data was the Chiang Mai University library's Lanna Cultural Collection. These archival sources offer scant information on my study communities, and the newspaper clippings contained therein are not collected systematically. Because the information contained in the archive was no better for other villages it described in terms of organization, I have no reason to believe that the organization or scope of the information about the villages in the archives reflects the quality or authenticity of those villages. It most likely reflects resource constraints.

Newspapers and Magazines

In Costa Rica the two national newspapers, *Nación* and *El Diario,* have featured my study communities in articles alerting the nation to the cultural heritage of Guaitil and San Vicente and the threat of losing this national resource because the artisans' clay is located on privately owned land. From these newspaper articles spanning from October 2002 to the present, one finds information about the artisans in the two communities and the histories of each locale.

In Thailand, a flurry of newspaper articles have appeared in the English-language dailies, *The Bangkok Post* and *The Nation.* The Thai-language newspapers also feature different handicraft communities, with the Thawai village among them. I have obtained numerous articles from these national newspapers on the experiences of the handicraft sector. Rather than the stories of "jeopardy" found in the Costa Rican newspaper articles, these articles focus on dynamism. Such magazines as the *Far Eastern Economic Review* also feature Thai handicraft artisans and stories about the dynamism of the handicraft economy in the Thai countryside.

Direct Observation

Direct observation enabled me to accomplish two goals. On the one hand, I could confirm the economic performance of the enterprises by observing the volume of transactions that the enterprise had. If I saw numerous tourists visiting a workshop, saw buying agents making frequent trips with bulk orders, or noticed the movement of large volumes of handicraft objects in and out of the workshop, I would check the reported monthly sales figures for that workshop with other workshops where similar levels of activity could be observed.

In addition, I was able to follow artisans for entire days at a time and to sit in their workshops and watch them at work. From observing these artisans as they performed their daily tasks and interacted inside and outside of the workshops, I was able to develop ethnographic sketches of the production processes. In tandem with the interviews I conducted with the heads of the workshops and other key informants, I could sketch the social organization production and pinpoint the stages in which social capital and external interventions might matter most for the workshop's economic development.

References

Alexander, Jeffrey C. 2004. "Cultural pragmatics: Social performance between ritual and strategy." *Sociological Theory* 22:527–73.

Alexander, Jennifer, and Paul Alexander. 2000. "From kinship to contract? Production chains in the Javanese woodworking industries." *Human organization* 59:106–16.

Allen, Rob. 1983. "The myth of a redundant craft: Potters in Northern Nigeria." *Journal of Modern African Studies* 21:159–66.

Anuman Rajadhon, Phya. 1988. *Essays on Thai folklore*. Bangkok: Thai Inter-Religious Commission for Development and Santhirakoses Nagapradipa Foundation.

Appadurai, Arjun. 1986. "Introduction: Commodities and the politics of value." In *The Social Life of Things: Commodities in Cultural Perspective*, ed. A. Appadurai. New York: Oxford University Press.

Bandelj, Nina. 2002. "Embedded economies: Social relations as determinants of foreign direct investment in Central and Eastern Europe." *Social Forces* 81:411–44.

Bauman, Zygmunt. 1998. *Globalization: The human consequences*. New York: Columbia University Press.

Bello, Walden F., Shea Cunningham, and Kheng Poh Li. 1998. *A Siamese tragedy: Development and disintegration in modern Thailand*. New York: St. Martin's Press.

Benton, Lauren A. 1989. "Industrial subcontracting and the informal sector: Restructuring in the Madrid electronics Industry." In *The informal economy: Studies in advanced and less developed countries*, ed. A. Portes, M. Castells, and L. Benton. Baltimore: Johns Hopkins University Press.

Bernardin, John H. 1977. "Behavioral expectation scales versus summated scales: A fairer comparison." *Journal of Applied Psychology* 62:422–27.

Biesanz, Mavis Hiltunen, Richard Biesanz, and Karen Zubris Biesanz. 1999. *The Ticos: Culture and social change in Costa Rica*. Boulder: Lynne Rienner Publishers.

Biggart, Nicole W., and Mark Orrú. 1997. "Societal strategic advantage: Institutional structure and path dependence in the automotive and electronics industries of East Asia." In *State, market, and organizational form*, ed. A. Bugra and B. Usdiken. Berlin: Walter de Gruyter.

Biggart, Nicole Woolsey, and Mauro F. Guillén. 1999. "Developing difference: Social organization and the rise of the auto industries of South Korea, Taiwan, Spain, and Argentina." *American Sociological Review* 64:722–47.

Bonacich, Edna, and Richard P. Appelbaum. 2000. *Behind the label: Inequality in the Los Angeles apparel industry.* Berkeley: University of California Press.

Borman, Walter C. 1975. "Effects of instructions to avoid halo error on reliability and validity of performance evaluation ratings." *Journal of Applied Psychology* 60:556–60.

Bourdieu, Pierre. 1977. *Outline of a theory of practice.* Cambridge: Cambridge University Press.

Bourgois, Philippe. 1986. "The black diaspora in Costa Rica: Upward mobility and ethnic discrimination." *New West Indian Guide* 60:149–66.

Bowie, Katherine A. 1992. "Unraveling the myth of the subsistence economy: Textile production in nineteenth-century northern Thailand." *Journal of Asian Studies* 51:797–823.

Breckenridge, Carol A. 1989. "The aesthetics and politics of colonial collecting: India at the World Fairs." *Comparative Studies in Society and History* 31:195–216.

Brusco, Sebastiano. 1982. "The Emilian model: Productive decentralisation and social integration." *Cambridge Journal of Economics* 6:167–84.

Burawoy, Michael. 2000. *Global ethnography: Forces, connections, and imaginations in a postmodern world.* Berkeley: University of California Press.

Burt, Ronald S. 1992. *Structural holes: The social structure of competition.* Cambridge, MA: Harvard University Press.

Callon, Michel, Cécile Méadel, and Vololona Rabeharisoa. 2002. "The economy of qualities." *Economy and Society* 31:194–217.

Capecchi, Vittorio. 1989. "The informal economy and the development of flexible specialization." In *The informal economy: Studies in advanced and less developed countries,* ed. A. Portes, M. Castells, and L. A. Benton. Baltimore: Johns Hopkins University Press.

Carruthers, David V. 2001. "The politics and ecology of indigenous folk art in Mexico." *Human organization* 60:356–66.

Causey, Andrew. 2003. *Hard bargaining in Sumatra: Western travelers and Toba Bataks in the marketplace of souvenirs.* Honolulu: University of Hawaii Press.

Chalfin, Brenda. 2004. *Shea butter republic: State power, global markets, and the making of an indigenous commodity.* New York: Routledge.

Chamratrithirong, Apichat, Kritaya Archavanitkul, Kerry Richter, Philip Guest, Thongthai Varachai, Wathinee Boonchalaksi, Nittaya Piriyathamwong, and Panee Vong-ek. 1995. "National migration survey of Thailand." Institute for Population and Social Research, Mahidol University, Bangkok, Thailand.

Chiang Mai Provincial Statistical Office (CMPSO). Various years. "Regional Statistics for Chiang Mai Province." Chiang Mai, Thailand: Provincial Statistical Office.

Chibnik, Michael. 2000. "The evolution of market niches in Oaxacan woodcarving." *Ethnology* 39:225–42.

Clark, Mary A. 1995. "Nontraditional export promotion in Costa Rica: Sustaining export-led growth." *Journal of Inter-American Studies and World Affairs* 37:181–223.

Cohen, Erik. 2000. The commercialized crafts of Thailand: Hill tribes and lowland villages. Honolulu: University of Hawaii Press.

Cohen, Jeffrey H. 1998. "Craft production and the challenge of the global market: An artisans' cooperative in Oaxaca, Mexico." *Human Organization* 57:74–82.

Coleman, James S. 1993. "Social capital in the creation of human capital." *American Journal of Sociology* 94:S95–121.

Collins, Randall. 2004. *Interaction ritual chains*. Princeton, NJ: Princeton University Press.

Colloredo-Mansfeld, Rudi. 2002. "An ethnography of neoliberalism: Understanding competition in artisan economies." *Current Anthropology* 43:113–37.

Costa Rican Census Bureau. 1975. "Censo 1973." San José, Costa Rica: Imprenta Nacional.

———. 1987. "Censo 1984." San José, Costa Rica: Imprenta Nacional.

Costa Rican Tourism Board (ICT). 2000a. "Costa Rica: Ingresos por Turismo." San José, Costa Rica: Imprenta Nacional.

———. 2000b. "Encuesta aérea de no residentes en Costa Rica: Temporada turística alta 2000." Microsoft Word document, sent to me by email from Hazel Mendez, ICT, 5 May 2003.

———. 2002. "Costa Rica touristic map." San José, Costa Rica: Imprenta Nacional.

Cowen, Tyler. 2002. *Creative destruction: How globalization is changing the world's cultures*. Princeton, NJ: Princeton University Press.

Coxhead, Ian. 1999. "Research Note No. 1: Thailand's boom and bubble and the fate of agriculture." Webpage www.aae.wisc.edu/coxhead/projects/lamyai/, accessed on 15 February 2004.

Creamer, Winifred. 1987. "Mesoamerica as a concept: An archaeological view from Central America." *Latin American Research Review* 22:35–62.

Crispin, Shawn W. 2003. "Weaving entrepreneurs." *Far Eastern Economic Review*, 10 April, pp. 32–34.

Curtin, Philip D. 1984. *Cross-cultural trade in world history*. New York: Cambridge University Press.

Dixon, Chris J. 1999. *The Thai economy: Uneven development and internationalisation*. New York: Routledge.

Dobbin, Frank. 1994. *Forging industrial policy: The United States, Britain, and France in the railway age*. New York: Cambridge University Press.

Dore, Ronald. 1992. "Goodwill and the spirit of market capitalism." In *The sociology of economic life*, ed. M. Granovetter and R. Swedberg. Boulder: Westview Press.

Economist Intelligence Unit. 2003. *Country report: Thailand*. London: The Economist Intelligence Unit.

Edelman, Marc. 1985. "Back from the Brink." *NACLA Report on the Americas* 19:37–48.

Edelman, Marc, and Mitchell A. Seligson. 1994. "Land inequality: A comparison of census data and property records in twentieth-century southern Costa Rica." *Hispanic American Historical Review* 74:445–91.

Evans, Peter B. 1995. *Embedded autonomy: States and industrial transformation*. Princeton, NJ: Princeton University Press.

Fallas Venegas, Helio. 1989. "Economic crisis and social transformation in Costa Rica." In *The Costa Rican reader*, ed. M. Edelman and J. Kenen. New York: Grove Weidenfeld.

Fine, Gary Alan. 2003. "Crafting authenticity: The validation of identity in self-taught art." *Theory and Society* 32: 153–80.

García Canclini, Nestor. 1990. *Culturas híbridas: Estrategias para entrar y salir de la modernidad*. Grijalbo: Consejo Nacional para la Cultura y las Artes.

Garfinkel, Harold. 1967. *Studies in Ethnomethodolgy.* Englewood Cliffs, NJ: Prentice-Hall.

Geertz, Clifford. 1973. *The interpretation of cultures.* New York: Basic Books.

———. 1979. "Suq: The bazaar economy of Sefrou." In *Meaning and order in Moroccan society: Three essays in cultural analysis,* ed. C. Geertz, H. Geertz, and L. Rosen. Cambridge: Cambridge University Press.

Gereffi, Gary. 1989. "International trade and industrial upgrading in the apparel commodity chain." *Journal of International Economics* 48:37–70.

Goffman, Erving. 1959. *The presentation of self in everyday life.* Garden City, NY: Doubleday.

———. 1961. *Encounters: Two studies in the sociology of interaction.* Indianapolis, IN: Bobbs-Merrill.

———. [1974] 1997. "Frame analysis." In *The Goffman Reader,* ed. Charles Lemert and Ann Branaman. Malden, MA: Blackwell.

Graburn, Nelson H. H. 1976. *Ethnic and tourist arts: Cultural expressions from the fourth world.* Berkeley: University of California Press.

Granovetter, Mark. 1983. "The strength of weak ties: A network theory revisited." In *Sociological theory,* ed. R. Collins. San Francisco: Jossey-Bass.

———. 1985. "Economic action and social structure: The problem of embeddedness." *American Journal of Sociology* 91:481–510.

———. [1974] 1995. *Getting a job: A study of contacts and careers.* Chicago: Chicago University Press.

Grootaert, Christiaan, and Thierry van Bastelaer. 2002. "Introduction and overview." In *The role of social capital in development: An empirical assessment,* ed. C. Grootaert and T. v. Bastelaer. New York: Cambridge University Press.

Grootaert, Christian, Deepa Narayan, Veronica Nyhan Jones, and Michael Woolcock. 2004. "Measuring social capital: An integrated questionnaire." World Bank Working Paper No. 18, The World Bank, Washington, DC.

Harpelle, Ronald N. 1993. "The social and political integration of West Indians in Costa Rica, 1930–1950." *Journal of Latin American Studies* 25:103–120.

Harvey, David. 2001. *Spaces of capital: Towards a critical geography.* New York: Routledge.

Healy, Kieran. 2006. *Last best gifts: Altruism and the market for human blood and organs.* Chicago: Chicago University Press.

Hernández, Mireya, and Flora Marín. 1975. *Guaitil: Una Reserva Autóctona en Peligro.* San José, Costa Rica: Editorial Fernandez-Arce Limitada.

Hernández Cerdas, Kenneth. 2002. "Artesans de Guaitil y San Vicente, Guanacaste: Emergencia por falta de ancilla." *Diario Extra,* 25 October, p. 6.

Herzfeld, Michael. 2004. *The body impolitic: Artisans and artifice in the global hierarchy of value.* Chicago: University of Chicago Press.

Hirschman, Albert O. 1984. *Getting ahead collectively: Grassroots experiences in Latin America.* New York: Pergamon Press.

Hough, Walter. 1893. "The ancient Central and South American pottery in the Columbina Historical Exhibition at Madrid in 1892." In *The World's Fair, being a pictorial history of the Columbian Exposition with a description of Chicago,* ed. W. E. Cameron. Boston, MA: MacConnell Brothers.

International Financial Corporation. 2001. *SME: World Bank Group review of small business activities 2001*. Washington, DC: The World Bank, www.ifc.org/sme/acrobat/sme_annual_2001_intro.pdf April 21, 2002.

Jacobs, Rick, and Steve W. J. Kozlowski. 1985. "A closer look at halo error in performance ratings." *Academy of Management Journal* 28:201–12.

Jamaree, Pitackwong. 1996. "Disorganized development: Changing forms of work and livelihood in rural northern Thailand." London: School of Oriental and African Studies, University of London.

Karp, Ivan, and Steven Lavine. 1991. *Exhibiting cultures: The poetics and politics of museum display*. Washington, DC: Smithsonian Institution Press.

Kincaid, Douglas A. 1989. "Costa Rican peasants and the politics of acquiescence." In *The Costa Rican reader*, ed. M. Edelman and J. Kenen. New York: Grove Weidenfeld.

Kopytoff, Igor. 1986. "The cultural biography of things: Commoditization as process." In *The social life of things: Commodities in cultural perspective*, ed. A. Appadurai. Cambridge: Cambridge University Press.

Krishna, Anirudh, and Elizabeth Shraeder. 1999. "Social capital assessment tool." Conference on Social Capital and Poverty Reduction, June 22–24, The World Bank, Washington, DC.

Kyle, David. 2000. *Transnational peasants: Migrations, networks, and ethnicity in Andean Ecuador*. Baltimore: Johns Hopkins University Press.

Lines, José A. 1978. "Distribución racial." *Esbozo Arqueologico de Costa Rica* 24:217–22.

Little, Walter E. 2002. "Selling strategies and social relations among mobile Maya handicrafts vendors." *Research in Economic Anthropology* 21:61–95.

Lowe, Gareth W. 1989. "The heartland Olmec: Evolution of material culture." In *Regional Perspectives on the Olmec*, ed. R. J. Sharer. New York: Cambridge University Press.

Lozano, Wilfredo. 1997. "Dominican Republic: Informal economy, the state, and the urban poor." In *The Urban Caribbean: Transition to the new global economy*, ed. A. Portes, C. Dore-Cabral, and P. Landolt. Baltimore: Johns Hopkins University Press.

Luechai, Chulasai, and Nataworn Siroros. 2002. "Networks and clusters development in northern Thailand." Chiang Mai, Thailand: SMEs Institute of Chiang Mai University working paper.

Luechai, Chulasai, and Frederick F. Wherry. 2003. *SMEs competitive strategy: Lessons learned in northern Thailand*. Chiang Mai: SMEs Institute of Chiang Mai University.

Luxner, Larry. 2000. "Microchips with macro power." *Américas ¡Ojo!* 52:3–4.

MacCannell, Dean. 1976. *The Tourist: A new theory of the leisure class*. New York: Schocken.

Malinowski, Bronislaw. 1961. *Argonauts of the western Pacific: An account of native enterprise and adventure in the Archipelagoes of Melanisian New Guinea*. New York: Dutton.

Maquet, Jacques. 1993. "Objects as instruments, objects as signs." In *History from things: Essays in material culture*, ed. S. Lubar and W. D. Kingerly. Washington, DC: Smithsonian Institution Press.

March, James P., and Johan G. Olson. 2004. "The logic of appropriateness." Arena Working Papers WP 09/2004, Centre for European Studies, the University of Oslo.

www.arena.uio.no/publications/working-papers2004/papers/wp04_9.pdf, accessed 15 March 2005, Oslo.

Mazurkewich, Karen. 2002. "From chalets to chairs." *Far Eastern Economic Review*, 3 October, p. 69.

Meisch, Lynn. 2002. *Andean entrepreneurs : Otavalo merchants and musicians in the global arena.* Austin: University of Texas Press.

Merton, Robert King. 1957. *Social theory and social structure.* Glencoe, IL.: Free Press.

Meyer, John W., John Boli, George M. Thomas, and Francisco O. Ramírez. 1997. "World society and the nation-state." *American Journal of Sociology* 103:144–81.

MIDEPLAN, Ministry of Planning. 2001. "2001 Índice de Desarrollo Social, Serie de Estudios Especiales, No. 3." Ministerio de Planificación Nacional y Política Económica Área Análisis del Desarrollo, San José, Costa Rica.

Mitchell, Timothy. 1989. "The world as exhibition." *Comparative Studies in Society and History* 31:217–36.

Molina, Ivan, and Steven Palmer. 1990. *The history of Costa Rica.* San José, Costa Rica: Editorial de la Universidad de Costa Rica.

Narayan, Deepa, and Lant Pritchett. 1999. "Cents and sociability: Household income and social capital in rural Tanzania." *Economic Development and Cultural Change* 47:871–97.

Nash, June. 1993. "Maya household production in the world market: The potters of Amatenango del Valle, Chiapas, Mexico." In *Crafts in the world market: The impact of global exchange on Middle American artisans,* ed. J. Nash. Albany, NY: State University of New York Press.

Nee, Victor G. 1973. *Longtime Californ': A documentary study of an American Chinatown.* New York: Pantheon Books.

Nesbitt, Richard D., and Timothy D. Wilson. 1977. "The halo effect: Evidence for unconscious alteration of judgments." *Journal of Personality and Social Psychology* 35:250–56.

Pasuk, Phongpaichit. 1980. "The open economy and its friends: The 'development' of Thailand." *Pacific Affairs* 53:440–60.

Pasuk, Phongpaichit, and Christopher John Baker. 1995. *Thailand, economy and politics.* New York: Oxford University Press.

Payung, Chaiyawong. Ca. 2001. "A guide to wood carving in the Thawai village [Makuteknoiyaan maiy ker salak baan Thawai]." Chiang Mai Province, Thailand.

Peleggi, Maurizio. 2002. *The politics of ruins and the business of nostalgia.* Bangkok: White Lotus Press.

Peralta, Manuel M. de, and D. Anastasio Alfaro. 1893. "Etnología Centro-Americana catálago razonado de los objetos arquelógicos de la República de Costa Rica en la Exposición Histórica Americana de Madrid—1892." In *The World's Fair, being a pictorial history of the Columbian Exposition with a description of Chicago,* ed. W. E. Cameron. Boston, MA: MacConnell Brothers.

Pérez-Sáinz, Juan Pablo. 1996. *Neoinformalidid en Centroamérica.* San José, Costa Rica: FLACSO.

———. 1997. "Guatemala: The two faces of the metropolitan area." In *The urban Caribbean: Transition to the new global economy,* ed. A. Portes, C. Dore-Cabral, and P. Landolt. Baltimore: Johns Hopkins University Press.

Pérez-Sáinz, Juan Pablo, and Allen Cordero. 1994. *Sarchí: Artesanía y capital social.* San José, Costa Rica: FLACSO.

Pérez-Sáinz, Juan Pablo, and Katharine Andrade-Eekhoff. 2003. *Communities in globalization: The invisible Mayan Nahual.* Lanham, MD.: Rowman and Littlefield.

Phipatseritham, Krirkkiat, and Kunio Yoshihara. 1983. "Business groups in Thailand." Institute of Southeast Asian Studies Discussion Paper No. 41, Singapore.

Pohorilenko, Anatole. 1981. "The Olmec style and Costa Rican archaeology." In *The Olmec and their neighbors: Essays in memory of Matthew W. Stirling,* ed. E. P. Benson. Washington, DC: Dumbarton Oaks Research Library and Collections.

Polanyi, Karl. [1944] 1957. *The great transformation.* Boston: Beacon Press.

Portes, Alejandro. 1995. "Economic sociology and the sociology of immigration: A conceptual overview." In *The economic sociology of immigration: Essays on networks, ethnicity, and entrepreneurship,* ed. A. Portes. New York: Russell Sage Foundation.

———. 1997. "Immigration theory for a new century: Some problems and opportunities." *International Migration Review* 31:799–825.

———. 1998. "Social capital: Its origins and applications in modern sociology." *Annual Review of Sociology* 24:1–24.

Portes, Alejandro, Manuel Castells, and Lauren A. Benton, eds. *The informal economy: Studies in advanced and less developed countries.* Baltimore: Johns Hopkins University Press, 1989.

Portes, Alejandro, Carlos Dore-Cabral, and Patricia Landolt. 1997. *The Urban Caribbean: Transition to the new global economy.* Baltimore: Johns Hopkins University.

Portes, Alejandro, and José Itzigsohn. 1997. "Coping with change: The politics and economics of urban poverty." In *The urban Caribbean: Transition to the new global economy,* ed. A. Portes, C. Dore-Cabral, and P. Landolt. Baltimore: Johns Hopkins University Press.

Portes, Alejandro, and Patricia Landolt. 2000. "Social capital: Promise and pitfalls of its role in development." *Journal of Latin American Studies* 32:529–47.

Portes, Alejandro, and Margarita Mooney. 2002. "Social capital and community development." In *The new economic sociology: Developments in an emerging field,* ed. M. F. Guillen, R. Collins, P. England, and M. Meyer. New York: Russell Sage Foundation.

Portes, Alejandro, and Ruben G. Rumbaut. 1996. *Immigrant America: A portrait.* Berkeley: University of California Press.

Portes, Alejandro, and Julia Sensenbrenner. 1993. "Embeddedness and immigration: Notes on the social determinants of economic action." *American Journal of Sociology* 98:1320–50.

Portes, Alejandro, and John Walton. 1981. *Labor, class, and the international system.* New York: Academic Press.

Powell, Walter W., and Paul DiMaggio. 1991. *The new institutionalism in organizational analysis.* Chicago: University of Chicago Press.

Powell, Walter W., and Laurel Smith-Doerr. 1994. "Networks and economic life." In *The handbook of economic sociology,* ed. N. J. Smelser and R. Swedberg. New York and Princeton: Russell Sage Foundation and Princeton University Press.

Przeworski, Adam, and Henry Teune. 1970. *The logic of comparative social inquiry.* New York: Wiley-Interscience.

Purcell, Trevor, and Kathleen Sawyers. 1993. "Democracy and ethnic conflict: Blacks in Costa Rica." *Ethnic and Racial Studies* 16:298–322.

Putnam, Robert D. 2000. *Bowling alone: The collapse and revival of American community.* New York: Simon and Schuster.

Putnam, Robert D., Robert Leonardi, and Raffaella Nanetti. 1993. *Making democracy work: Civic traditions in modern Italy.* Princeton, NJ: Princeton University Press.

Quijano, Aníbal. 2000. "Coloniality of power and Eurocentrism in Latin America." *International Sociology* 15:215–32.

Ragin, Charles C. 1987. *The comparative method: Moving beyond qualitative and quantitative strategies.* Berkeley: University of California Press.

Reskin, Barbara F. 2002. "Rethinking employment discrimination and its remedies." In *The new economic sociology: Developments in an emerging field,* ed. M. F. Guillén, R. Collins, P. England, and M. Meyer. New York: Russell Sage Foundation.

Ritzer, George. 2003. "Rethinking Globalization: Glocalization/Grobalization and Something/Nothing." *Sociological Theory* 21:193–209.

Román, S. Dennis. 1994. "San Vicente: Tradición cerámica y modernización." Unpublished prospectus, Department of Anthropology, University of Costa Rica, San José, Costa Rica.

Rovine, Victoria. 2001. *Bogolan: Shaping culture through cloth in contemporary Mali.* Washington, DC: Smithsonian Institution Press.

Rydell, Robert W., Nancy E. Gwinn, and James Burkhart Gilbert. 1994. *Fair representations: World's fairs and the modern world.* Amsterdam: Vrije University Press.

Sabel, Charles. 1993. "Studied trust: Building new forms of cooperation in a volatile economy." In *Exploration in economic sociology,* ed. R. Swedberg. New York: Russell Sage Foundation.

Schudson, Michael. 1989. "How culture works: Perspectives from media studies on the efficacy of symbols." *Theory and Society* 18:153–80.

Schumpeter, Joseph A. 1976. *Capitalism, socialism, and democracy.* London: Allen and Unwin.

Scott, James C. 1998. *Seeing like a state: How certain schemes to improve the human condition have failed.* New Haven: Yale University Press.

Scott, John F. 1999. *Latin American art: Ancient to modern.* Gainesville: University Press of Florida.

Sharer, Robert J. 1989. "The Olmec and the southeast periphery of Mesoamerica." In *Regional perspectives on the Olmec,* ed. R. J. Sharer and D. C. Grove. New York: Cambridge University Press.

Simmel, Georg. 1955. *Conflict: The web of group-affiliations.* Glencoe, IL: Free Press.

Skinner, G. William. 1957. *Chinese society in Thailand: An analytical history.* Ithaca: Cornell University Press.

Smith, Charles W. 1989. *Auctions: The social construction of value.* New York: New York Free Press.

Solinas, Giovanni. 1982. "Labour market segmentation and workers' careers: The case of the Italian knitwear industry." *Cambridge Journal of Economics* 6:331–52.

Somers, Margaret R., and Fred Block. 2005. "From poverty to perversity: Ideas, markets, and institutions over two hundred years of welfare debate." *American Sociological Review* 70:260–87.

Soustelle, Jacques. 1984. *The Olmecs: The oldest civilization in Mexico.* Garden City, NY: Doubleday.

Spooner, Brian. 1986. "Weavers and dealers: The authenticity of an oriental carpet." In *The social life of things: Commodities in cultural perspective,* ed. A. Appadurai. New York: Cambridge University Press.

Stone, Doris. 1950. "Notes on present-day pottery making and its economy in the ancient Chorotegan area." *Middle American Research Records* 1:269–80.

Sujintana, Hemtasilpa 2005. "Retailing: Consuming with a difference." *Bangkok Post Year-End Economic Review 2004,* www.bangkokpost.com/ecoreviewye2004/retailing.html, accessed 10 February 2005.

Swedberg, Richard. 2005. "We need more ideas!" *Accounts: AA Economic Sociology Section Newsletter* 5:2–3.

Swenson, James. 2001. "A Central American standout." *LatinFinance* (July):45.

Swidler, Ann. 1986. "Culture in action: Symbols and strategies." *American Sociological Review* 51:273–86.

Terrio, Susan J. 1996. "Crafting grand cru chocolates in contemporary France." *American Anthropologist* 98:67–79.

Thongchai, Winichakul. 1994. *Siam mapped: A history of the geo-body of a nation.* Honolulu: University of Hawaii Press.

———. 2000. "The quest for 'Siwilai': A geographical discourse of civilization thinking in the late nineteenth and early twentieth-century Siam." *Journal of Asian Studies* 59:528–49.

Thorndike, Edward L. 1920. "A constant error in psychological ratings." *Journal of Applied Psychology* 4:25–29.

Unger, Danny. 1998. *Building social capital in Thailand: Fibers, finance, and infrastructure.* New York: Cambridge University Press.

Uzzi, Brian. 1999. "Embeddedness in the making of financial capital: How social relations and networks benefit firms seeking financing." *American Sociological Review* 64:481–505.

Van Esterik, Penny. 2000. *Materializing Thailand.* Oxford: Berg.

Velthuis, Olav. 2003. "Symbolic meanings of prices: Constructing the value of contemporary art in Amsterdam and New York galleries." *Theory and Society* 32(2): 181–215.

Waldinger, Roger D., and Michael I. Lichter. 2003. *How the other half works: Immigration and the social organization of labor.* Berkeley: University of California Press.

Warr, Peter G. 1993. *The Thai economy in transition.* New York: Cambridge University Press.

Weber, Max. [1922–23] 1978. *Economy and society: An outline of interpretive sociology,* ed. Guenther Roth and Claus Wittich. Berkeley: University of California Press.

Weil, Jim. 2001. "Un ecomuseo para San Vicente: Artesanos de cerámica y turismo cultural en Costa Rica." *Herencia* 13:137–54.

Wherry, Frederick F. 2006a. "The nation-state, identity management, and indigenous crafts: Constructing markets and opportunities in Northwest Costa Rica." *Ethnic and Racial Studies* 29:124–52.

———. 2006b. "The social sources of authenticity in global handicraft markets: Evidence from northern Thailand." *Journal of Consumer Culture* 6:5–32.

Wilson, Bruce M. 1998. *Costa Rica: Politics, economics, and democracy.* Boulder: Lynne Rienner.

Woolcock, Michael, and Deepa Narayan. 2000. "Social capital: Implications for development theory, research, and policy." *World Bank Research Observer* 15:225–49.

World Tourism Organization. 2005. "World tourism: Highlights." Madrid, Spain: World Tourism Organization.

Wuthnow, Robert. 1996. *Poor Richard's principle: Recovering the American dream through the moral dimension of work, business, and money.* Princeton, NJ: Princeton University Press.

Wyatt, David K. 2003. *Thailand: A short history.* New Haven: Yale University Press.

Yashar, Deborah J. 1997. *Demanding democracy reform and reaction in Costa Rica and Guatemala, 1870s–1950s.* Stanford: Stanford University Press.

Zelizer, Viviana A. 2001. "Circuits of commerce." In *Self, social structure, and beliefs: Explorations in the sociological thought of Neil Smelser,* ed. J. Alexander, G. T. Marx, and C. Williams. Berkeley: University of California Press.

———. 2005a. "Circuits within capitalism." In *The Economic sociology of capitalism,* ed. V. Nee and R. Swedberg. Princeton, NJ: Princeton University Press.

———. 2005b. *The purchase of intimacy.* Princeton: Princeton University Press.

Zhou, Min. 1992. *Chinatown: The socioeconomic potential of an urban enclave.* Philadelphia: Temple University Press.

Index